Marc Beaumont has practised at the Bar of England and Wales for 35 years. He specialises in professional disciplinary law, defending barristers, solicitors, surveyors and other professionals against investigations and prosecutions brought by their regulators. In the barrister field, he has conducted, appeared in or advised in a number of leading and significant cases against the Bar Standards Board including, *JR v Bar Standards Board* [2012] EWCA Civ 320 and all ten associated cases, *O'C v Bar Standards Board* (2012) Visitors, unrep., all of the appeals and judicial review applications culminating in *Regina (CR) v Bar Standards Board* [2014] EWCA Civ 1630, *JS v Bar Standards Board* [2016] EWHC 3015, *SH v Bar Standards Board* [2017] 4 WLR 54 and *FK v Bar Standards Board* [2018] EWHC 2184, as well as *Regina (K) v Institute of Legal Executives* [2012] 1 All ER 1435, which extended *Re P, a barrister* [2005] 1 WLR 3019 (in which he appeared at trial). He has often been the draftsman of legal submissions, or adviser, in cases that do not mention his name or disclose his full role. Marc's unique commitment to this work, his tenacity and his skill as an advocate, received national recognition otherwise hitherto withheld from a litigation adversary of the BSB, when the BBC Radio 4 *Today Programme* described him as *"the Barrister's Barrister"*. Marc was the architect of the blueprint for the Bar's Public Access scheme, which has dovetailed with this area of work to enable professionals to instruct barristers directly in disciplinary cases without incurring the cost of solicitors. Marc invented the Barristers' Complaints Advisory Service in the mid-1990s (recently sadly abolished by the Bar Council and BSB) and has campaigned for 25 years for a proper, non-discretionary system of funded defence for the Bar in BSB cases. Marc also has a busy Chancery/Commercial practice and is a Fellow of the Chartered Institute of Arbitrators.

Beaumont on Barristers
A Guide to Defending Disciplinary Proceedings

Beaumont on Barristers
A Guide to Defending Disciplinary Proceedings

Marc Beaumont
Barrister-at-Law, Gray's Inn,
LLB Hons (Manch), FCIArb

Law Brief Publishing

© Marc Beaumont

All rights reserved. No part of this publication may be reproduced, stored in a retrieval system, or transmitted, in any form or by any means, electronic, mechanical, photocopying, recording or otherwise, without the prior permission of the publisher.

Excerpts from judgments and statutes are Crown copyright. Any Crown Copyright material is reproduced with the permission of the Controller of OPSI and the Queen's Printer for Scotland. Some quotations may be licensed under the terms of the Open Government Licence (http://www.nationalarchives.gov.uk/doc/open-government-licence/version/3). BSB Handbook quotations are reproduced with permission from the General Council of The Bar and The Bar Standards Board. The handbook is available at https://www.barstandardsboard.org.uk/the-bsb-handbook.html. The 2012 Final Report From The Council of the Inns of Court Disciplinary Tribunals and Hearings Review Group by Desmond Browne QC (the 'Browne Report') is available at https://www.tbtas.org.uk/wp-content/uploads/2015/06/Final-Report-From-The-Council-Of-The-Inns-Of-Court-COIC-Disciplinary-Tribunals-And-Hearings-Review-Group.pdf. The BTAS publications are copyright and available at https://www.tbtas.org.uk/policies-guidance-and-publications/. Quotations from BTAS are reproduced in accordance with their terms.

Cover image © iStockphoto.com/baona

The information in this book was believed to be correct at the time of writing. All content is for information purposes only and is not intended as legal advice. No liability is accepted by either the publisher or author for any errors or omissions (whether negligent or not) that it may contain. Professional advice should always be obtained before applying any information to particular circumstances.

Published 2020 by Law Brief Publishing, an imprint of Law Brief Publishing Ltd
30 The Parks
Minehead
Somerset
TA24 8BT

www.lawbriefpublishing.com

Paperback: 978-1-913715-00-7

*To my best barrister friend from 'the trenches',
Joe Rich, who first encouraged me to think of
myself as a disciplinary law specialist.*

FOREWORD BY LORD HENDY QC

For those involved in disciplinary proceedings against barristers, particularly for those who defend them, this book is the invaluable resource which has been lacking to date. It maps the explosion of litigation in this area since the advent of the Bar Standards Board in 2006. That is not a coincidence: the BSB has adopted an active prosecutorial role which flows from its conception of the public interest in exercising its discretion deriving from the Legal Services Act 2007.

It is thus particularly important that the knowledge required to defend barristers in BSB proceedings has been gathered together in this vital handbook. Barristers against whom BSB proceedings are brought often feel that the odds are weighted against them. This book, without doubt, will help to level those odds.

The book is an accessible companion but is no less learned for that and it achieves that tricky balance between erudition and readability. Marc Beaumont probably has the leading practice at the Bar in the defence of barristers (though his extensive practice takes him to other areas too). His knowledge of the field reveals much unreported material (some of which is anonymised so as not further to embarrass those who have been prosecuted by the BSB). This is an excellent and well written textbook and I highly commend it.

Lord Hendy QC
Old Square Chambers
London

PREFACE

This book has been written several times in the interstices of brain tissue without being committed to paper. It has been a challenge, finally, to turn thought into the written word, whilst conducting a busy practice at the Bar. The exercise has left me in admiration of those who write far more extensive academic works. I have been very slow and I thank Tim Kevan and Garry Wright sincerely for their forbearance.

The aim of this book is to be rather more than an idiot's guide, but, intentionally, less than a textbook. The books that occupy that space between those polar extremes have been my frequent saviours in practice – Sir David Bean's evergreen work on Injunctions, Gary Webber's brilliant little books on landlord and tenant and, in this field, the late Andrew Hopper QC and Greg Treverton-Jones QC's book on solicitors. These are books that hit the pressure points because the authors know the issues that tend to arise in real practice. So I have tried to hit the pressure points. Whether my objective is attained, I shall leave you, dear reader, to judge. I hope, at least, to share valuable knowledge I have gained from a niche area of practice.

Disciplinary law is still not really regarded by some judges, or those who come to evaluate barrister performance, as a specialism. That is why it attracts some practitioners who may think, mistakenly, that it is the same as professional negligence, or just like a criminal trial, where the default position is that a quick guilty plea will reap dividends. I have seen such dilettantist attitudes end in catastrophe, (usually when reading the trial transcript before advising on appeal).

No garlands are handed out to those who get a barrister off some squalid charge on a wet Wednesday evening at Gray's Inn. Indeed, some of the issues I have taken in cases discussed in this book have been positively, politically toxic. Fewer waves might have been made defending the most prolific of serial criminals, than some of those barristers whose cases I have fought. This was particularly so when the BBC Radio 4 Today programme dubbed me "the Barrister's Barrister" on national radio in 2013, just at the time when the Bar's disciplinary system was under the judicial microscope in some of my cases due to serious systemic failures in some 700 past cases.

Disciplinary proceedings inflict emotional suffering on many barristers far more profound than the BSB would ever believe. I do not wish to make that worse for those who have been caught up in them. So, save where otherwise agreed, all case names have been abbreviated, even where cases have been reported in law reports or elsewhere. Whilst this area of the law wins no popularity contests, it does require courageous advocacy, some ingenious applications of the law and, most importantly, a strong sense of the need to confront a more powerful adversary to prevent injustices, and hypocrisy, and to minimise the long term consequences of human folly.

Finally, John Hendy has written a foreword. I dedicate Chapter 8 to him. He has given me any instinct that I have gained for human rights law. John is by far the most generous-hearted person I have met in 35 years at the Bar. It has been a privilege to have worked with him.

The law, both reported and unreported, is stated as known to me to be relevant on 31st March 2020. Of course, any errors or omissions are entirely mine.

> Marc Beaumont
> Windsor
> 31st March 2020

TABLE OF CASES

A-M.V. v Finland (2017) Application no. 53251/13	*8.52*
Adetoye v Solicitors Regulation Authority [2019] EWHC 707 (Admin)	*5.16; 7.27*
Agrokompleks v Ukraine (2012) Application no. 23465/03)	*8.31*
Akodu v Solicitors Regulation Authority [2009] EWHC 3588 (Admin)	*5.25; 5.27*
Al-Rawi v Security Service [2011] UKSC 34	*6.39*
Albert and Le Compte v Belgium [1983] 5 EHRR 533	*7.57*
Ali v United Kingdom [2016] 63 EHRR 20	*8.43*
André v France (2008) Application no. 18603/03	*8.57*
APEH Üldözötteinek Szövetsége v Hungary [2002] 34 EHRR 34	*8.15*
AQ v Bar Standards Board (2013) Visitors to the Inns of Court, unrep.	*6.76; 9.12*
Arthur J S Hall & Co v Simons [2002] 1 AC 615	*6.46*
Attorney General's Reference (No.2 of 2001) [2004] 2 AC 72	*8.25*
AV v Bar Standards Board [2011] All ER (D) 223	*6.25*
AW v Bar Standards Board (2013) Visitors to the Inns of. Court, unrep.	*4.2; 8.89*
Azumi v Vanderbilt and others [2017] EWHC 45 (IPEC)	*6.15*
Balani v Spain (1994) 19 EHRR 565	*6.74*
Baldock v Webster [2006] QB 315	*2.23; 2.25*
Bar Standards Board v AK (2020) unrep.	*6.6*
Bar Standards Board v JD (2016) unrep.	*8.49; 8.77; 11.6*
Bar Standards Board v JS (2014) unrep.	*4.4; 12.15*

Bar Standards Board v LC [2017] EWHC 3101 (Admin)	*8.45; 11.9; 11.12*
Bar Standards Board v RC (2016) unrep.	*4.5; 4.6*
Bar Standards Board v RM (2019) unrep.	*8.60-8.62; 8.91*
Bar Standards Board v MW (2014) unrep.	*6.67*
Bărbulescu v Romania [2017] IRLR 1032	*8.52*
Barlow Clowes International v Eurotrust International [2005] UKPC 37	*5.10; 5.11*
Barthold v Germany [1985] 7 EHRR 383	*8.68*
Baxendale-Walker v Law Society [2008] 1 WLR 426 CA	*9.2; 9.3; 9.9*
Baxendale-Walker v Law Society. [2006] EWHC 643 (Admin)	*9.2; 9.3; 9.9*
Biagioli v San Marino (2014) 59 EHRR SE13	*2.18*
Blake v United Kingdom [2007] 44 EHRR 29	*8.24*
Boddington v British Transport Police [1999] 2 AC 143	*6.32; 12.16*
Bolton v Law Society [1994] 1 WLR 512	*7.17-7.19; 7.24; 7.45; 11.21*
Bradford & Bingley Building Society v Seddon [1999] 1 WLR 1482	*6.31*
Brett v Solicitors Regulation Authority [2014] EWHC 2974	*5.13*
Brown v Stott [2003] 1 AC 681	*8.25*
Brown v United Kingdom [1998] 28 EHRR 233	*8.9*
Bruce v Odhams Press Ltd [1936] 1 KB 697	*6.39*
Brumărescu v Romania [2001] 33 EHRR 35	*8.12*
Bryan v United Kingdom [1996] 21 EHRR 342	*8.43*
Bultitude v Law Society [2004] EWCA Civ 1853	*7.24*
Burrowes v Law Society [2002] EWHC 2900	*7.24*
Campbell v Hamlet [2005] 3 All ER 1116	*6.48*
Chambers v DPP [2013] 1 WLR 1833	*8.67*

Clarke v United Kingdom (2005) Application no. 23695/02	*8.32*
Coeme v Belgium [2000] ECHR 32492/96	*2.18*
Comingersoll S.A. v Portugal [2001] 31 EHRR 31	*8.24*
Copland v United Kingdom (2007) 45 EHRR 37	*8.52*
Coppard v Customs and Excise Commissioners [2003] QB 1428	*2.23-2.25*
Cosmos Maritime Trading & Shipping Agency v Ukraine (2019) Application no. 53427/09	*8.35*
Council of Civil Service Unions v Minister for the Civil Service [1985] AC 374	*6.40*
Council of the Law Society of Scotland v Scottish Legal Complaints Commission [2010] CSIH 79	*4.2*
CR v Bar Standards Board (2013) Visitors to the Inns of Court, unrep.	*6.20; 6.73; 8.29; 11.18; 11.25*
D v Bar Standards Board [2018] EWHC 2762 (Admin)	*11.6*
Darnell v United Kingdom [1993] 18 EHRR 205	*8.24*
Davidson v Scottish Minsters [2004] UKHL 24	*6.8-6.9*
Davies v United Kingdom [2002] 35 EHRR 29	*8.24*
Demir v Turkey [2009] 48 EHRR 54	*2.26*
Denisov v Ukraine (2018) Application no. 76639/11	*8.39*
Deweer v Belgium [1980] 2 EHRR 439	*8.23*
DM v Bar Standards Board [2017] EWHC 969 (Admin).	*6.12; 6.18; 7.57*
DMD Group A.S. v Slovakia [2010] ECHR 19334/03	*2.18*
Dyer v Watson [2004] 1 AC 379, PC	*8.22*
Eastaway v United Kingdom [2005] 40 EHRR 17	*8.24*
Fawdry v Murfitt [2003] QB 104	*2.23; 2.25*
Felix v General Dental Council [1960] 2 AC 707	*4.2*
Fisher v Keane (1878) 11 Ch D	*6.39*

FK v Bar Standards Board [2018] EWHC 2184 (Admin)	4.13; 7.35; 7.53; 8.52-8.53; 8.63-8.64; 8.77; 8.86; 11.22-11.23; 11.26
Fredin v Sweden (no. 2) (1994) Application no. 18928/91	8.17
G v United Kingdom (1988) 55 DR 251.	8.9
General Medical Council v Adeogba [2016] EWCA Civ 162	6.62
General Medical Council v Hayat [2018] EWCA Civ 2796.	6.66
Gestmin SA v Credit Suisse (United Kingdom) Ltd [2013] EWHC 3560	6.23; 6.56
Gouriet v Union of Post Office Workers [1977] QB 729	6.28
Hashman & Harrup v United Kingdom [2000] 30 EHRR 241	8.76
Helow v Home Secretary [2008] 1 WLR 2417	6.10; 8.82
Henderson v Henderson (1843) 3 Hare 100.	6.30
HG v Bar Standards Board [2018] EWHC 1409 (Admin).	8.89
Hill v Institute of Chartered Accountants in England and Wales [2013] EWCA Civ 555	10.13
Hoodless v Financial Services Authority [2003] UKFTT 007	5.14
Ighalo v Solicitors Regulation Authority [2013] EWHC 661 (Admin)	6.12
In Re H and others (Minors) (Sexual Abuse: Standard of Proof) [1996] AC 563	6.50
In re Medicaments & Related Classes of Goods (No.2) [2001] 1 WLR 700	6.17
Investors Compensation Scheme Ltd v West Bromwich Building Society [1998] 1 WLR 896	2.13

Ivey v Genting Casinos (United Kingdom) Ltd t/a Crockfords [2017] UKSC 67	5.11
J v Bar Standards Board (2017) unrep.	3.21
JH v Bar Standards Board (2011) Visitors to the Inns of Court, unrep.	2.15; 6.32
John v Rees [1970] 1 Ch 345	6.38; 6.40
JR v Bar Standards Board [2012] EWCA Civ 320	3.15
JS v Bar Standards Board [2016] EWHC 3015 (Admin)	5.17; 6.42; 6.47; 9.5
JS v Bar Standards Board [2016] EWHC 3015 (Admin) (costs)	9.5
Kanda v Government of Malaya [1962] AC 322	6.39
Kelly v BBC [2001] Fam 59	8.79
König v Germany [1979/80] 2 EHRR 170	8.23-8.24
Koottummel v Austria [2011] 52 EHRR 9	8.17
Le Compte v Belgium [1982] 4 EHRR 1	8.8; 8.20; 8.37; 8.43
Livingstone v Adjudication Panel for England [2006] EWHC 2533	8.63-8.64; 8.66; 8.80
Locabail (U.K.) Ltd. v Bayfield Properties Ltd [2000] QB 451	6.11; 6.18
Lockyer v Ferryman (1877) 2 App.Cas. 519	6.29
Malhous v Czech Republic [GC] (2001) Application no. 33071/96	8.17
Matthews v Solicitors Regulation Authority [2013] EWHC 1525 (Admin)	7.41
McCartan Turkington Breen v Times Newspapers [2001] 2 AC 277	8.79
McFadden v UNITE the Union (2019) UKEAT/0147/19/D	6.27; 6.29
McGinley & Egan v United Kingdom [1999] 27 EHRR 1	8.13
MD v Bar Standards Board [2020] EWHC 467 (Admin)	8.81

Meek v Birmingham City Council [1987] IRLR 250	6.78
Meerabux v A-G of Belize [2005] UKPC 12	6.9
Micallef v Malta [2010] 50 EHRR 37	8.36; 8.38
Moreira de Azevedo v Portugal [1991] 13 EHRR. 721	8.12
Mutu & Pechstein v Switzerland (2018) Application nos. 40575/10 and 67474/10	8.18
N v Bar Standards Board [2014] EWHC 2681	6.63
N v Finland [2004] 38 EHRR 45	8.89
Neill v North Antrim Magistrates' Court [1992] 1 WLR 1220	6.40
Nicholas v Cyprus [2018] 67 EHRR 40	8.34
Nideröst-Huber v Switzerland. [1998] 25 EHRR 709	8.14
Niemietz v Germany [1992] 16 EHRR 97	8.52; 8.57
O'C v Bar Standards Board (2012) Visitors to the Inns of Court, unrep.	4.14; 6.76; 11.15; 11.18-11.19
O'C v Bar Standards Board [2017] UKSC 78	11.16
O'Reilly v Mackman [1983] 2 AC 237	6.39
Piechowicz v. Poland [2015] 60 EHRR 24	8.54
Porter v Magill [2002] 2 AC 357	6.8-6.9; 6.13; 7.57;
Postermobile v Brent LBC (1997) *The Times* 8th December	6.31
Preiss v General Dental Council [2001] 1 WLR 1926	4.2
Pretto v Italy [1983] 6 EHRR 182	8.12
R v Bar Standards Board (2013) Visitors to the Inns of Court, unrep.	7.26
Raheem v Nursing and Midwifery Council [2010] EWHC 2549 (Admin)	6.39; 6.61
Ramos Nunes de Carvalho e Sá v Portugal (2018) Application 55391/13	8.17; 8.28

Rao v General Medical Council [2002] UKPC 65	4.2
RC v Bar Standards Board (2014) Visitors to the Inns of Court, unrep.	5.21; 8.53
Re Carecraft Construction Company Limited [1994] 1 WLR 172	10.14
Re King and Co's Trade Mark [1892] 2 Ch 462	6.39
Re P (a barrister) [2005] 1 WLR 3019	2.7; 2.14; 3.21; 6.9; 6.34
Re S (a Barrister) [1970] 1 QB 160	2.2; 11.1
Redmond-Bate v DPP (1999) BHRC 375	8.67
Regina ([DM]) v Visitors to the Inns of Court [2015] EWCA Civ 12	6.3; 6.24
Regina (AR, a barrister) v Legal Ombudsman [2014] EWHC 601 (Admin)	12.17
Regina (Bar Standards Board) v NS [2016] EWCA Civ 478	4.2; 9.8
Regina (Bonhoeffer) v General Medical Council [2011] EWHC 1585	6.39
Regina (British Sky Broadcasting) v Central Criminal Court [2011] EWHC 3451	6.39
Regina (Calhaem) v General Medical Council [2007] EWHC 2606 (Admin)	4.11; 5.17
Regina (Coke-Wallis) v Institute of Chartered Accountants in England & Wales [2011] 2 AC 146	6.30
Regina (CR) v Visitors to the Inns of Court & Bar Standards Board [2014] EWCA Civ 1630	2.2; 6.7; 8.9; 8.41; 11.1; 11.3
Regina (Evans) v Chief Constable of Sussex [2011] EWHC 2329	6.39
Regina (Green) v Police Complaints Authority [2004] 1 WLR 725 HL	6.22
Regina (JS, a barrister) v Legal Ombudsman [2016] EWHC 612 (Admin)	12.17
Regina (K) v Institute of Legal Executives [2012] 1 All ER 1435	6.9; 6.13

Regina (LC, a barrister) v Legal Ombudsman [2014] EWHC 182 (Admin)	*12.16*
Regina (Mandic-Bozic) v British Association for Counselling & Psychotherapy & United Kingdom Council for Psychotherapy [2016] EWHC (Admin) 3134	*6.30*
Regina (Raheem) v Nursing and Midwifery Council [2010] EWHC 2549	*6.39; 6.61*
Regina (Remedy UK Ltd) v General Medical Council [2010] EWHC 1245 (Admin)	*4.6; 8.60-8.61*
Regina (YM) v Bar Standards Board [2013] EWHC 3097 (Admin)	*2.13-2.15; 2.17; 2.22; 2.24; 2.26-2.28;*
Regina v Adaway [2004] EWCA Crim 2831	*6.33; 8.49*
Regina v Army Board of the Defence Council, ex parte Anderson [1992] QB 169	*6.39*
Regina v Askov [1990] 2 SCR 1199	*8.26*
Regina v Bloomfield [1997] 1 Cr App R 135	*6.31*
Regina v Bow Street Magistrate, Ex p. Pinochet (No. 2) [2000] 1 AC 119	*6.9*
Regina v Central Television Plc [1994] 3 All ER 641	*8.66*
Regina v Civil Service Appeal Board, ex parte Cunningham [1992] ICR 816	*6.77*
Regina v Croydon Justices ex parte Dean [1994] 98 Cr App R 76	*6.31*
Regina v G [2004] 1 AC 1034	*5.12*
Regina v Galbraith [1981] 1 WLR 1039	*6.67*
Regina v Ghosh [1982] QB 1053	*5.8; 5.11*
Regina v Goodyear [2005] 2 Cr App Rep 20	*10.13-10.14*
Regina v Gough [1993] AC 646	*6.13*
Regina v Maxwell [2010] UKSC 48	*6.21; 6.23-6.24; 6.26; 6.31; 8.25*

Regina v Metropolitan Police Disciplinary Tribunal, ex parte Police Complaints Authority (1993) 5 Admin LR 225	6.21
Regina v Ministry of Defence, ex parte Murray [1997] EWHC Admin 1136	6.77
Regina v Momodou [2005] 1 WLR 3442	6.22; 6.24; 6.56
Regina v Rimmington [2006] 1 AC 459	8.62
Regina v Robert Thomas [1995] Crim LR 938	6.31
Regina v Shayler [2003] 1 AC 247	8.68; 8.78
Regina v Visitors to the Inns of Court, Ex parte [RC] [1994] QB 1	11.15-11.16
Regner v Czech Republic [GC] [2018] 66 EHRR 9	8.14
RICS v Kelly (2019) unrep.	10.13
RICS v Wells (2018) unrep.	10.13
Roberts v Bank of Scotland [2013] EWCA Civ 882	8.67
Robins v United Kingdom [1997] 26 EHRR 527	8.24
Royal Brunei Airlines v Tan [1995] 2 AC 378	5.9; 5.11
Roylance v General Medical Council [2000] 1 AC 311	8.61
Ruiz-Mateos v Spain [1993] 16 EHRR 505	8.14
Rustavi 2 Broadcasting Company Ltd et al v Georgia (2019) Application no. 16812/17	8.37
S v General Council of the Bar [2005] EWHC 844	6.5; 8.51
Sacilor Lormines v France [2012] 54 EHRR 34	8.32
Salsbury v Law Society [2008] EWCA Civ 128	7.24;11.21-11.22
Sanders v Kingston [2005] LGR 719	8.68
Scott v Solicitors Regulation Authority [2016] EWHC 1256 (Admin)	5.14
SH v Bar Standards Board [2017] 4 WLR 54	4.6; 5.14; 11.14
Sharp v Law Society of Scotland [1984] SC 129	4.2
Siddiqui v Oxford University Chancellor, Masters and Scholars [2016] EWHC 3451	6.15

Silver v General Medical Council [2003] UKPC 33	4.2
Sokurenko & Strygun v Ukraine [2006] ECHR 29458/04	2.18
Solicitors Regulation Authority v Bass & Ward [2012] EWHC 2457 (Admin)	9.9
Solicitors Regulation Authority v Chan [2015] EWHC 2659 (Admin)	5.14
Solicitors Regulation Authority v Davis & McGlinchey [2011] EWHC 232 (Admin)	7.41
Solicitors Regulation Authority v Leigh Day and others [2018] EWHC 2726 (Admin)	4.8; 4.10
Solicitors Regulation Authority v RS (2019) 28th November, unrep.	6.51
Solicitors Regulation Authority v Sharma [2010] EWHC 2022 (Admin)	7.24
Sovtransavto Holding v Ukraine [2004] 38 EHRR 44	6.28
Sramek v Austria [1985] 7 EHRR 351	8.32
Starrs v Ruxton (2000) SLT 42	8.29
Steel & Morris v United Kingdom [2005] 41 EHRR 22	8.16
Stocker v Stocker [2019] UKSC 17	8.82-8.83
Strouthos v London Underground Limited [2004] EWCA Civ 402	6.39
Sumakan Ltd v Commonwealth Secretariat (No 2) [2007] EWCA Civ 1148	2.24; 2.27
Tariq v Home Office [2012] 1 AC 452	6.39
TR v Bar Standards Board [2016] EWHC 2023 (Admin)	6.63; 6.65
Twinsectra Limited v Yardley [2002] 2 AC 164	5.10; 5.13
Virdi v Law Society [2010] EWCA Civ 100	2.14; 10.13; 10.14

Virgin Atlantic v Zodiac Seats [2014] 1 AC 160	*6.28; 6.30*
Vogt v Germany [1995] 21 EHRR 205	*8.67*
Volkov v Ukraine [2013] 57 EHRR 1	*8.42*
Watts v Watts [2015] EWCA Civ 1297	*6.15*
Werner v Austria [1998] 26 EHRR 310	*8.14*
Wingate & Evans v *Solicitors Regulation Authority* [2018] EWCA Civ 366	*4.11; 5.15; 5.17; 8.44; 8.80*
Wingrove v United Kingdom [1997] 24 EHRR 1	*8.68*
Wiseman v Borneman [1971] AC 297	*6.40*
Xavier Da Silveira v France (2010) Application no. 43757/05	*8.57*
Yat Tung Investment Co Ltd v Dao Heng Bank Ltd [1975] AC 581	*6.30*
Zeynalov v Azerbaijan (2013) Application no. 31848/07	*8.41*

TABLE OF STATUTES

Communications Act 2003	*8.92*
Courts and Legal Services Act 1990 21	 *12.4*
Crime and Courts Act 2013 24	 *4.6; 11.2; 11.9; 11.10*
Equality Act 2010	*5.19*
Human Rights Act 1998 4 6 8	*8.3-8.5* *11.6* *8.4* *8.25*
Legal Services Act 2007 1 14 20 21 136 137(1) 137(5) 159 176 Schedule 4	*1.05; 1.10; 2.1; 2.13; 3.6;* *11.8; 11.24; 12.5* *5.5* *4.5* *2.3* *2.3; 2.14; 2.17* *12.12* *12.9* *12.10* *12.5* *2.14* *2.3*

Protection from Harassment Act 1997	*8.92*
Sexual Offences (Amendment) Act 1992 1	*6.58*
Solicitors Act 1974 49	*11.5*

CONTENTS

Chapter One	The Effect of Disciplinary Proceedings	1
Chapter Two	How Barrister Self-Regulation Failed	7
Chapter Three	Investigating Barristers – Traps and Tips	53
Chapter Four	What is Professional Misconduct?	61
Chapter Five	The Conduct Standards	75
Chapter Six	Trial Preparation and Conduct	87
Chapter Seven	Sanctions	153
Chapter Eight	Barristers and Human Rights	179
Chapter Nine	Costs in Disciplinary Cases	223
Chapter Ten	Consent Orders	231
Chapter Eleven	Appeals	239
Chapter Twelve	The Legal Ombudsman	269

CHAPTER ONE
THE EFFECT OF DISCIPLINARY PROCEEDINGS

1.1 The profession's concern for the maintenance of standards and their enforcement overlooks the human reality of disciplinary investigations and proceedings. Nothing prepares a barrister for his or her first experience of them. There is no training of young barristers in how to field complaints or even as to what happens when one is made. A professional complaint is an assault on everything the barrister has worked to achieve: reputation, self-confidence, status. Suddenly, all that seems to be questioned and, perhaps, to be in real jeopardy.

1.2 There has been no survey of the effect of disciplinary proceedings on barristers. However, in 2015, the British Medical Journal reported[1] on a survey of almost 8000 doctors who had faced or were facing disciplinary investigations or proceedings. 16.9% of doctors with current/recent complaints reported moderate / severe depression compared to doctors with no complaints (9.5%). 15% reported moderate / severe anxiety compared to doctors with no complaints (7.3%). Distress increased with complaint severity, with highest levels after General Medical Council referral (26.3% depression, 22.3% anxiety). Doctors with current / recent complaints were 2.08 times more likely to report thoughts of self-harm or suicidal ideation. Most doctors reported defensive practice: 82–89% hedging and 46–50% avoidance. 20% felt victimised after whistleblowing. 38% felt bullied and 27% spent over 1 month off work. Over 80% felt processes would improve with transparency, managerial competence, capacity to claim lost earnings and action against vexatious complainants.

---

1 *"The impact of complaints procedures on the welfare, health and clinical practice of 7926 doctors in the UK: a cross-sectional survey"*

1.3 A 2016 study sponsored by the American Bar Association, the *Commission on Lawyer Assistance Programs,* surveyed nearly 13,000 currently practising US attorneys and found that approximately 28% of lawyers were struggling with some level of depression, approximately 19% were struggling with anxiety and 21% to 36% qualified as problem drinkers. [2] But in England, there is a school of thought that suits the agenda of the BSB that barristers are robust people, who should be accountable for their behaviour and so should submit willingly to BSB scrutiny. In reality, the incidence of depressive illness and anxiety disorders both generally and caused or exacerbated by BSB investigations and proceedings will be just as high as in the UK medical profession and the US legal profession.

1.4 Understanding, capturing, defining and explaining something unpleasant can be difficult. Underlying the regulation of barristers until the advent of the BSB in 2006, was a somewhat confused, barrister-driven interpretation of a post-Victorian and pseudo-public school attitude, manifesting itself as stigma attaching to the mere *making* of an allegation of professional misconduct. That attitude surfaced in the way in which the old PCC, which for years vested tremendous investigatory power in a retired NCO, treated barristers accused of professional misconduct. It was also revealed by the way in which tribunals processed cases. This was on occasion carried out in an environment that was certainly as, if not, more, tensile and unpleasant, than any courtroom.

1.5 After 2006, and particularly after the placing of regulation on a statutory footing by the Legal Services Act 2007, which endowed the Bar Council with the means both to create the Bar Standards Board and invest it with a mission and high-level objectives blessed with the imprimatur of Parliament, the old attitudes changed, at least ostensibly, in motivation and in presentation. Regulation became conducted as part of a consumerist ideology

---

2 see: *Journal of Addiction Medicine* (Feb 2016).

with a strong lay element. Whilst before, an unpleasant and damaging process was imposed by barristers on barristers, but without a headline cause, now it was done by barristers and non-lawyers, in the name of philosophical principles. In one high profile case conducted by the author, a senior barrister faced some 10 hopeless complaints generated by the RSPCA against him from cases in which he acted as defence counsel in animal welfare cases. His practice was destroyed by these complaints, but in a 2012 interview reported in the Law Society's Gazette[3] in response to questions about the failed complaints, the BSB Chair said: *'It doesn't surprise me that sometimes barristers, who are themselves under investigation don't like it, but I think that shows we're doing a good job.'*

1.6 Whilst the powers and funding of the Bar Standards Board have increased greatly since its inception in 2006, the organisation of barrister defence has remained static and may well now have gone into reverse. The author's personal efforts in the mid-1990s resulted in the creation of the Barristers' Complaints Advisory Service ("BCAS"), a panel of volunteers from all parts of the Bar and from all disciplines. The BSB agreed to signpost BCAS on all initial complaints letters. However, at some stage, the BSB stopped doing this. The parent body, the Bar Council, appears, in secret, to have either endorsed or instigated this on some flimsy, if any, basis. As a consequence, the benevolent role and important work of BCAS, has been severely retarded. This could only happen within a professional body dominated by those concerned with prosecuting and punishing their brethren to the extent that they would so readily sacrifice a worthy and cost-free way of redressing the gross inequality of arms that besets the Bar's system of discipline. The spectacle of one party outgunning the other and winning an uneven contest just because it has clandestinely exploited its historic control of the profession's governance and

---

3 https://www.lawgazette.co.uk/news/deech-hits-back-over-bar-tribunal-collapse-claim/66662.article

assets, is as far from any notion of justice as a coliseum blood sport.

1.7 Barristers are obliged to purchase professional indemnity insurance from a monopoly insurer, the Bar Mutual Indemnity Fund ("BMIF"). However, cover for the defence of disciplinary proceedings is limited to those cases where a complaint may give rise to an action for professional negligence and is in any event discretionary. Representation at the majority of disciplinary hearings is not backed by BMIF. This leaves a huge gap in the protection of barristers. Accused barristers tend to depend on the benevolence of colleagues to assist them or, the worst of all options, to represent themselves. This has the effect that there is no community of expert defence counsel and no pooling of knowledge and experience of barrister disciplinary proceedings. However, an accused barrister represented by counsel making perhaps his or her one and only appearance at BTAS, is prosecuted by the BSB, an organisation with substantial resources at its command and a corps of paid and trained advocates, for whom acting for the BSB, even without charge, has for many years been perceived at least, to be prestigious and career advancing.

1.8 Until very recently, there was no publication of key decisions. Now, at least, some key modern decisions are accessible on the website of the Bar Tribunals and Adjudication Service and, more recently, the BSB has begun to publish important decisions too, although that is properly the task of the Tribunal and not of the regulator, who may be thought (rightly or wrongly) to be tempted not to publish decisions that are critical of it.

1.9 One feature of barrister defence being so lacking in organisation is that defending barristers in disciplinary cases is sometimes perceived to be second-rate work performed for largely troublesome individuals. It is often not regarded, as it should be, as a specialist area of practice. These perceptions could not be further from the truth. Any barrister accused of professional misconduct is entitled to the best possible representation, as the taint of mere accusation can end a career. Moreover, it is vital by specialising in this work to build up both a legal and anecdotal knowledge of past cases and of the BSB's own practices in such cases. For example, equipped with knowledge of internal processes as to disclosure, the arguments of the author in several cases since 2010 eventually resulted in a much more transparent BSB process of investigating complaints and in much better disclosure of case examination materials.

1.10 As at March 2020, there is still no organised system of defence over 23 years after the author first proposed a "Barristers Defence Association" to the Bar Council as one of its elected members in 1996. No statute requires the Bar to organise defence. Indeed, it is argued (wrongly) by the BSB that the Legal Services Act 2007 requires the Bar Council *not* to do so. It is not obligatory to carry PII for disciplinary proceedings. BMIF does not wish to be obliged to offer cover in every disciplinary case. There are no political votes to be gained from enabling barristers better to defend themselves. The oversight regulator, the Legal Services Board, is not concerned with this topic. The profession that is uniquely and exclusively concerned, above any other, with the administration of justice, paradoxically operates a system of disciplinary adjudication that fails to guarantee equality of arms in its own procedures. Given the professional and personal consequences of such proceedings for those subject to them, this system is still badly in need of reform.

1.11 Under the rules, a fine can be up to £50,000 imposed on an individual barrister, or £250,000 on a regulated BSB legal services entity. Even a reprimand can retard, or even irrevocably ruin, future prospects of judicial elevation or appointment to the rank of Queen's Counsel. Sanctions have to be declared in Chambers' bids for bulk work and to any Chambers to which a barrister may wish to apply. The BSB's publication of the sanction online may remain on the internet indefinitely. Tribunal convictions of barristers, as with solicitors, appear to be attended nowadays by press releases by the BSB itself, which are in turn published in online blogs or other legal newsletters such as *Legal Futures* (apparently now enjoying some 60,000 site visits per month), which is e-mailed to and seen or read weekly by thousands of subscribing solicitors and barristers.

1.12 Hearings are in public but the public generally displays little interest in barrister disciplinary proceedings. But the internet is a phenomenon of untold catalytic power for regulators. Even proven misconduct, which may only have affected the conduct of a single case, several years earlier, will become a public event broadcast across the globe by the BSB after the case concludes. It is no exaggeration that a finding of professional misconduct is made into a national and international event. Once on the internet with the fanfare of a BSB press release, anyone can know about it or can discover it, if they wish, for years to come. The effect on most men and women, trying to carry on and make their way, perhaps earning a living in an already very difficult job, with a young family to keep, may be catastrophic.

CHAPTER TWO
HOW BARRISTER SELF-REGULATION FAILED

2.1 The Bar's machinery of disciplinary regulation is governed by the Legal Services Act 2007. As will be explained in the analysis below, that statute established (or, more accurately, endorsed) the General Council of the Bar as the Bar's regulator. That body created the Bar Standards Board ("BSB") from 2006, which is the Bar's statutory regulator, albeit it remains an agent of the General Council of the Bar. Cases are investigated and prosecuted by the Professional Conduct Committee ("PCC") of the BSB just as, before 2006, the PCC of the General Council of the Bar conducted investigations and prosecutions. Until January 2014, there was no functionally and physically independent tribunals system, but from that date an independent tribunal, the Bar Tribunals and Adjudication Service ("BTAS") was created under the auspices of the Council of the Inns of Court ("COIC"). Before 2014, tribunals were arranged by COIC and usually took place in rooms in a set of barristers' chambers. Now they take place in bespoke premises at Gray's Inn.

2.2 In the seminal decision in *Regina (CR) v Bar Standards Board* [2014] EWCA Civ 1630, the Court of Appeal, took the opportunity to summarise these arrangements in this way:

> "11. From the thirteenth century onwards the judges of the King's courts determined who was entitled to appear before them as advocates. At an early date it became the normal practice of the judges to grant rights of audience to persons who had been called to the Bar by one of the Inns of Court. By the mid-seventeenth century that practice had become invariable. Every person called to the Bar by one of the Inns of Court was entitled to practise in the courts. Accordingly it was the function of the Masters of the Bench

("benchers") of each Inn to determine (a) who was fit to be called to the Bar and (b) who should be disbarred, alternatively temporarily suspended from practising, by reason of misconduct. The benchers of each Inn exercised these powers on behalf of and with the consent of the judges: see the excellent historical summary in *In re S (A Barrister)* [1970] 1 QB 160.

12. These arrangements remained in place following the enactment of the Judicature Acts 1873 to 1875, which established the Court of Appeal and the divisions of the High Court. In 1966 each of the Inns of Court passed a resolution creating a new body, the Senate of the Four Inns of Court ("the Senate"). By those resolutions the Inns transferred to the Senate their former function of disciplining barristers. At the same time the judges of the three divisions of the High Court passed a resolution confirming that the Senate should exercise disciplinary powers over barristers. In this way all the powers to discipline barristers, which historically had been exercised first by judges and then by benchers, devolved upon the Senate. The Senate established a Disciplinary Committee to consider allegations of misconduct and to determine the appropriate punishment for any misconduct which was proved. The only residual role of the benchers of each Inn was to promulgate and give effect to any punishments which the Senate's Committee may impose upon errant members of that Inn.

13. In 1986/7 there was another upheaval. The Senate was dissolved and a new body, the Council of the Inns of Court ("COIC"), was created. COIC's constitution has been amended from time to time. It currently includes the following provisions:

' COMPOSITION OF THE INNS' COUNCIL

2. The Inns' Council shall be composed of the following members:

(a) The President

(b) (i) The Treasurers of the Inns

(ii) Eight members to be appointed by the Inns

(c) The Officers

(d) The Chairman of the Bar Council's Training for the Bar Committee.

(e) The Chair and Vice Chair of the Bar Standards Board.

(f) The Chair of the Bar Standards Board's Education and

Training Committee.

THE PRESIDENT

3. The President shall be elected by the members of the Inns' Council specified in clause 2(b) hereof. The President shall be a Bencher of one of the Inns, but shall not be one of the members specified in such clause 2(b), (c) or (d). The President shall hold office for three years and shall be eligible for re-election. The President shall be entitled to vote on any matter at any meeting of the Inns' Council. If the President resigns or ceases for any reason to be able to act, a successor shall be elected as soon thereafter as practicable.

....

THE BAR COUNCIL AND THE BAR STANDARDS BOARD

7. The Bar Council and Bar Standards Board members specified in Clause 2 (c), (d), (e) and (f) shall not be entitled to vote."

14. During 1986 the four Inns of Court passed resolutions transferring the disciplinary powers of the Senate to COIC. On 26th November 1986 the Lord Chancellor and the three heads of divisions of the High Court (on behalf of all High Court judges) signed a resolution confirming the transfer of disciplinary powers to COIC.

15. I turn now to clause 1 (f) of COIC's constitution. It will be necessary to trace the history of that provision. Clause 1 (f) (as originally drafted) stated that one of COIC's functions was "to appoint Disciplinary Tribunals in accordance with the provisions of Schedule A hereto". Clause 1 of Schedule A provided that the Professional Conduct Committee of the Bar Council should have the duty of preferring charges of misconduct against barristers. Clause 4 (a) of Schedule A provided that a Disciplinary Tribunal should consist of a judge as chairman, a lay representative "from a panel appointed by the Lord Chancellor" and three barristers. Clause 4 (b) of Schedule A provided that the President may appoint two barristers to fill any vacancies on the Tribunal before the start of the hearing. Clause 4 (c) of Schedule A gave the President power to make further changes to the membership of the Tribunal before the hearing began.

16. In 2000 COIC resolved that Schedule A should be replaced by the Disciplinary Tribunals Regulations 2000 ("the 2000 Regulations"). Clause 1 (f) of COIC's constitution was duly amended to refer to the 2000 Regulations, which became an annex to the Bar's Code of Conduct.

CHAPTER TWO – HOW BARRISTER SELF-REGULATION FAILED • 11

Regulation 2 of the 2000 Regulations required a Disciplinary Tribunal to consist of a judge or retired judge, two barristers and two lay representatives. The requirement that the lay representatives be drawn from a panel appointed by the Lord Chancellor was dropped. A new requirement was added, namely that retired judges were only eligible for nomination if they were on a panel of retired judges appointed by the President.

17. The Disciplinary Tribunals Regulations 2000 were amended on a number of occasions over the years. An amendment made in 2005 removed the requirement that any retired judge had to be drawn from a panel appointed by the President. The version of the Disciplinary Regulations which is most relevant for present purposes is the Disciplinary Tribunals Regulations 2009 ("the 2009 Regulations").

18. The Bar Standards Board ("BSB") was established under the 2007 Act. The BSB has replaced the Bar Council as the body which prosecutes cases of alleged misconduct by barristers before Disciplinary Tribunals. The BSB has entrusted some of its functions in that regard to the Professional Conduct Committee of the BSB.

19. Regulation 2 of the 2009 Regulations provides:

'Composition of Disciplinary Tribunals

(1) A Disciplinary Tribunal shall consist of either three persons or five persons.

(2) A five-person panel shall (subject to paragraph (4) below) consist of the following five persons nominated by the President:

(a) as Chairman, a Judge; and

(b) two lay members; and

(c) two practising barristers of not less than seven years' standing.

(3) A three-person panel shall consist of the following three persons nominated by the President:

(a) as Chairman, one Queen's Counsel or a Judge; and

(b) one practising barrister of not less than seven years' standing; and

(c) one lay member'…..

20. Regulation 8 of the 2009 Regulations provides that, after receiving charges against a barrister from the BSB representative, the President shall issue a convening order. The convening order will set out the names of the members of the Tribunal, the date of the hearing and other details. Thereafter the Tribunal will proceed in the manner prescribed by the Regulations. ' "

2.3 The current position is that the BSB and the Professional Conduct Committee ("the PCC") have regulatory functions delegated to them by the Bar Council, which is an approved regulator under the Legal Services Act 2007 (see, paragraph 1 of Part 1 of Schedule 4 to the 2007 Act). Prior to 2010, disciplinary powers over barristers were exercised mainly by the BSB in investigating complaints and bringing prosecutions (under the Complaints Rules) and by COIC which made arrangements for the Disciplinary Tribunals to sit and determine charges (under the Disciplinary Tribunals Regulations). From 1st January 2010, these arrangements were treated as having been approved by the Legal Services Board (paragraph 2(1) of Part 1 of Schedule 4 to the Legal Services Act 2007).

2.4 In July 2013, the Legal Services Board approved an application by the BSB for an alteration in its regulatory arrangements, by the replacement of the Bar Code of Conduct with the "BSB Handbook" as from January 2014. The Complaints Regulations 2014 and the Disciplinary Tribunals Regulations 2014 comprise Sections A and B respectively of Part 5 of the Handbook.

2.5 In modern times, there have been two, standout cases that have marked a systemic breakdown in the Bar's disciplinary arrangements followed by systemic reform. In the first, *Re P, a barrister* [2005] 1 WLR 3019, a challenge was mounted to the role of a lay member of an appeal panel who was simultaneously a serving member of the PCC. It was held that she was automatically disqualified from sitting on the basis that she could not be a judge in her own cause, alternatively the doctrine of apparent bias prevented her from sitting. The Visitors to the Inns of Court (Chair: Colman J.) uttered what was then the unfashionable and perhaps even heretical view, that the decision by the PCC to institute proceedings against a barrister imposed upon the PCC as agent for the Bar Council a duty to prosecute that person and to present the case against the barrister in a manner designed to procure conviction and that those representing the Bar Council did not have the function of a neutral *amicus*, but had an interest in procuring conviction, or in the case of appeals before Visitors, in defeating an appeal. Until *Re P,* even the suggestion that the regulator was a "prosecutor", was regarded as mildly offensive and in some circles, still is. But it is important to understand that the BSB clearly *is* a prosecutor and that its function is to procure convictions of barristers.

2.6 In the 6 years that followed *Re P,* the issue of the need for the objective independence of the Bar's disciplinary 'judges' should have been a matter of historical interest only, with no risk of the problem recurring. However, by late 2011, a new problem had emerged – that of 'time expiry'. It had been discovered by COIC that a number of disciplinary judges' terms had expired, but that in spite of this, they had carried on sitting in disciplinary cases, thought to be as many as 700. An internal enquiry was set up and it reported in the form of the 2012 *Final Report From The Council of the Inns of Court Disciplinary Tribunals and Hearings Review Group* by Desmond Browne QC (the so-called 'Browne Report').

2.7 The multiplicity of embarrassing problems portrayed by Mr Browne QC are not merely worthy of being recalled, but must not be forgotten. The fact that they occurred despite *Re P* is an eye-opening example of how an unaccountable prosecutor with no organised opposition defence body can, by a process of accretion, arrogate to itself irregular systemic advantages that eventually serve to undermine the fairness of the entire disciplinary process:

3. Irregularities in appointments to panels

3.1 Shortly after commencing work, it became apparent to the Group that there were problems with the appointment of persons to the COIC lists. In particular, a number of panels included amongst their membership barrister and lay representatives whose appointments were time expired or who were ineligible for other reasons.

3.2 The Group uncovered the following deficiencies in appointments:

(1) Time Expiry

The COIC lists of barrister volunteers and lay representatives who sit as panel members had not been properly maintained. Persons appointed to the lists remained beyond the time at which they ought to have been re-appointed or removed.

The appointments can be grouped into cohorts as follows:

Group 1

Chronologically, the first members of the lists to become time expired were the lay representatives appointed in autumn 2005. These individuals were appointed for a 3-year term. The exact date of some of their appointments is unclear. Some who had, in effect, been transferred from the Bar Council to COIC received an appointment letter from the President of COIC dated 11 November 2005, whilst others who had been recruited by COIC during summer 2005 appear to have received a letter dated 19 September 2005 from [The Under Treasurer responsible at the time for disciplinary matters]. stating that "the President of COIC, has approved your placement" [sic]. This letter was then followed by a letter dated 11 November 2005 from [The Under Treasurer]. This second letter is not entirely clear about the date of appointment, either when read on its own or together with the 19 September letter. In the absence of any clear appointment instrument for the summer 2005 COIC recruits, 19 September 2005 has been taken as their starting date.

All those who received a letter dated 11 November 2005 (whether from the President of COIC or The Under Treasurer were re-appointed by a letter from the President of COIC [Dame Janet Smith]. The hard-copies of this letter are dated 11 December 2005, but it is believed that this is a typographical error and the letter ought to have been dated 11 December 2008. This conclusion is consistent with the draft versions stored on the Tribunals Secretary's harddrive. Re-appointment on 11 December 2008 would mean that the Bar Council transferees were time expired for up to one month and the summer 2005 COIC recruits were time expired for just under two months immediately prior to their re-appointment.

There is no evidence that the re-appointments in December 2008 were ever considered by the Tribunals Appointments Body ("the TAB") and COIC is currently seeking advice on the consequences (if any) of this omission.

The re-appointments in December 2008 were for 3 years and, consequently, the lay representatives became time expired again on 11 December 2011. They were re-appointed for 12 months on 18 January 2012 by a resolution of COIC.

Group 2

The next group to become time expired are those barrister volunteers appointed to the list prior to the adoption of the TAB Terms of Reference ("TOR") on 10 May 2006. Prior to the formation of the TAB, it is believed that barrister volunteers were added to COIC's list for an indefinite period and that there were no requirements for any particular appointment procedures to be followed. By virtue of clause 19(b) of the TOR, these barrister volunteers had their appointments made subject to a 3-year maximum term from that date and consequently became time expired on 10 May 2009.

Group 3

Barrister volunteers were appointed to the list in June or July 2007 and appear never to have received an appointment letter or any indication of their terms of office. In the absence of an appointment instrument, it is unclear whether they were validly appointed and, if so, whether they were appointed for 3 years, which would be consistent with the appointments of lay representatives in 2005 and non-judicial panel members in 2009, or whether they were appointed for five years in accordance with clause 19(b) of the TAB TOR. COIC is currently taking advice on both these issues.....

(2) Bar Council Appointees

Amongst the lay representatives used by COIC for approximately the last seven years are a number of lay representatives who were appointed by the Bar Council just prior to the decision in *Re P (A Barrister)*, [2005] 1 WLR 3019 ("the Bar Council Appointees"). The Bar Council Appointees attended a Professional Conduct and Complaints Committee ("the PCCC") meeting for the purpose of training but due to *Re P* never sat on the PCCC.

Following judgment in *Re P* in January 2005, it appears that a decision was taken that the Bar Council Appointees would not be used by the Bar Council and they were transferred to COIC to sit on Disciplinary Tribunals. Defendants were asked to sign a waiver, as an interim measure, to guard against any challenge for apparent bias stemming from the fact that the initial appointments had been made by the Bar Council. In an attempt to regularise their position, the Bar Council Appointees were invited to attend a familiarisation session with the intention that this would serve to negate any apparent bias that may have attached itself to them by reason of the manner of their initial appointment. Most of the Bar Council Appointees attended that familiarisation session on 31 October 2005 and received an appointment letter from the President of COIC dated 11 November 2005. Four of the Bar Council Appointees did not attend the familiarisation session and did not receive an appointment letter, but continued to sit as lay representatives and received the same re-appointment letter in December2008 as the other Bar Council Appointees and the COIC recruits of 2005 (see Issue (1), group 1 above).

Difficult questions arise as to whether the Bar Council Appointees were tainted by bias and, if so, whether the familiarisation session was effective in negating that bias.

(3) Committee Membership

Prior to 10 October 2005, Disciplinary Tribunal panel members were prohibited by the Disciplinary Tribunals Regulations 2000 from sitting on the Bar Council's PCCC. Following *Re P*, this was extended by the Disciplinary Tribunals Regulations 2005 to prohibit membership of other Bar Council Committees and membership of the Bar Council itself. It was amended again following the creation of the BSB. Today, the Disciplinary Tribunals Regulations 2009 prohibit panel members from being members of the Bar Council, the BSB or any of those organisations' committees.

Two issues have arisen in connection with this:

(1) Some members of COIC's lists were concurrently members of the Bar Council, the BSB and/or one or more of those organisations' committees, in breach of the Disciplinary Tribunals Regulations. Arguably this could give rise to a claim of apparent bias.

(2) Some members of COIC's lists joined the Bar Council, the BSB and/or one or more of those organisations' committees subsequent to their appointment to the lists. This would appear to have invalidated their appointment and as such may have affected their eligibility to sit as panellists even after they had resigned the conflicting membership.

We do not believe that this issue goes back beyond 10 October 2005, since that was the date that the Disciplinary Tribunals Regulations 2005 came into force. This was the first set of regulations which extended the prohibition on membership of the Bar Council and its committees beyond the PCCC. If the rule was broken in a case before 10 October 2005, it would seem that a line was drawn under it by *Re P*. *Re P* provided notice to anyone who might have been affected by a breach of this rule to challenge the validity of their panel. Accordingly, a pre-10 October 2005 defendant could not sensibly be heard to say that he/she ought now to be allowed to bring an appeal or seek a judicial review out-of-time.

If any pre-10 October 2005 defendant wished to assert that the Disciplinary Tribunals Regulations 2000 were in themselves deficient – i.e. that the exclusion ought to have applied to other committees and the Bar Council – it is again too late to do so since what would then be being challenged would not be the eligibility of the panel but the compliance of the Disciplinary Tribunals Regulations with the common law and Article 6 of the European Convention on Human Rights. The terms of the Disciplinary Tribunals Regulations were known to pre-10 October 2005 defendants and if a defendant desired to challenge them, he/she could and should have done so at the time of their hearing.

(4) Practising Status

Under the terms of the Disciplinary Tribunals Regulations, barristers sitting on Disciplinary Tribunals have always been required to be practising, although not necessarily in self-employed practice. However, prior to the coming into force of the Disciplinary Tribunals Regulations 2009, if a non-practising barrister was being prosecuted, reg. 2(1)(c)(i) of the Disciplinary Tribunals Regulations 2000 and

2005 provided for a non-practising barrister to sit on the panel. It has not been practical to discover whether the defendant in all the cases involving non-practising panel members was a non-practising barrister. Accordingly, it has been decided to identify all those cases involving non-practising panel members and alert the defendant barristers in those cases to the non-practising status of the panel member and, where the case was heard prior to the coming into force of the Disciplinary Tribunals Regulations 2009, also to alert the defendant barristers to the exception in reg. 2(1)(c)(i).

(5) Honorary Silks

Those barristers who are honorary Queen's Counsel do not hold a working rank. It therefore seems more than likely that they are not eligible to sit as chairs of 3-person panels. This affects two Queen's Counsel who were members of the COIC lists.

(6) Tribunal Appointments Body Irregularities

Two issues have come to light regarding the original membership of the TAB. The first is that one of the barrister members of the TAB, DA was concurrently a member of the BSB's Conduct Committee. Although this was not specifically prohibited by the TOR adopted in 2006, it is possible that this dual membership could give rise to a charge of apparent bias and hence that appointments made following approval by the TAB were invalid. The second issue is that the original members of the TAB were due to expire in rotation over the first 3 years of the TAB. This never took place and the original members of the TAB were only stood down by the President of COIC in February 2012. This could give rise to an argument concerning the eligibility of those panel members approved by members of the TAB who should have stepped down and been replaced during those first 3 years.

(7) Prosecutors Sitting as Panel Members

Amongst those appointed to COIC's lists are two barristers who are, or have been, members of the BSB's Prosecutors' Panel. Research in this area has been limited as the BSB has not been able to provide records of the membership of its Prosecutors' Panel before 2009. However, it is known that both barristers have been BSB prosecutors since before their appointment to COIC lists.

(8) Sufficient Standing

Under the Disciplinary Tribunals Regulations 2009, rr.2(2)(b) & 2(3)(c), barrister members of Disciplinary Tribunal Panels must be of at least seven years' standing. Upon completing the initial assessment in March 2012, it was found that 3 barristers fell foul of this rule. However, these sittings all occurred prior to 2009 and the Disciplinary Tribunals Regulations of that time only required barrister members to be of five years' standing. The 3 individuals concerned were all of five years' standing at the relevant time. It is therefore hoped that this issue will disappear after completion of the final assessment, but some uncertainty remains because the initial assessment looked at the date of call, rather than the date of commencing practice.

(9) Unilateral Appointment

Another discovery was that one of the Queen's Counsel members of the lists was unilaterally appointed by the Tribunals Secretary in October 2006. The correspondence which evidences the unilateral appointment also reveals that this individual was a BSB prosecutor at the time.

The individual concerned remains a member of the BSB Prosecutors' Panel.

(10) Clerks

Under the terms of the job description annexed to the 2006 TAB TOR, clerks were expected to be in independent practice and of at least five years' call. They also needed to hold a practising certificate. One of the current clerks never completed pupillage, whilst others were not of five years' call. This is far from satisfactory but it is not thought to be capable of threatening the validity of any decisions, since clerks are not responsible for making decisions.

3.3 Of the above issues, only the failure properly to maintain the list of clerks is considered not to give rise to the possibility of invalidity. In some instances, COIC is seeking further advice from counsel.

3.4 The policy adopted as to notifying barristers convicted in disciplinary proceedings is that they will be contacted by COIC whenever it is arguable that one of the issues identified could have affected the eligibility of the members of the panels which heard their cases and thus potentially undermine the validity of the verdict. The initial assessment conducted between 30 March and 4 April 2012 revealed:

- 516 time expired hearings

- 51 hearings conflicted by committee membership

- 105 hearings with unregistered barristers

- 12 hearings where a barrister panellist was not seven years call

CHAPTER TWO – HOW BARRISTER SELF-REGULATION FAILED • 23

These were preliminary figures subject to final verification."

2.8 It was extraordinary that despite the decision in *Re P*, another 51 disciplinary decisions against barristers were at risk of invalidation due to the conflicted status of decision-makers and a conflation of the roles of prosecutor and disciplinary judge in those cases.

2.9 The Browne Report led to firm recommendations for change in the form of a more professionally administered disciplinary tribunal operating from its own premises in Gray's Inn under the supervision of a full-time administrator. This new structure was up and running from early 2014.

CR, a barrister

2.10 However, the issue of time-expiry gave rise to a legal challenge and the second seminal modern case in this area, namely *Regina (CR, a barrister and others) v Bar Standards Board* [2014] EWCA Civ 1630. The outcome of up to 516 past cases depended on the decision.

2.11 The late CR was convicted by a Bar Disciplinary Tribunal in June 2010 based on a prior finding by the Solicitors Disciplinary Tribunal relating to the conduct of CR as a Registered Foreign Lawyer. The DT found proved a single charge that on 14th September 1998, when CR was practising as a solicitor, having set up her own firm, which required an English solicitor partner, she told a Law Society investigator that a solicitor called Mr R had been in partnership with her at the firm until 1st September 1998, when that was untrue.

2.12. One of the barrister panellists in her 2010 case, Mr JS, was time-expired, unbeknown to any of the panel members or trial counsel. This was disclosed by COIC only after CR had appealed to the Visitors to the Inns of Court on other grounds. In early 2012, Sir Anthony May gave directions for the determination of the issue, the first indication to the defence that this problem had occurred. Even once those directions were given, the defence still had no idea that there had been any invalidity in JS's appointment, still less the scale of the problem as revealed later on in 2012 by the Browne Report.

2.13 Once this problem had been disclosed, the point was taken as a preliminary issue before the Visitors and then by way of judicial review to the Divisional Court and to the Court of Appeal. CR argued that a time-expired panel member was not a tribunal "established by law" as required by ECHR Article 6. The compelling submission of John Hendy QC (as he then was),[1] was that:

> (a) By the Legal Services Act 2007, a requirement was imposed for an approved Regulator for barristers (amongst others) involved in "reserved legal activities." The General Council of the Bar was duly approved as the approved Regulator (s.20 and Schedule 4, paragraph 1). By s.20 and Schedule 4, paragraph 2, the Act deemed the existing *regulatory arrangements* of the General Council of the Bar as approved by the Legal Services Board for the purposes of the Act. S.21 of the Act specified that references to the *regulatory arrangements* of a body were references to, "(e) its disciplinary arrangements in relation to regulated persons (including its *discipline rules*)" and that:
>
>> "*discipline rules*, in relation to a body, means any rules or regulations (however they may be described) as to the disciplining of regulated persons."
>
> (b) No part of the Bar's regulatory arrangements was constituted by primary or secondary legislation. The *regulatory arrangements* for the disciplinary regime for barristers were thus constituted by a series of documents ("however they

---

[1] Leading the author

may be described"). Together they constituted a set of rules which had the deemed approval required by the Act;

(c) As the Divisional Court had accepted in the earlier case of in *Regina (YM) v Bar Standards Board* [2013] EWHC 3097 (Admin), the *disciplinary rules* included at the date of both his and CR's disciplinary trials, the following:

- The *Terms of Reference of the Tribunals Appointments Body* of COIC 2006 adopted by COIC in 2006;

- The *Disciplinary Tribunals Regulations* adopted by the Bar Standards Board ("BSB") in 2009;

- A *Memorandum of Understanding* between the BSB and COIC dated 2010;

- The *Constitution of COIC* 2011;

(d) The regulatory arrangements of the disciplinary rules had since changed in response to the Browne Report. The *Terms of Reference of the Bar Tribunals and Adjudication Service* ("BTAS") 2012 and the *Appointments Protocol of COIC*, 2013, were intended to obviate several of the issues giving rise to the *CR* appeal;

(e) After the advent of the BSB in January 2006, the procedure for selecting and appointing panel members to sit on disciplinary hearings was codified. Before 2006, panellists had been appointed by the Chairman of the Bar Council and/or by the Bar Council's "Complaints Commissioner", or by the President of COIC. There was apparently little attempt to insulate COIC from the prosecutor or to identify the dangers of a close relationship between the two bodies. After *Re P, a barrister*, that system was plainly inappropriate given the prosecutorial status of the Bar Council as the parent body of the BSB. So COIC formulated a new procedure for selecting panellists. Henceforth, they would be chosen by a body to be known as the Tribunals Appointments Body ("TAB") in accordance with *Terms of Reference* ("TOR") drawn up by COIC;

(f) The court held in *YM* at [27] that the Bar's "discipline rules" were to be found in a series of separate documents. These documents, the court accepted at [19], included the rules which prescribed that COIC should maintain (through its TAB) a "pool of barristers", assessed against specific criteria, interviewed, approved, and listed (subject to annual review) for a fixed term of 5 years (for new appointments) or 3 years (existing pool members), a term which was renewable once only. These COIC rules (adopted by the BSB) prescribed that COIC convened the members of each Disciplinary Tribunal and Visitors' panel, that the President of COIC formally made the appointments to the Disciplinary Tribunal panels and that the Lord Chief Justice formally made the appointments to the Visitors' panels. These points were reiterated in several of the "discipline rules" documents by the BSB and COIC: see *YM* at [20-22]. As the Divisional Court held at [23]:

> "All of these declarations reinforce the distinction between the responsibilities of the BSB and COIC and that, as part of its responsibility for appointment of members of Disciplinary Tribunals and Visitors' Hearings, COIC has established a pool of those it has vetted as suitable for membership of such panels."

(g) But in a most surprising legal analysis, Moses LJ had held in *YM* at [24], that the COIC rules themselves did not require the President of COIC to choose members of a Disciplinary Tribunal from the vetted pool set up for that very purpose. Nor did they require the LCJ to choose members of a Visitors' Panel from that pool. The powers of appointment of the President of COIC and the LCJ were

CHAPTER TWO – HOW BARRISTER SELF-REGULATION FAILED • 27

contained in the Disciplinary Tribunal Regulations ("DTR"), which were also part of the s.21 approved disciplinary rules ("however they may be described"). The DTR, in turn, did not expressly require selection from the pool [30] with the consequence, the court held, that selection was unconfined by COIC's "elaborate procedure for vetting those suitable to sit on a disciplinary panel" (as Moses LJ had described it at [24]. He had held that the elaborate procedure of criteria, vetting, and the time limits for serving as a panel member were all therefore otiose and could be disregarded. This was so notwithstanding that the court accepted at [27] that "COIC's constitution, its creation of the Tribunals Appointments Body in 2006 and the Memorandum of Understanding with the Bar Standards Board" were all included in the disciplinary rules of the Bar Council pursuant to s.21;

(h) It was submitted by *CR* that any failure to confine the selection of panel members to the pool of qualified candidates from whom it was intended selection should be made, was in breach of the "disciplinary rules" and "regulatory arrangements". It was thus unlawful and in breach of Article 6 of the ECHR, Article 47 of the EU Charter of Fundamental Rights and of Article ("EUCFR") 14.1 International Covenant of Civil and Political Rights ("ICCPR");

(i) The court held at [33] in *YM* that, *"the legal authority to sit is derived from [The Disciplinary Tribunals Regulations 2009 and the Hearings before the Visitors Rules 2005] and not from [the other Disciplinary Rules] constituting the pool."* However, the DTR and the Visitors Rules (selected from amongst the other Discipline Rules) did *not* constitute the *sole* requirements for appointment. The Disciplinary Rules documents which required the, "constituting [of] the pool" had no different status or value than the DTR and/or the Visitors' Rules; and the "constituting the pool" documents established precisely the legal authority *to be qualified* to sit –

there was no other legal authority bestowing that qualification on anyone or, indeed, removing the need for such qualification. Neither the DTR nor the Visitors Rules were statutory instruments and neither had any higher legal status or superior provenance than any of the other Discipline Rules approved under the 2007 Act;

(j) The court in *YM* accepted that the TOR were part of the *regulatory arrangements* approved under the 2007 Act. The BSB did not purport to overrule, displace or seek the withdrawal of the TOR when it introduced the DTR. Indeed the DTR were presumably drafted on the basis and in the knowledge of the pre-existing TOR. The DTR evidently left gaps which were filled by the TOR (such as in relation to qualification of members of panels and their security of tenure). The TOR continued (with the DTR) to be applicable as part of the *regulatory arrangements* until COIC introduced the *Appointments Protocol* of 2013 to replace the TOR. The administrators of the scheme (who *in reality* made the selection) evidently considered the TOR valid and binding and sought only to select from the pool (although in CR's case they failed to note that Mr JS was time-expired). Indeed, the BSB publicised to barristers that members of Disciplinary Tribunals were drawn from the pool;

(k) Taken together, the TOR and the DTR formed the essential *regulatory arrangements* before January 2013. It was not tenable to read them separately and give separate effect to them. Together they constituted a code for the proper appointment of panels;

(l) Yet Moses LJ held in *YM* at [30] and [31], that, *"none of the provisions of COIC require the President or the Lord Chief Justice to make appointments from the pool."* But, submitted CR to the CA, so to conclude was to disregard the juxtaposition of passages in the "Discipline Rule" called the

CHAPTER TWO – HOW BARRISTER SELF-REGULATION FAILED • 29

Memorandum of Understanding (paragraph 27) and cited by the Court at [22]:

> "7.1 COIC will retain a pool of suitably qualified clerks and Panel members to meet the needs **of all relevant hearings** for any one year. ...
>
> 11.1 COIC will be responsible for appointing all Panel members **for all relevant hearings**. Such appointments will be made by the President of COIC.... Where appropriate, COIC will delegate authority to the Tribunals Administrator to undertake this task...
>
> 14.1 COIC will be responsible for the appointment of the barrister member and the lay member of Visitors Panels..."

(m) The words did not *expressly* state the requirement to select only from the pool; but they surely said as much in the passages cited above. The intention to maintain a pool to meet the needs, "of *all* relevant hearings" could mean nothing else;

(n) It was submitted to be self-evident that if the set of Disciplinary Rules provided both for the vetting, appointment and regular review of a suitably qualified pool by COIC and for the selection of panel members by the President of COIC or by its administrator, then the selection was required to be from the pool. The fact that each process was regulated by a separate document could, without more, make a difference. If both were intended to be of effect, then both had to be read together. If not, the document containing the rules regulating the establishment of a qualified and certified pool had no effect;

(o) It was submitted that the words of the various Discipline Rules, read together, bore a simple, straightforward, ordinary and natural meaning. Whether one applied, by analogy, the canons of contractual construction stated by Lord Hoffmann in *Investors Compensation Scheme Ltd v West Bromwich Building Society* [1998] 1 W.L.R. 896 at 912-3, or the first principles of statutory interpretation set out in *Bennion on Statutory Construction*, or even Article 31 of the *Vienna Convention on the Law of Treaties*, the result was the same;

(p) As the Administrative Court held at [34], *"anyone reading the regulations and rules themselves would gain the clearest impression that the qualifications devised by COIC for eligibility to the pool were themselves the qualifications for appointment to panels."* The contrary conclusion was counterintuitive and was held by the Court itself to be discernible only, *"by a process bordering on Talmudic analysis;"*

(q) But if the language of the rules was not compelling enough, the requirement to draw only from the pool was implicit. In contractual terminology, it was an implied term, both giving effect to the clear intention of the parties who drafted the documents and necessary to give them business efficacy. As to intention, it was submitted that it was the plain intention of COIC and the BSB in setting up the rules for, and seeking to maintain, a pool of suitably qualified persons available for selection as panel members that selection should be confined to the pool. There was no evidence of any contrary intention and it was significant that until *YM* and *CR,* in the wake of the devastating revelations of the *Browne Report*, all parties had assumed that the requirement to select from the pool was both the intention and the meaning of the rules. Tellingly, no appointment had ever been made from outside of the pool and no rational explanation of why such an appointment might be desirable had been thought of. Moses LJ held at [36] in *YM* that the explanation put forward in his case by the BSB "borders on sophistry." In *CR*, the panel members were drawn and intended to be drawn, from the pool, albeit it turned out that Mr JS was no longer qualified to be in it [36];

(r) As to business efficacy, the necessity of the requirement to draw only from a pool of qualified people was obvious. The disciplinary system needed suitable people to sit judicially and the pool system was devised precisely to ensure that need was fulfilled. It was necessary to select panel members only from the pool if the rules establishing and maintaining the latter were not to be rendered otiose. Furthermore, COIC and the BSB had concluded that the qualified pool system constituted a necessary protection for barristers and the public. That protection was lost if the President of COIC and the Lord Chief Justice were not required to draw from the qualified pool;

(s) As the judgment in *YM* stated at [37]:

> "COIC's functions in vetting those eligible were of great importance. They established and maintained standards for appointment designed to fulfil the requirements of Art. 6 of the European Convention on Human Rights. There was no dispute that Art.6 applied to disciplinary hearings in relation to barristers. Art. 6.1 of the Convention requires the disciplinary tribunals and Visitors' panels to be "established by law" and to be "independent." Their composition must comply with the rules by which they are composed... Independence requires guarantees against outside pressure, in relation to appointment and term of office, and requires the appearance of independence..."

(t) So, argued *CR*, it was an implicit and necessary requirement of the Discipline Rules deemed approved by Parliament, that those of them which provided for, "vetting those eligible" and which, "established and maintained standards for appointment designed to fulfil the requirements of Art. 6" should not be disregarded. This was *a fortiori* when it was appreciated that Art. 14 of the ICCPR added "competence" to "independence "and "impartiality". So Art. 14 was wider than Art. 6 ECHR or Art. 47 EUCFR. The COIC system of quality-assured panellists was calibrated to create a corps of "competent" judges. Time-limited judges were not "competent." Furthermore, COIC had decided that it was necessary to have a continuous system for assessing competence, which required that reassessment was needed after 3 years. Since that period had plainly been exceeded in Mr JS's case, it was not possible for the BSB to prove that he was any longer "competent" when he came to sit on CR's case, the burden being on the BSB to do so.

2.14 Jackson LJ in the Court of Appeal followed Moses LJ in *YM* in the Administrative Court and held that:

> 51. I should begin by setting out the relevant background. The Visitors' decision in *In Re P (a barrister)* [2005] 1 WLR 3019 emphasised the separate roles of those who prosecute and those who adjudicate upon allegations of misconduct by members of the Bar. In *P* a Disciplinary Tribunal convened by the President of COIC pursuant to the 2000 Regulations found the appellant barrister guilty of misconduct and suspended her from practice for three months. The Visitors appointed to hear the barrister's appeal included N, who was also a member of the Bar's Professional Conduct and Complaints Committee. That Committee was responsible for prosecuting allegations of misconduct, although N had not been involved in prosecuting the current case. The appellant barrister objected to

CHAPTER TWO – HOW BARRISTER SELF-REGULATION FAILED • 33

N's participation and the Visitors upheld that objection. N was obliged to recuse herself both on common law principles and in order to secure compliance with ECHR article 6.

52. Following the decision in *P* COIC took steps to secure that only eligible persons would be appointed to serve on Disciplinary Tribunals or panels of Visitors. COIC decided to create a pool of suitable persons for that purpose. COIC set up the Tribunals Appointments Body ("TAB"), whose function was to appoint appropriate persons to the COIC pool. COIC also drew up terms of reference ("TOR") under which the TAB would operate.

53. The TOR included the following:

' TERMS OF REFERENCE

1. The Tribunals Appointments Body (the Body) is a COIC appointed body. It is established to vet the applications of those people desirous of being members of the panel of persons to sit and decide on issues of misconduct and inadequate professional service and fitness to practise brought by the BSB and certify that those they select to the panels are fit and properly qualified to conduct the business for which they have been selected.

Composition

2. The Body shall consist of a Chairman, two barristers one of whom should be in silk and a lay representative. The Body will be appointed by the President of COIC in consultation with the Treasurers of the four Inns after canvassing the Inns for volunteers....

Terms of Office

4. Persons appointed to the Body will normally serve three years, save that in the first three years of operation one barrister will change after one year, the lay representative and the other barrister member after two years and the chairman after three years....

Method of Operation

7. The Body will meet as necessary and at least once per year, as directed by the Chairman. They will consider applications to sit on disciplinary and other hearings from Barristers and Lay Representatives which will be made in response to advertisements in Counsel magazine and the national press respectively. Barristers may put themselves forward for consideration at other times and such applications may be reviewed as a paper exercise. The Body will be responsible for designing and amending as necessary an application form.

8. The Body's task will be to vet such applications, take up references as necessary to ensure that members of the Barristers and the Lay Representatives panels are representative of their groups and suitably qualified to sit on disciplinary and fitness to practise panels and hearings. A separate list will be maintained of those selected to be clerks to tribunals.

9. The Body will review the entire lists at least once each calendar year.

10. The Body will be assisted by the Tribunals Secretary who will maintain both lists.

....

19. The Tribunals Secretary will maintain the following lists:

a. Lay representatives available for hearings: 30-40 each appointed for five years, renewable once.

b. Barristers volunteering for hearings: approximately 150. Existing panel members will be permitted to remain on the panel for up to a further three years. Barristers once appointed may serve on the panel for five years, renewable once. It is intended that up to 50 new barristers will be recruited each year in the first three years to replace those who have taken no active part in the recent past. The aim should be to have completely vetted panels by October 2009.

c. Silks volunteering to sit on and chair hearing: approximately 30. Save for the numbers, recruitment and service will be as for barristers at paragraph 19.b above.

d. Clerks engaged by COIC on a case by case basis: 10. Clerks will be engaged for five years, renewable once.'

54. Unfortunately matters did not proceed in the manner envisaged by the TOR. In particular the initial members of TAB did not stand down in rotation, as required by clause 4 of TOR. Instead they all remained in post until February 2012. TAB did not annually review the four lists of persons who comprised the COIC pool, as required by clause 9 of TOR. Indeed TAB did not meet at all between November 2008 and February 2012. Numerous members of the COIC pool remained in the four lists after they had become time-expired under clause 9 of TOR. Such persons continued to be appointed to Disciplinary Tribunals or panels of Visitors, as and when the President or the Lord Chief Justice so decided. Between 2006 and 2011 one

member of TAB, [DA] was also a member of the BSB's Professional Conduct Committee.

55. For a fuller account of the administrative mishaps which occurred, reference should be made to the Browne Report. These matters did not come to light during the period 2006-2011.

56. In the meantime, unaware of the mishaps, on 29th September 2010 the President of COIC and the chairman of the BSB signed a memorandum of understanding ("MOU"). This set out the arrangements between COIC and the BSB for arranging and administering disciplinary proceedings. Paragraph 1 of the MOU defined panel members as:

> 'Judges, barristers and lay people appointed by COIC to determine a proceeding under the relevant provisions of the Annexes to the Code of Conduct namely: the Complaints Rules, the Disciplinary Tribunal Regulations and the Adjudication Panel and Appeal Rules, the Fitness to Practise Rules, the Interim Suspension Rules and the Hearings before the Visitors Rules.'

57. Paragraph 3.2 said that the MOU was not intended to be legally binding. Thereafter the MOU provided:

> '6.1 COIC will have the responsibilities set out in this paragraph and outlined in more detail in the relevant sections below:
>
> a) Recruitment of clerks and Panel members;
>
> b) Induction and training of Panel members and clerks;

CHAPTER TWO – HOW BARRISTER SELF-REGULATION FAILED • 37

c) Providing hearing venues for all relevant hearings;

d) Recording of relevant hearings;

e) Appointment of Panel Members for all relevant hearings....

Recruitment of Panel Members and Clerks

7.1 COIC will retain a pool of suitably qualified clerks and Panel Members to meet the needs of all relevant hearings for any one year.

7.2 In determining the size of the pool of clerks and Panel Members required, COIC will liaise with the BSB on an annual basis, early in the second half of each calendar year, to forecast the number of hearings for the year ahead and thereby assess whether that pool is sufficient to meet the projected demand.

7.3 COIC will also conduct an assessment every three years to determine whether all clerks and Panel Members in the current pool wish to remain and whether they are suitable to continue to do so....

11.1 COIC will be responsible for appointing all Panel Members for all relevant hearings. Such appointments will be made by the President of COIC in accordance with the relevant provisions of the Code of Conduct. Where appropriate, COIC will delegate authority to the Tribunals Administrator to undertake this task....

Appeals to the Visitors

14.1 COIC will be responsible for the appointment of the barrister member and the lay member of Visitors' panel, appointed under Rule 10 of the Hearings before the Visitors Rules 2005, to hear appeals against decisions of Disciplinary Tribunals.' "

58. On 23rd November 2011 COIC appointed a Review Group, chaired by Desmond Browne QC, to review the current disciplinary arrangements. Once the Review Group had started work it uncovered the problems to which I have referred above.

59. I turn now to the impact of those matters on the applications before this court. In [YM's] case two members of the Disciplinary Tribunal, namely Mr [F] and Mr [S] were time-expired members of the COIC pool. One of the Visitors who heard Mr [YM's] appeal, Mr [J] was a time-expired member of the COIC pool.

60. In Miss [H's] case, it is not entirely clear to me which members of the Disciplinary Tribunal and/or the Visitors were time-expired, but it is at least established that one of the Visitors was: see paragraph 4 of the Divisional Court's judgment, to which there has been no challenge on the facts.

61. In [CR's] case one member of the Disciplinary Tribunal, Mr [JS] was time- expired. By the time [CR's] appeal came on before the Visitors, the earlier administrative errors had come to light. [CR] was therefore able to rely upon the expiry of [JS's] tenure as one of her grounds of appeal to the Visitors. The Visitors rejected that ground, holding that the 2009 Regulations did not require members of the Disciplinary Tribunal to be drawn from the COIC pool.

62. Mr Hendy submits that the court should read all the relevant documents together. These are the TOR, the 2009

Regulations, the MOU, the 2010 Rules and the Constitution of COIC. It was, he submits, the clear intention that both the President and the Lord Chief Justice should only nominate persons from the COIC pool to hear disciplinary cases or appeals.

63. Regard should also be had to the information packs and guidance documents given to members of the COIC pool. I take those lengthy documents into account, but will not extend this judgment with quotations from those sources.

64. I have carefully considered all of the materials upon which Mr Hendy relies. The MOU and the TOR lead the reader to expect that both the President and the Lord Chief Justice will make appointments from the COIC pool, but they do not impose any express obligation to that effect. On the contrary they simply set out procedures for securing that each person in the COIC pool would be suitable to serve as a Tribunal member or Visitor, in the event that he or she is nominated for any particular case.

65. I turn now to COIC's constitution and the 2009 Regulations. Clause 1 (f) of COIC's constitution requires COIC to appoint Disciplinary Tribunals in accordance with the Disciplinary Tribunals Regulations. Regulation 2 of the 2009 Regulations provides that the President shall nominate the members of Disciplinary Tribunals. Neither COIC's constitution nor the 2009 Regulations place any limit on which judges, barristers and lay representatives the President may select. Earlier versions of the Disciplinary Tribunals Regulations did impose such restrictions (as recited in Part 2 above) but those restrictions were subsequently dropped. There was once an express requirement that lay representatives should be drawn from a panel appointed by the Lord Chancellor, but that requirement has been deleted. Likewise there was once a requirement

that retired judges be drawn from a panel appointed by the President, but that requirement has been deleted.

66. I turn next to the Hearings before Visitors Rules. Rule 12 of the 2010 Rules provides that the Lord Chief Justice is to nominate the persons who are to hear appeals as Visitors. The Rules place no limit on which judges, barristers and lay representatives the Lord Chief Justice may select.

67. Since there is no express obligation upon the President or the Lord Chief Justice to make nominations from the COIC pool, the real question becomes whether any such obligation is to be implied. Mr Hendy submits that, when the various regulatory documents are read together, it was plainly the intention that nominations should only be made from the COIC pool; indeed the documents must be read in this way in order to give them efficacy: see the reasoning of the Court of Appeal in *Virdi v Law Society* [2010] EWCA Civ 100...... Mr Hendy argues that if a Disciplinary Tribunal or Panel of Visitors is appointed from outside the COIC pool, it could not be independent or guaranteed to be free from outside pressure. Thus any Disciplinary Tribunal or Panel of Visitors appointed from outside the COIC pool would not comply with ECHR article 6.

68. I do not accept these submissions. It is helpful to begin by considering the position in 2006. The decision in *P* alerted COIC and the Bar Council to the fact that things could not go on as before. Steps had to be taken to prevent persons vulnerable to accusations of apparent bias from being appointed to hear disciplinary matters. The result was (i) the creation of the TAB and the COIC pool and (ii) the drafting of the TOR. If it had been intended to restrict appointments to members of the COIC pool, both the Disciplinary Tribunals Regulations and the Hearings before

CHAPTER TWO – HOW BARRISTER SELF-REGULATION FAILED • 41

Visitors Rules would have been amended at that time to say so. But this did not happen.

69. In my view the only possible conclusion to be drawn from the documents is this. The architects of the new scheme in 2006 were creating a pool of barristers, lay representatives and others from which nominations could safely and properly be made for the purpose of disciplinary hearings and appeals. They were not placing an absolute ban on appointing persons from outside the pool as members of Disciplinary Tribunals or as Visitors. To imply such a ban would be contrary to the express provisions of the documents. It would also be surprising if there were such a prohibition, because some barristers do very specialist work; on occasions it may be appropriate to appoint a barrister or lay representative with particular expertise which is not available within the COIC pool. Furthermore there was no need for a complete ban. The court or the Visitors would step in to protect a defendant barrister, if an ineligible person were appointed to sit. This is precisely what happened in *P*.

70. I do not accept the proposition that a Disciplinary Tribunal or a panel of Visitors appointed from barristers or lay representatives outside the pool would not be independent or would not be guaranteed to be free from outside pressure.

71. If the President of COIC or the Lord Chief Justice nominated barristers or lay representatives who in his or her opinion were suitable to hear a disciplinary charge or appeal, that would constitute compliance with ECHR article 6. The discharge of this function by the President or the Lord Chief Justice is in itself a sufficient guarantee that the Disciplinary Tribunal members or Visitors would be independent and free from outside pressure. The President and the Lord Chief Justice are senior members of the Judi-

ciary and Inns of Court, to whose jurisdiction the barrister submitted upon call to the Bar. It goes without saying that if the President or the Lord Chief Justice had any personal connection with the case he or she (like any other judicial office-holder) would stand aside, so that a deputy could perform the function.

72. Mr Hendy submits that all the documents referred to above form part of the Bar's "regulatory arrangements" as defined in section 21 of the 2007 Act. Barristers are "regulated persons" under the Act. Section 176 requires that all barristers comply with the Bar's regulatory arrangements. Therefore the time-expired barristers in the COIC pool were prohibited from serving as members of Disciplinary Tribunals or as Visitors.

73. The Divisional Court did not accept this argument. Nor do I. If the 2009 Regulations, the 2010 Rules, the TOR, the MOU and COIC's constitution have the meaning which I attribute to them, then the regulatory arrangements for the Bar do not prevent barristers outside the COIC pool from sitting on Disciplinary Tribunals or as Visitors. Therefore there is no breach of section 176.

2.15 As stated by Jackson LJ at [52], following the 2005 decision in *Re P*, COIC took steps to secure that "only eligible persons" would be appointed to serve on Disciplinary Tribunals or panels of Visitors. So COIC decided to create a pool of "suitable" persons for that purpose and set up the Tribunals Appointments Body, whose function was to appoint "appropriate" persons to the COIC pool. Jackson LJ stated the purpose of the pool at [52], but then held that it was not necessary *only* to select from the pool for example, as expertise might be required from outside it. In fact, this had never been done and the BSB did not submit that it ever had. The truth is that none of the time-expired panellists in the conjoined appeals of *CR, YM or JH* were selected from outside of the pool due to their expertise, but merely due to mal-administration.

2.16 The question was not whether the rules and allied texts imposed a general ban on all and any appointment of *ad hoc* panellists from outside of the pool, but whether the rules and allied texts, all of which had equal value as sources of disciplinary regulation, imposed a ban on formerly legitimate panellists after their time-expiry. The obvious answer to that question was surely that they did.

2.17 The Court's approach to s. 21 of the 2007 Act impacted on the other professions governed by the 2007 Act. The Solicitors Disciplinary Tribunal ("SDT") has a codified system for appointments to the SDT. It is set out in the, *Solicitors Disciplinary Tribunal Appointment Protocol* (2012). The tenure is for a fixed 5 years. The Master of the Rolls formally appoints those selected against fixed criteria. This is done after an open competition. There is no suggestion that he could, if he wished, select *ad hoc*, a disciplinary judge for a single case from outside of the pool of members, such that a time-expired SDT judge could lawfully sit. It is clear that the Protocol, like the TAB TOR is, as Moses LJ accepted in *YM*, a "regulatory arrangement" and, as such, defines the legality of the right and power of any disciplinary judge to exercise the powers of the SDT over a prosecuted solicitor. This point was made to the CA, who ignored it.

2.18 The requirement that a tribunal be "established by law" is a vital ingredient of ECHR Article 6, which requires courts and tribunals adjudicating on civil rights and obligations and/or criminal "charges" to have a proper constitutional legitimacy. This expression reflects the principle of the rule of law, which is inherent in the system of protection established by the Convention and its Protocols: *Biagioli v San Marino* (2014) 59 EHRR SE13. The phrase "established by law" covers not only the legal basis for the very existence of a "tribunal", but also compliance by the tribunal with the particular rules that govern it:

Sokurenko and Strygun v Ukraine [2006] ECHR 29458/04; *Coeme v Belgium* [2000] ECHR 32492/96. "Law", within the meaning of Art 6(1) comprises not only legislation providing for the establishment and competence of judicial organs, but also any other provision of domestic law which, if breached, would render the participation of one or more judges in the examination of a case irregular: *DMD Group A.S. v Slovakia* [2010] ECHR 19334/03 at [59]. A breach by a court of such domestic legal provisions gives rise to a violation of Art 6(1): *DMD Group* at [61]. A court which, without any explanation, oversteps the usual limits of its jurisdiction is not a, "tribunal established by law" in the proceedings in question: *Sokurenko v Ukraine* at [27-28]. It is submitted that the decision of the CA in *CR* failed to engage adequately with these principles.

2.19 An appeal to the European Court of Human Rights was drafted [2] and awaited Ms CR's signature. Tragically, in the process of contacting her to obtain that signature, it was discovered that she had passed away. That meant that there was no further judicial consideration of the issue. This was perhaps a reprieve for the UK given the issues that were so properly castigated by Desmond Browne QC's group and the arguably controversial judicial findings set out above. For the decision of the CA in *CR* is baffling. A cynic might say that it bears all the unsatisfactory hallmarks of a policy decision designed to prevent the re-opening of so many past appeals, as adumbrated in the Browne Report. It is true that had the CR appeal succeeded, there would have been a number of possibly ill-deserved re-trials. But that is a small price to pay for observing due process.

De facto judges

2.20 The BSB also argued in *CR* that even if disciplinary judges were time-expired, the '*de facto* judge' principle ensured that the

---

[2] By Mr Hendy QC and the author

CHAPTER TWO – HOW BARRISTER SELF-REGULATION FAILED • 45

decisions of time-expired panel members nevertheless had legitimacy as "*de facto* judges".

2.21 It was submitted that that common law doctrine was not compatible with Article 6 of the ECHR, Art 47 of the EU's Charter of Fundamental Rights ("EUCFR") or Article 14 of the International Covenant on Civil and Political Rights ("ICCPR"), because a tribunal containing time-expired judges is not a tribunal, "established by law" and no *ex post facto* fiction could make it so. Nor could a tribunal be treated as "competent" under Art.14 of the ICCPR, when it was plainly *no longer* competent.

2.22 The common law *de facto* judge doctrine serves to ratify the legality of public decisions made by those who, albeit unknown at the time, did not have legal authority to make a decision. It was submitted in *CR* that the Divisional Court was in error in *YM* in regarding this doctrine as unaffected by the incorporation of Art. 6 of the ECHR and/or Art. 47 of the EUCFR into English law.

2.23 The legality of the acts of a judge reputed to have an authority that in truth had not been conferred on him at all, is treated at common law as saved by this doctrine: *Fawdry v Murfitt* [2003] QB 104; *Coppard v Customs and Excise Commrs* [2003] QB 1428; Baldock v Webster [2006] QB 315). But this also raises the question whether Art. 47 EUCFR, which is drafted identically to Art. 6, save that it requires a tribunal to be "*previously* established by law," renders unlawful the common law doctrine of *de facto* judge.

2.24 The court in *YM* at paragraphs [47]-[48], accepted the submission that Art. 47 is now binding and of direct effect in England. But Moses LJ held that the word "*previously*" adds nothing to the otherwise identical test in Art. 6 of the ECHR of, "...*established by law.*" However, Sedley LJ in *Sumakan Ltd v Commonwealth Secretariat (No 2)* [2007] EWCA Civ 1148 at [51] suggested that the *de facto* doctrine may not survive Art. 47 due to the use of the word "....*previously*" in, "...**previously** established by law." That was at a time at which it was not thought that Art. 47 was of direct effect. But now it does have direct effect in the UK, as the court in *YM* readily accepted.

2.25 Sedley LJ said this:

> "51 The *de facto* doctrine is an escape from the ordinary consequences of a defective or non-existent judicial appointment, adopted by the common law in the interests of legal certainty. It has been applied at least three times in recent years by this court (*Fawdry v Murfitt* [2003] QB 104; *Coppard v Customs and Excise Comrs* [2003] QB 1428 and Baldock v Webster [2006] QB 315); but it is a remedy of last resort.
>
> It sails close to the wind of article 6(1) of the European Convention on Human Rights, which entitles litigants to "an independent and impartial tribunal established by law".
>
> The second paragraph of article 47 of the (non-binding) EU Charter of Fundamental Rights, it is worth noting, expands this to "previously established by law", a provision which, as noted in *Coppard's case* [2003] QB 1428, para 38, could, if made binding, spell the end of the *de facto* doctrine."

2.26 It was submitted in *CR* that:

    a. the word "previously" *does* "expand" and add something to Art. 47 and that it is plainly not otiose. Art. 47 of the EUCFR of 2000 represents the contemporary "international law background" for the modern scope and application of Art. 6 of the ECHR, against which Art 6 thus falls to be viewed and construed: see *Demir v Turkey* [2009] 48 EHRR 54 at [76];

CHAPTER TWO – HOW BARRISTER SELF-REGULATION FAILED • 47

b. the prefix *"previously"* means that for a tribunal to be lawful, it has to exist in the eyes of the law as a tribunal *before* it sits in judgment on the citizen. An un-certificated UK judge can have no authority or power over a citizen, save as is restored to him *ex post facto* by a future court or tribunal (or even by the *de facto* judge himself or herself) invoking the common law doctrine of *de facto* judge in a legal contest over the status of the earlier court or tribunal. Thus the doctrine works retrospectively, not prospectively. It was submitted to the CA that, in effect, *"previously…"*, must logically mean, or be read down to mean, "pre-scribed", which, in its literal English meaning, suggests something "*pre*-written," which the *de facto* judge doctrine, as a retroactive judicial construct, plainly cannot be;

c. Whilst in *YM*, Moses LJ had expressed the view that "established" in Art. 6 of the ECHR and "previously established" in Art 47 meant the same thing, this was untenable as a matter of ordinary language. The guidance in the EU Charter's interpretative document, the *Explanations relating to the Charter of Fundamental Rights* (2007/C 303/02), relied on heavily by the court in *YM*, that Art. 47, "corresponds to" Art. 6 of the ECHR, was not that it, *precisely* corresponded to it. It would have been very simple for the framers of the later EUCFR to cut and paste Article 6 of the ECHR into the EU Charter, but they did not do so;

d. the EUCFR signalled a modern declaration that is at the core of the rule of law itself, namely that *ad hoc* courts and judges adjudicating on criminal charges, civil rights and the rights protected by EU legislation are unlawful and that, for their decisions to be lawful, they must be the product of an *anterior* matrix of appropriate rules, however those rules might be created. This being so, the common law doctrine of *de facto* judge, which is based on the pretence that something that is irregular was regular all along, could not be regarded as compatible with Art.47 or thus with Art.6;

e. it was impossible to understand how a court or tribunal that had not passed through the laid down, threshold requirements for establishing "competence" within the meaning of Art 14 ICCPR could somehow be assumed to be "competent", when it was not "competent". ECHR Art 6 and the need for a disciplinary tribunal to be "established by law" had to be interpreted according to Article 31(3) of the Vienna Convention on the Law of Treaties, that is, compatibly with the need for "competence" expressed by Art 14 of the ICCPR. The practice of the Strasbourg court is to read all international instruments together: *Demir supra* at [76]. Thus for a disciplinary judge to be "established by law" under Art 6, he also had to be "competent" and to be "competent", his authority had to be without retrospective creation. Since Art. 6 had to be read together with Art. 14 ICCPR, time-expired panel member Mr JS was not "established by law" under Art 6. The TAB pool was a system of quality control. It was a vetting system that, so long as it was not deviated from, achieved Art 14 "competence." By the time he sat on CR's case, Mr JS was no longer "competent" in this sense;

f. Therefore, the *de facto* judge doctrine could not survive Art 14 ICCPR: merely because people might *assume* a judge to be "competent", could not *make* him or her "competent".

2.27 Unfortunately, the CA at [75]-[78] did not consider it necessary to decide this issue, given its decision that the rules did not *require* disciplinary judges to be from the time-limited pool. But it would otherwise have granted permission to move for judicial review on this point, which Jackson LJ stated at [77] raised "formidable arguments". That suggests, as in *Sumakan*, that the Divisional Court's decision in *YM* on the issue of *de facto* judges may not survive future argument.

2.28 The BSB sought permission to cross-appeal against the decision of the Divisional Court making no order as to costs. Moses LJ was

CHAPTER TWO – HOW BARRISTER SELF-REGULATION FAILED

highly critical of the BSB despite their technical success on the issue about the COIC pool. Jackson LJ said this:

> 99. In the course of his judgment Lord Justice Moses, though finding in favour of the Visitors and the BSB on the issues of law, was strongly critical of the situation which COIC and the BSB had created. He criticised the apparent mismatch between different sets of rules which had given rise to the current litigation. He also criticised the administrative errors which the Browne Report had revealed.
>
> 100. I see force in the criticisms which Lord Justice Moses has made and with which Mr Justice Kenneth Parker has agreed.
>
> 101. It would be much better all round if (a) TAB comply properly with the TOR and (b) the Disciplinary Tribunals Regulations and the Hearings before Visitors Rules are amended so as to require nominations to be made from the COIC pool, save where there is good reason to look outside the pool. If COIC and the BSB take these obvious steps, the disciplinary arrangements of the Bar and the Inns of Court will be more transparent and more satisfactory.
>
> 102. Lord Justice Moses said that the Bar should be at the forefront of setting standards as to how institutions should regulate themselves. I agree. I would add that instead of being at the forefront, the Bar and COIC seem to have been lagging behind. That is not acceptable.
>
> 103. Mr Nicholls submits that any criticisms of this nature should be directed against COIC, not the BSB. In my view the BSB cannot shirk its responsibilities so easily. The BSB carries out functions on behalf of the Bar Council, which is the statutory regulator under the 2007 Act. Furthermore the BSB writes the Bar's Code of Conduct, to which the Disciplinary Regulations form an annexe. In this litigation

the BSB has assumed the burden of defending the position of both COIC and itself, whilst not denying the series of administrative errors which have occurred.

104. It is also significant that the BSB has obtained a decision of the Divisional Court, which clarifies the law in an area that has been the subject of much controversy ever since the publication of the Browne Report. There is a case for saying that the BSB (in the unusual circumstances of this case) should bear the cost of obtaining that benefit.

2.29 The decision in *CR* is reflected in the current rules rE142 and rE143:

"rE142

With the exception of judicial Chairs, the persons nominated by *the President* to sit on a *Disciplinary Tribunal* must be selected from the pool appointed by the *Tribunal Appointments Body*.

rE143

In deciding who will sit on the panel, the *President* may have regard to the nature of the charge(s) and/or application(s) being determined and to the identity of the *respondent*(s) against whom the charges have been made......"

2.30 But just as at the time of *CR,* the BSB was unable to point to a single case in which the President of COIC had had to select a panellist from outside the pool, so the author is unaware of a single case since rE143 came into force in which anyone has been selected from outside of the pool. The pool of pre-approved panellists was always key. JS's time expiry was always fatal to his right to sit in *CR*. Mr Hendy QC's submissions, set out in detail above, were unanswerable. The judgments of Moses LJ and Jackson LJ denied CR a successful appeal before she sadly died. Policy was all. The alternative was chaos.

CHAPTER THREE
INVESTIGATING BARRISTERS – TRAPS AND TIPS

3.1   Some barristers tend to come out fighting. But this is precisely the wrong way to go about responding to a BSB complaint. Moreover, many barristers will be up to capacity, or beyond it, with professional commitments. So the temptation not only to be aggressive, but perfunctory, is often irresistible. Other barristers suffer another extreme reaction to complaints: they fall apart completely and appear over-willing to fall on their proverbial sword for no good reason.

3.2   The Bar equips barristers from a young age with almost complete independence of thought and action. This too is the wrong mindset for an effective response to complaints. Its reverse side is both self-importance and a tendency to play the victim card – both unattractive traits in a respondent to a complaint. Modesty and measured detachment are the name of the game, but such a tone is often hard to attain without professional draftsmanship.

3.3   The perfect response to a complaint is thus, in the author's view, beyond the majority of barristers to formulate alone, because the traits that stand them in such good stead as advocates and champions of the causes of their clients – assertiveness, celerity and opinionated thinking, become handicaps. What is required is time, reflection, thoughtfulness, patience and the wisdom of an objective adviser.

3.4   Unfortunately, most barristers have no access to independent legal advice unless they can obtain it *pro bono*. PII with BMIF only provides cover for advice and the drafting of responses to complaints where the complaint is made by a client who may have a parallel negligence claim. BMIF exercises a discretion in other cases. The exercise of that discretion, which is usually exercised against providing cover, can be challenged before the Financial Services Ombudsman, but such proceedings are ponderous. Many barristers are unable to fund legal advice on their own for the length of an entire case, whilst the Bar Standards Board has comparatively limitless funds. The current position is indefensible as it plays straight into the BSB's hands by giving it grossly unfair tactical, financial and psychological advantages.

3.5. The machinery of investigation within the BSB is set out at rE12 *et seq*. The investigation, unlike any future trial, is confidential: rE63. Any limitation period, formerly as low as 6 months, has been abolished, leaving the Bar apparently potentially exposed to complaints of great antiquity about which memory may have long since faded and papers may have long since been destroyed. As time passes, this change is likely to prove to be a cause of great injustice if and to the extent that the BSB ignores a protest that it is impossible to answer a complaint due to the effluxion of time.

3.6 Assessment is in light of the "regulatory objectives" of the Legal Services Act 2007, which are: 1. protecting and promoting the public interest; 2. supporting the constitutional principles of the rule of law; 3. improving access to justice; 4. protecting and promoting the interests of consumers; 5. promoting competition in the provision of legal services; 6. encouraging an independent, strong, diverse and effective legal profession; 7. increasing public understanding of the citizen's legal rights and duties; and 8. promoting and maintaining adherence to the following professional principles: a that authorised persons act with independence and integrity; b that authorised persons maintain proper standards of work; c that authorised persons act in the best interests of their clients; d that authorised persons comply with their duty to the court to act with independence in the interests of justice; and e that the affairs of clients are kept confidential.

3.7 The BSB case officer, often not legally qualified, will carry out a "risk assessment". This is a tick-box proforma. It may well categorise even the most experienced practitioner as "high risk", given the nature of the allegation made, an entry made in reference to a barrister's reputation with his regulator as to which he or she has had no opportunity to make any representations at all. A copy of this document should be sought in all cases and if it is wrong, it should be challenged. Its conclusion may be very wounding indeed.

3.8 The case officer will summarise the complaint and send that summary to the barrister under investigation for his response. This is a matter of obligation: rE15. All correspondence with the complainant should be obtained if it is not provided and the BSB asked to confirm that its summary of the complaint is the last word in the matter, so that the goalposts cannot be moved later on in the investigation.

3.9 The response to the summarised complaints should be measured, although there will always be exceptions to this sound rule of thumb. A complaint brought by another barrister may call for a more rigorous response and a different style. As stated above, it ought to be drafted by specialist disciplinary law counsel. It must engage with the issues and only the issues. Background should be relevant and not prolix. The response document may well be produced at the tribunal as evidence and so should be entirely consistent with the barrister's true account of events. Poor drafting may prove to be unexpectedly costly later at trial.

3.10. The response is sent to the complainant for comment. It is rare for those comments materially to alter the complexion of the case by this stage. However, sometimes excessive indulgence is shown for complainants and this should be resisted. They should not be permitted to recast their cases once the complaint has been summarised and answered by the barrister.

3.11 The response and comments on it are sent to a Case Examiner, formerly known, a little oddly, as a 'sponsor' barrister. He or she produces a report summarising the facts, analysing the issues, suggesting an outcome and, if appropriate, drafting outline charges.

The name of the Case Examiner is known only to the relevant staff and members within the BSB. It was stated by the BSB in one case that this is to prevent disgruntled people from attacking the Case Examiner, a curious argument which does not explain why Disciplinary Tribunals (or even judges) are not anonymised. More worryingly, this lack of transparency means that there is no way for the barrister under investigation to determine if the Case Examiner might be conflicted, even unwittingly and in an objective sense, or if in some way the doctrine of apparent bias may operate. A Case Examiner barrister who acts for the accused barrister X's frequent litigation adversary, would not be the right person to be seen to be making recommendations about the disposal of a serious complaint against X. This has actually happened. This is not obviously the kind of public service that commands such secrecy and is in contrast to the opportunity for challenge to panel members that *is* afforded at a full trial.

3.12 The report is discussed in a committee, now called an "Independent Decision-Making Body" or "IDB", but until 2019, the PCC (Professional Conduct Committee). In many cases, but not all, the committee follows the outcome proposed by the Case Examiner. One criticism of this procedure has been that the case papers, including the barrister's response to the complaint, including a response which may, on occasion, have been professionally drafted at some expense, are not read by the committee members in advance of the committee meeting, or at all. The case papers are not even copied for each committee member, but one bundle is available in the room for anyone who may wish to read it. It is thought that nobody usually does so. So the accuracy and comprehensiveness of the report of the Case Examiner is critical because it is usually the only document read by the other decision-makers.

3.13 If not provided, disclosure of that report should be sought in every case, at least to ensure that it was accurate when laid before the committee. The report used to be withheld altogether and, after several challenges,[1] changes were gradually made by the BSB, resulting first in partial disclosure of the report and, later, in the current position, whereby the report is disclosable in full. It can be a valuable resource.

3.14 The committee meeting is attended by the Case Officer. He or she takes notes. It is denied by the BSB that these are minutes properly so-called. But they should still be sought in every case. The BSB may strain not to provide them. So in most cases there will be no evidence of any discussion whatsoever, giving the impression that the Case Examiner's report is both the beginning and the end of any rational thought about the issues. If it is deficient – and some *are* deficient – or if it is jaundiced – and some *are* a little sarcastic, or even palpably dismissive of the barrister's explanation, without any forensic basis for being so, the barrister concerned may well become subject unjustly to public disciplinary proceedings.

3.15 A decision to prosecute is, in principle, susceptible to judicial review. This was tacitly accepted in *JR v BSB* [2012] EWCA Civ 320. In that case, the concern of JR (against whom all Charges were eventually withdrawn), was that the 'sponsor' report failed accurately to set out the true context of his discussions with the opposition advocate. So, in principle, if a Case Examiner's report has significantly misled the IDB, judicial review would lie (at least) to compel a freshly constituted IDB to consider a fresh Case Examiner's report.

3.16 The committee reaches a decision as to dismissal of the complaint, or whether to refer the matter to a Tribunal, whether 5-person or 3-person, or as to whether, say, to proffer advice. In doing so, it applies a two-fold test: (1) is there is a realistic prospect of a finding of 'professional misconduct' being made and (2) having regard to the regulatory objectives, is it in the public interest to pursue disciplinary action? Test (1) is understood to be

---

1 In cases argued by the author

determined on the civil standard even in cases where the criminal standard still applies.

3.17 In moving to a new system with a smaller decision-making committee, it remains to be seen whether the problems above will be eliminated or compounded. Presumably, a smaller committee can more readily be furnished with all of the case papers and so will not need to be so reliant on the work of one person. And a smaller group can more readily minute its necessarily shorter discussions.

Administrative Sanctions

3.18 A possible outcome short of referral to a Tribunal is an "administrative sanction" under rE19. This could be a fine of up to £1,000 for an individual, or £1,500 for a BSB entity, or a warning or fixed penalty. After *Re P, a barrister* [2005] 1 WLR 3019, where it was held that an appeal panel could not lawfully include a serving PCC member, the Bar Council's PCC (the BSB's microcosmic precursor), had to disband its so-called summary panels. These were committees of three PCC members, who would conduct an inquisitorial process, held in private, at the end of which they had the power to reprimand a barrister. The illegality of that process, conceived before Article 6 of the ECHR was enacted into UK law by the Human Rights Act 1998, was that the Bar Council played investigator, prosecutor, judge and jury. As "judge", it was obviously not "independent" within Article 6.

3.19 By way of the "administrative sanction" procedure, the BSB has introduced something resembling the Bar Council's anachronistic and illegal summary panels. It is impossible to see how any sanction imposed by the BSB itself, thereby acting as investigator, prosecutor and judge, can be lawful. The *availability* of an appeal to an independent panel under rE54 *et seq* is a public lawyer's answer to this criticism, but at the point of investigation and imposition of the administrative sanction, the obvious illegality is not counteracted. The legality of a procedure for barristers should not depend on them having to appeal in every case.

3.20 It is not possible to understand how, given the *Re P* embargo in r.E144 on disciplinary decision-makers being concurrent Bar Council or BSB officers or advocates, that can be circumvented by the simple expedient of removing decision-making about internally imposed sanctions to the BSB's PCC, or to the PCC in its reincarnation, of the "Independent Decision-Making Body" and/or its staff, and away from the BTAS tribunals. The BSB labelling a BSB committee "Independent", does not make it independent of the BSB, although the nomenclature clearly recognises the legal obligation to *try* to achieve independence. From what the "Independent Decision-Making Body" is *meant* to be independent is far from clear. If it is intended that this new body is the Bar's Crown Prosecution Service, whilst the case officers are the Bar's Police, then rather more than a mere change of name would be required to achieve substantive independence.

3.21 The author's written submissions to the above effect in *J v BSB* (2017) resulted in these remarks being made by the panel:

> "…the Appeal Panel recognised that as an approved regulator, the BSB should have robust regulations and procedures enabling it to impose administrative sanctions without the risk of unnecessary challenge on procedural or natural justice grounds. It therefore observed (but without making any findings in that regard) that the BSB might wish to re-consider the processes and operation of the Administrative Sanction procedure; in particular the applicability of the common law to the processing of a *complaint* up to and before a decision is made to lay a charge with reference to the principles set out in the case of *In re P (a Barrister)* [2005] 1 WLR 3019."

CHAPTER FOUR
WHAT IS PROFESSIONAL MISCONDUCT?

4.1 In practice as in life we regularly use language that we do not pause to define. For those who practise in the field of professional discipline, we speak of "professional misconduct". Cast your eye down the list of the kinds of issues prosecuted by regulators and you will find a spectrum of offences from dishonesty to the most footling breach of a professional code. Many regulators will assert that all of these are cases of "professional misconduct". But if that is right, then we have systems of control that are based on strict liability, where intent and degree are irrelevant. It is right that save in respect of breaches of the Solicitors Accounts Rules, no such system pervades. What is required is a working definition of "professional misconduct" that sufficiently ensures that the full weight of a disciplinary process is brought to bear only on the most serious cases and that less serious cases are dealt with in some other way, such as a system of advice-giving. That is surely the essence of "outcomes focussed" and proportionate regulation.

4.2 The BSB Handbook, like the Code of Conduct before it, defines many things, but says little about the meaning of "professional conduct". It is defined as a breach of the Handbook by an applicable person which is not appropriate for disposal by way of the imposition of "administrative sanctions". This is despite judicial tests having been developed since 2013. These have set the bar for "professional misconduct" at a high level, but the Handbook appears not to reflect binding authority. It is to be found first in *AW v Bar Standards Board* (2013) unreported, an appeal to the Visitors to the Inns of Court, in which Sir Anthony May adopted and applied the Scottish test for professional misconduct:

12. Ms. Foster has helpfully assembled the authorities and direct reference to her skeleton argument for this appeal is appropriate and duly acknowledged. What follows comes, in the main, directly from paragraphs 18 to 28 of her skeleton argument. She submits as follows:

"18. The case law shows the courts have been astute to differentiate the isolated, albeit negligent, lapse from acceptable conduct from the serious kind of culpability which attracts the opprobrium of a finding of professional misconduct.

19. This consistent thread may be discerned throughout reported disciplinary law from the early cases. Thus in *Felix v. The General Dental Council* [1960] 2 AC 707 Lord Jenkins, speaking for the Board of Privy Council, said this of three examples of mistaken, over-charging by a dentist:

"To make good a charge of 'infamous or disgraceful conduct in a professional respect' in relation to such a matter as the keeping of the prescribed dental records it is not in their Lordships' view enough to show that some mistake has been made through carelessness or inadvertence in two or even three cases out of ... 424 patients treated during the period in which the mistakes occurred whether the carelessness or inadvertence consisted in some act or omission by the dentist himself or in his ill-advised delegation of the making of the relevant entries to a nurse or receptionist and omitting to check the forms to see that she had done as she was told."

"20. In that case the prosecution submitted:

'It is not contended that an isolated, careless mistake should come within the range of professional misconduct at all. Equally, it is not necessary to go so far as to prove fraud before an element of infamous or disgraceful conduct is important. An element of recklessness or complete irresponsibility in regard to these matters would equally amount to infamous or disgraceful conduct ...'

21. Likewise, 40 years later in *Preiss v. The General Dental Council* [2001] 1 WLR 1926 Lord Cooke of Thorndon said at paragraph 28 on page 1936C:

'It is settled that serious professional misconduct does not require moral turpitude. Gross professional negligence can fall within it. Something more is required than a degree of negligence enough to give rise to civil liability but not calling for the opprobrium that inevitably attaches to the disciplinary offence.'

And at paragraph 29:

'That for every professional man whose career spans, as this appellant's has, many years and many clients, there is likely to be at least one case in which for reasons good and bad everything goes wrong – and that this was his, with no suggestion that it was in any way representative of his otherwise unblemished record."'

Ms. Foster goes on:

"22. This passage was adopted and the reasoning applied in the case of a doctor who had failed, when answering an emergency call, to recognise the serious clinical signs of cyanosis in a severely depressed patient treated with Diazepam and Dihydrocodeine required an immediate visit or a 999 call. In that case the patient in fact died from a drug overdose; the Privy Council declined to say this was inevitably misconduct. The Board said in *Rao v.*

The General Medical Council (GMC) [2002] UKPC 65 at paragraph 17:

'For the purposes of the outcome of this appeal, their Lordships proceed on the basis that this was a borderline case of serious professional misconduct. It was based on a single incident. There was undoubted negligence but something more was required to constitute serious professional misconduct and to attach the stigma of such a finding to a doctor of some 25 years standing with a hitherto unblemished career.'

22. In the case of *Silver v. The General Medical Council* [2003] UKPC 33 the same reasoning was applied and the Privy Council replaced the finding of professional misconduct with a finding of none in a case where they recognised the importance of the fact that the events occurred in an isolated incident relating to one patient (albeit over a number of days) as compared with a number of patients over a longer period of time. They also reflected that it was relevant to take account of the professional's long period (some 40 years) of unblemished professional conduct"

24. More recently in *Nandi v. The GMC* [2004] EWHC 2317 (Admin) the same principles have been applied and the clear distinction between negligently falling below standards and misconduct upheld. It has been re-emphasised in that case by the High Court *per* Collins J that the court must:

'51. bear in mind and look at the whole picture. I have to look at the doctor's record as a whole, practising for 30 years. These were two instances some three years or more apart in a 30 year period. It may well be, and indeed it no doubt is the case on the findings of the Committee, which, as I have said, I regard as appropriate, that there was a falling below the standards, which no doubt Dr Nandi sets himself as well as being the standards that one would expect from a general practitioner, but I do not think that it can properly be regarded as serious within the appropriate test. It seems to me that the Committee has taken altogether too harsh a view of what happened here and, as their reasons show, have given more weight than they should to the matters which they refer to and have regarded a falling below the standards of practice set out in the guidance as itself sufficient to amount to serious professional misconduct.'

25. The cases", says Ms. Foster, "are not confined to the medical sphere. A finding of professional misconduct is a very serious matter for a legal professional. In recent consideration of the phrase in *Council of the Law Society of Scotland v. Scottish Legal Complaints Commission* [2010] CSIH 79 is [she suggests] a compelling authority. It emphasises the well established meaning:

' ... although professional misconduct is not defined, these words have long been understood to have the broad meaning attributed to them by Lord President (Emslie) in *Sharp v. The Law Society of Scotland* [1984] SC 129, where he said, delivering the opinion of the court, at pages 134 and 135:

'There are certain standards of conduct to be expected of competent and respectable solicitors. A departure from these standards which would be regarded by competent and reputable solicitors as **serious and reprehensible** may properly be categorised as professional misconduct.'"

13. Ms. Foster submits that:

> "26. 'Professional Misconduct' is clearly not, it is suggested, a phrase that is apt within legal practice to cover a mere slip, a single isolated error of judgment, or an act that does not infringe the spirit of the rule.
>
> 14. Ms. Foster then goes on to refer to two BSB Tribunal cases, one called [NS] and the other called [*In Re M*] where she abstracts quotations on the subject of discreditable conduct which she suggests not only support the submissions she is making but also, I think she would say, are inconsistent to an extent with the findings of the Tribunal in the present appeal. I do not set those out in detail.
>
> 15. We note that Mr. Tatford has drawn to our attention to a recent decision of The Visitors called [*TR*] *v. The Bar Standards Board* where Sir Raymond Jack, sitting with a Visitors Panel, has referred to the case of [NS] and questioned whether it can be taken quite as far as is suggested.
>
> 16. That does not, however, detract from the quite plain theme that comes from the other authorities to which Ms. Foster and now we have referred which are consistent and compelling and, in our judgment, require us to modify the literal effect of paragraph 907. I at least when it applies to paragraph 708(i) but in reality and logic the modification needs to apply throughout. The reason for this is the concept of **professional misconduct carries resounding overtones of seriousness, reprehensible conduct which cannot extend to the trivial.**"

4.3 So the conjunctive test of "serious and reprehensible" emerged from *AW*, a decision that received almost no publicity at the time and was not thereafter cited at disciplinary trials by the BSB at all in accordance with the duty, applicable to all barristers, to cite all authorities, even where they undermine one's case.

CHAPTER FOUR – WHAT IS PROFESSIONAL MISCONDUCT? • 67

4.4 Two unreported, public decisions of Bar Disciplinary Tribunals[1], applied the *Walker* test. In both, the barristers were acquitted. In the first decision, *BSB v JS* (2014), what was a technical breach of the old Code of Conduct by a barrister who declined to cooperate fully with the Legal Ombudsman's investigation of him, was excused by way of a complete acquittal by a panel chaired by Mr. Alan Steinfeld QC. The panel considered that the barrister had some considerable justification in requiring disclosure from the LeO *before* he replied to the complaint, rather than after the case officer had written her report.

4.5 In the second decision, *BSB v RC* (2016), conducted after the coming into force of the BSB Handbook, a Panel chaired by Mr. Rhodri Davies QC, had to consider the case of a barrister who had practised for 15 months without a practising certificate, (which, *prima facie*, is a criminal offence under section 14(1) of the Legal Services Act 2007). RC managed successfully to invoke the *AW* test by showing that the Bar Council's online renewal system had been defective and had led to him wrongly assuming that he had paid his certification fee, when in fact he had not. This was not mere mitigation, but was held to be a complete defence by applying *AW*. In neither case, did the BSB, as opposed to the defence, volunteer *AW* to the tribunal, which did not otherwise know about that case. However, in *BSB v RC*, the BSB expressly conceded through counsel appearing before the Disciplinary Tribunal, that *AW*, decided under the old Code of Conduct, also applied to the BSB's Handbook as the high threshold of misconduct that has to be reached before breaches of the Handbook will amount to 'professional misconduct'. This being so, one might have thought that by 2020, the definition of "professional misconduct" would have been amended accordingly in the Handbook, but not so. That appears to be intentional.

4.6 By late 2016, whilst the Visitors and two disciplinary tribunals had now adopted and applied the new test, the High Court had not done so in the context of the then new route of statutory

---
1 In which the author defended both of the barristers concerned.

appeal in section 24 of the Crime and Courts Act 2013. The appeal[2] in *SH v Bar Standards Board* [2017] 4 WLR 54 came before Lang J., two months after *BSB v RC*. In that case, the conduct involved alleged irritating and anti-social behaviour at a Chambers' party, but behind all this was, as the court found, a serious medical condition that reacted adversely with alcohol. Lang J said this:

> Ground 6: Did the Tribunal err in concluding that the facts proved against Mr *SH* met the high threshold of serious professional misconduct
>
> 49 The Tribunal correctly directed themselves that they had to be sure that the conduct proved amounted to professional misconduct, applying the criminal standard of proof ie beyond reasonable doubt.
>
> 50 The Handbook defines professional misconduct as follows: "(161) professional misconduct means a breach of this Handbook by a BSB regulated person which is not appropriate for disposal by way of the imposition of administrative sanctions, pursuant to section 5A."
>
> 51 In *[AW] v Bar Standards Board* (unreported) 19 September 2013, Sir Anthony May, the former Lord Justice of Appeal, sitting as a Visitor to the Inns of Court, considered the meaning of "professional misconduct" in an earlier edition of the Bar's Code of Conduct which was in similar terms. He concluded that on a literal interpretation, any breach of the Code however trivial would constitute professional misconduct. He held that this could not be the correct approach, saying:
>
> "11. consistent authorities (including, it appears, other decisions of Bar Standards Board Tribunals) have made clear that the stigma and sanctions attached to the concept

---

2 Drafted by the author

of professional misconduct across the professions generally are not to be applied for trivial lapses and, on the contrary, only arise if the misconduct is properly regarded as serious."

"16. the concept of professional misconduct carries resounding overtones of seriousness, reprehensible conduct which cannot extend to the trivial."

52 In *R (Remedy UK Ltd) v General Medical Council* [2010] EWHC 1245 (Admin); [2010] ACD 72 Elias LJ reviewed the authorities and said, at para 37:

"(1) Misconduct is of two principal kinds. First, it may involve sufficiently serious misconduct in the exercise of professional practice such that it can properly be described as misconduct going to fitness to practise. Second, it can involve conduct of a morally culpable or otherwise disgraceful kind which may, and often will, occur outwith the course of professional practice itself, but which brings disgrace upon the doctor and thereby prejudices the reputation of the profession."

53 Curiously, the Handbook does not contain any guidance on the meaning of professional misconduct, in particular, there is no reference to the requirement that the misconduct must be serious. However, it appears that the Tribunal was aware of this requirement, and applied it, since they dismissed the charges in respect of complainant D on the grounds that "we are not satisfied that the conduct in relation to these charges was sufficiently serious to meet the threshold of professional misconduct."

54 The Tribunal accepted that Mr SH did not intend his actions to cause offence to the complainants or to make them feel uncomfortable, however, they concluded that the lack of intent in his drunken state did not excuse his conduct. The Tribunal found that excessive consumption

of alcohol drove him to act as he did and his medical condition did not make a significant contribution to his conduct.

55 As I have already said, in the light of the further medical evidence adduced on appeal, I have concluded that the Tribunal misunderstood and misapplied the medical evidence, and thus assessed Mr SH's conduct on an erroneous basis. The medical evidence established, on the balance of probabilities, that his inappropriate, and at times offensive, behaviour was a consequence of his medical condition. It also established that his excessive consumption of alcohol was very likely to have been a response to the onset of his medical condition, and it probably had the unfortunate consequence of exacerbating his disinhibition and loss of judgment. In these circumstances, Mr SH's behaviour plainly was not reprehensible, morally culpable or disgraceful, as it was caused by factors beyond his control. In my judgment, it did not reach the threshold for a finding of serious professional misconduct.

4.7 *SH* places an obligation on the defence to explore with one's client the possible availability of factors which might at first blush appear to be mere mitigation. The availability of psychiatric and psychological expert evidence means that it may be possible in exceptional cases like *SH,* to achieve a much better understanding of the sometimes complex and subtle reasons for what might bluntly be termed "misconduct". The *AW* test is a conduit through which such matters may lead to an acquittal. The Bar is a profession made up of complex, highly strung individuals. They suffer from a high rate of mental illness. They are very vulnerable to complaints. Their job requires them, at times, to test the boundaries of what is regarded as the conventional. The job involves frequent judgment calls. Judgment may be clouded by mental ill-health. So it is vital that what is seen as 'misconduct' is flexible enough to respond benevolently in suitable cases.

4.8 The *AW / SH* approach was followed by a 3-judge Divisional Court in *SRA v Leigh Day and others* [2018] EWHC 2726 (Admin) at [157]-[158], [200] and [236].

4.9 The *AW / SH* test impacts on investigations as well as trials. Regulators regularly fail to test projected prospects of success according to a test of "serious reprehensibility". They are frequently not challenged to do so by those who advise professionals at the investigatory stage. This is mistaken.

Strict liability?

4.10 The much lamented leading expert on legal services law, the late Andrew Hopper QC, explained in a lecture jointly presented with the author in 2012[3], that the Solicitors Regulation Authority tended to view the disciplinary world as one in which any breach of a code required a sanction, in other words that the entire disciplinary regime ought to be one of strict liability. The question-begging definition of "professional misconduct" in the BSB's Handbook, which still chooses to ignore the above case-law definitions, suggests that the BSB is of a similar mindset, where what matters most is not guilt, but the scale of punishment. If so, this is a dangerous approach to professional discipline, because it would mean that every single act of negligence, for example, is not only actionable in damages, but should in parallel be prosecuted before a disciplinary tribunal. That view has now been held to be wrong: see, *SRA v Leigh Day & others* [2018] EWHC 2726 (Admin) at [158].

Negligence cases

4.11 Jurisprudentially, the only species of professional negligence that may warrant a disciplinary prosecution is in respect of acts or omissions by professionals that are both "serious" and "reprehensible" in all of the three pre-requisites of: (a) mental element,

---

3 *Public Access Bar Association,* Middle Temple (2012)

(b) deficient performance and (c) practical impact. This is reflected in the principles espoused by Jackson J. (as he then was) in *R (Calhaem) v General Medical Council* [2007] EWHC 2606 (Admin) at [39]. Not all instances of negligence are "professional misconduct." In *Wingate & Evans* v *SRA* [2018] EWCA Civ 366, Jackson LJ said this:

> 105. [SRA] Principle 6 is aimed at a different target from that of [SRA] Principle 2. Principle 6 is directed to preserving the reputation of, and public confidence in, the legal profession. It is possible to think of many forms of conduct which would undermine public confidence in the legal profession. Manifest incompetence is one example. A solicitor acting carelessly, but with integrity, will breach Principle 6 if his careless conduct goes beyond mere professional negligence and constitutes "manifest incompetence"; see *Iqbal* and *Libby*.

> 106. In applying Principle 6 it is important not to characterise run of the mill professional negligence as manifest incompetence. All professional people are human and will from time to time make slips which a court would characterise as negligent. Fortunately, no loss results from most such slips. But acts of manifest incompetence engaging the Principles of professional conduct are of a different order.

4.12 In the most serious cases, it will often be pointless to make submissions about "serious reprehensibility". But many disciplinary cases occupy a position at the equator of professional discipline. A case that has crossed that equator in the investigator's eyes may not have crossed it by any great distance, if at all. It is in those cases that the defence invocation of the *AW / SH* test is likely to be of most significance. The deployment of such an argument will often be made in the face of strong objection (even threats of dire consequences, in the author's experience) from the prosecutor. It requires courage and mettle to advance such points, but as can be seen from *JS* and *RC*, tribunals will give the issue serious consideration if the point is well taken, sometimes with positive results.

Triviality

4.13 As Warby J. put it in *FK v BSB* [2018] EWHC 2184 (Admin) at [36]:

> The authorities make plain that a person is not to be regarded as guilty of professional misconduct if they engage in behaviour that is trivial, or inconsequential, or a mere temporary lapse, or something that is otherwise excusable, or forgivable.

There will be cases where the triviality or even the vexatiousness of the allegation cries out for a robust application of the *AW / SH* test in a strike-out application under rE127. Examples of the kind of such vexatiousness that would respond to the test are the barrister who referred to local authority prosecutors as "Little Hitlers" in a private conversation and a barrister who, in a dispute with his gardener, threatened him with an order for costs. The BSB took these allegations very seriously, but neither case ever reached a trial.

4.14 But unchallenged, some cases will reach such trials, when they should not do so. So what was reported as the ludicrous prosecution by the BSB in 2019 of the senior law officer for Scotland, also a QC, for leaving his shotgun out of its cabinet, but within the confines of his own home, appears to have fallen into this category. A prosecution for doing something that is perfectly lawful, as in *O'C v BSB* (2012) Unrep. (barrister signing a statement of truth), despite the BSB earnestly trying to argue otherwise, would also fall into this category.

4.15 These are all examples of cases where a strike out application either did succeed, could have succeeded, or the BSB discontinued. If the BSB is unafraid to bring such cases, the defence should be unafraid to test them before the directions judge. Baker J helpfully articulated the relevant test at a strike-out application, as:

> Taking the case at its highest, is there a realistic prospect that a disciplinary tribunal, adopting the criminal standard of proof [or the civil standard, where now applicable], would find the case amounted to misconduct?

CHAPTER FIVE
THE CONDUCT STANDARDS

5.1 The structure of the BSB's Handbook is based on Core Duties supplemented by Conduct Rules which are accompanied by Guidance. Parts 1-3 of the Handbook list at the beginning the outcomes that the rules in that section are designed to achieve. The Core Duties and the rules are mandatory, whereas the Guidance is not. Failure to comply with the Guidance is not in itself a breach of the Handbook, but the barrister or authorised body may need to show how their obligations have been met if they depart from the Guidance. The outcomes are also not mandatory, but will be taken into account by the BSB when considering how to respond to alleged breaches.

The Core Duties

5.2 The BSB Handbook is based on an outcomes-focused and a risk-based approach to regulation. The code contained within Part 2 of the Handbook includes the ten Core Duties ("CD") applicable to all barristers:

> CD 1: You must observe your duty to the court and the administration of justice.
>
> CD 2: You must act in the best interests of each client.
>
> CD 3: You must act with honesty and with integrity.
>
> CD 4: You must maintain your independence.
>
> CD 5: You must not behave in a way which is likely to diminish the trust and confidence which the public places in you or the profession.

CD 6: You must keep the affairs of each client confidential.

CD 7: You must provide a competent standard of work and service to each client.

CD 8: You must not discriminate unlawfully against any person.

CD 9: You must be open and co-operative with your regulators.

CD 10: You must take reasonable steps to manage your practice, or carry out your role within your practice, competently and in such a way [as] to achieve compliance with your legal and regulatory obligations.

5.3 These Core Duties underpin the Handbook and the BSB's entire regulatory framework

5.4 Charges of professional misconduct are brought under the Core Duties and/or the rules, usually both.

Regulatory Objectives

5.5 The Handbook also refers to "Regulatory objectives". These have the meaning given to them by section 1 of the Legal Services Act 2007 and consist of the following objectives:

(a) protecting and promoting the public interest;

(b) supporting the constitutional principle of the rule of law;

(c) improving access to justice;

(d) protecting and promoting the interests of consumers;

(e) promoting competition in the provision of legal services;

(f) encouraging an independent, strong, diverse and effective legal profession;

(g) increasing public understanding of the citizen's legal rights and duties; and

(h) promoting and maintaining adherence to the professional principles.

The professional principles

5.6 The "professional principles" are

(a) that authorised persons should act with independence and integrity,

(b) that authorised persons should maintain proper standards of work,

(c) that authorised persons should act in the best interests of their clients,

(d) that persons who exercise before any court a right of audience, or conduct litigation in relation to proceedings in any court, by virtue of being authorised persons, should comply with their duty to the court to act with independence in the interests of justice, and

(e) that the affairs of clients should be kept confidential.

CD 3: Dishonesty cases

5.7 A finding of dishonesty is almost always likely to result in a disbarment. So the determination of the meaning of dishonesty may be vital, although experience suggests that contesting the facts is usually more significant than technical tests.

5.8 The approach to dishonesty cases has recently changed. The old two-stage test in *R v Ghosh* [1982] QB 1053 was: (1) were D's actions dishonest by the standards of ordinary and honest people? If yes, then (2), did D realise that what he was doing was by those standards dishonest? If yes, then D would be convicted. That test was adopted in disciplinary cases until the 1990s.

5.9 In the mid-1990s, disciplinary tribunals began to follow the lead of the House of Lords in breach of trust cases, where third parties are sued for dishonestly assisting in a breach of trust. In *Royal Brunei Airlines v Tan* [1995] 2 AC 378, the House adopted an objective test. Dishonesty meant not acting as an honest person would act in the circumstances of the case.

5.10 In *Twinsectra Limited v Yardley* [2002] 2 AC 164, the House appeared to approve a subjective element and the requirement of a guilty mind on the part of the defendant. In *Barlow Clowes International v Eurotrust International* [2005] UKPC 37, the Privy Council disavowed any subjective element to the test.

5.11 In *Ivey v Genting Casinos (UK) Ltd t/a Crockfords* [2017] UKSC 67, at [74], the Supreme Court approved the test in *Royal Brunei Airlines* and *Barlow Clowes*:

> 74. ......the second leg of the test propounded in *R v Ghosh* [1982] QB 1053 does not correctly represent the law and that directions based upon it ought no longer to be given. The test of dishonesty is as set out by Lord Nicholls in *Royal Brunei Airlines.. v Tan* [1995] 2 AC 378 and by Lord Hoffmann in *Barlow Clowes International Ltd v Eurotrust International Ltd* [2006] 1 WLR 1476, para 10: see para 62 above. When dishonesty is in question the fact-finding tribunal must first ascertain (subjectively) the actual state of the individual's knowledge or belief as to the facts. The reasonableness or otherwise of his belief is a matter of evidence (often in practice determinative) going to whether he held the belief, but it is not an additional requirement

that his belief must be reasonable; the question is whether it is genuinely held.

When once his actual state of mind as to knowledge or belief as to facts is established, the question whether his conduct was honest or dishonest is to be determined by the fact-finder by applying the (objective) standards of ordinary decent people. There is no requirement that the defendant must appreciate that what he has done is, by those standards, dishonest.

Recklessness cases

5.12 In the criminal law, (a) a person is reckless if he is aware of a risk which does exist, or would exist, or (b) is reckless in respect of a result, if he is aware of a risk that it would occur, and if it was in the circumstances known to him, unreasonable to take the risk: *R v G* [2004] 1 AC 1034.

5.13 In the regulatory context, a professional person will be reckless if he is aware of a risk that his conduct breaches the rules, but continues with it nonetheless: *Brett v SRA* [2014] EWHC 2974; or takes a blinkered approach to risk: *Twinsectra supra* at [44]. As in the tort of deceit, the BSB may plead recklessness as a serious, but secondary, form of dishonesty, especially where the alleged dishonesty involved some written or oral misrepresentation. But it is rare for these cases to be fought other than on their facts.

Disintegrity cases

5.14 In CD3 honesty and integrity are bedfellows. As in paragraph 301 of the old Code of Conduct, where dishonesty and discreditability were bracketed together, there is a strong argument that "integrity" takes its colour from and so should be read *ejusdem generis* with "honesty". In *SH v BSB* [2017] 4 WLR 54 at [43], Lang J. accepted the author's written submissions to this effect and held:

43 Mr SH submitted that the Tribunal misconstrued the meaning of "integrity" in CD3. It was intended to cover professional integrity not personal/sexual morality. The term "integrity" must take its colour from the term "honesty" in CD3. An analogous submission was accepted in [*Bar Standards Board v S*] (unreported) 2009 by the Disciplinary Tribunal, chaired by Mr John Hendy QC, when considering paragraph 301 of an earlier iteration of the Code of Conduct which provided that a barrister must not engage in conduct which is "dishonest or otherwise discreditable to a barrister". The Tribunal held, at para 17:

'The juxtaposition of dishonesty and discreditableness is, in our view, significant. We do not think that the word discreditable has to be construed, as the lawyers would say, *ejusdem generis*, but we do think that the gravity of the conduct takes colour from the fact that the first description of the untoward conduct is 'dishonest'.'

44 Both parties relied upon the definition of "integrity" in the New Oxford English Dictionary as "the quality of being honest and having strong moral principles: moral uprightness". The BSB referred to *Scott v Solicitors Regulation Authority* [2016] EWHC 1256 (Admin) in which the Divisional Court upheld a finding that the financial irregularities committed by a solicitor were not dishonest but lacked integrity. Sharp LJ referred, at paras 37–39 to *Hoodless v FSA* [2003] UKFTT 007 (FSM) in which the Financial Services and Markets Tribunal said, at para 19:

'In our view 'integrity' connotes moral soundness, rectitude and steady adherence to an ethical code. A person lacks integrity if unable to appreciate the distinction between what is honest or dishonest by ordinary standards. (This presupposes, of course, circumstances where ordinary standards are clear. Where there are genuinely grey areas, a finding of lack of integrity would not be appropriate.)'

Sharp LJ agreed with the approach taken in *Solicitors Regulation Authority v Chan* [2015] EWHC 2659 (Admin) where Davis LJ declined to define integrity, concluding that a lack of integrity could be identified by reference to the facts of a particular case. I do not consider that this line of authorities assists the BSB since they concerned financial irregularities in the course of professional practice, and the charges of lack of integrity undoubtedly did "take their colour" from dishonesty. The issue raised in this case was not before the court in *Scott* or *Chan*.

45 I agree with the construction [of Mr Hendy QC] and, reading the core duties and rules as a whole, I consider that Mr SH's construction of CD3 is correct. "Integrity" in CD3 takes its colour from the term "honesty" in CD3 and connotes probity and adherence to ethical standards, not inappropriate and offensive social or sexual behaviour. In support of his construction chapter C2 is headed "Behaving ethically" and Rule rC9, which supplements CD3, only lists requirements which accord with Mr SH's construction, and does not list requirements which accord with the BSB's wider use of the term integrity to cover personal conduct unrelated to honesty or probity.

5.15. In *Wingate v Solicitors Regulation Authority* [2018] EWCA Civ 366, the Court of Appeal, summarised the law on integrity:

(1) Integrity is a broader concept than honesty. In professional codes of conduct, the term "integrity" is a useful shorthand to express the higher standards which society expects from professional persons and which the professions expect from their own members. The underlying rationale is that the professions have a privileged and trusted role in society. In return they are required to live up to their own professional standards;

(2) It is not possible to formulate an all-purpose, comprehensive definition of integrity. On the other hand, it is a counsel of despair to say: "Well you can always recognise it, but you can never describe it." The broad contours of what integrity means in the context of professional conduct, are now clearer. Integrity connotes adherence to the ethical standards of one's own profession. That involves more than honesty alone. The duty to act with integrity applies not only to what professional persons say, but also to what they do;

(3) Neither courts nor professional tribunals must set unrealistically high standards. The duty of integrity does not require professional people to be paragons of virtue. In every instance, professional integrity is linked to the manner in which that particular profession professes to serve the public;

(4) Just as a jury in a criminal trial is drawn from the wider community and is well able to identify what constitutes dishonesty, so a professional disciplinary tribunal has specialist knowledge of the profession to which the respondent belongs and of the ethical standards of that profession.

Accordingly such a body is well placed to identify a want of integrity. The decisions of such a body must be respected, unless it has erred in law.

5.16 Despite *SH*, a finding of disintegrity can be made even where an allegation of dishonesty is not made, or is not upheld: *Adetoye v SRA* [2019] EWHC 707 (Admin).

CD 7: Manifest incompetence cases

5.17 The reader should refer to chapter 4 on the meaning of "professional misconduct" and especially the cases of *R (Calhaem) v GMC* [2007] EWHC 2606 and *Wingate & Evans* v *SRA* [2018] EWCA Civ 366. Cases such as *JS v BSB* [2016] EWHC 3015 (Admin), in which a barrister was accused, ultimately unsuccessfully, of what one might call, 'professional misconduct negligence' in the drafting of and advising on a matrimonial consent order, are still rare. The "manifest incompetence" test in *Wingate* should maintain the *status quo*. It is desirable in policy terms that the BSB does not allow itself to be a dry (and cost-free) run for every potential claim of negligence.

Poor Service

5.18 CD7 cases of poor "service" may tend to spring from Legal Ombudsman referrals.

CD 8

5.19 CD8 cases will be judged against the criteria in the Equality Act 2010. Some of these cases are very serious, albeit the use of racist language often appears to accompany the consumption of large quantities of alcohol. It is submitted that *race* discrimination must be clear and obvious: this is not an arena in which the BSB should advance fine distinctions or test novel contentions.

5.20. A trend in 2019 in the solicitors' profession was for the SRA to prosecute cases of younger women complaining about advances by older men. But these would more likely be CD5 cases than cases of sexual discrimination.

CD 5

5.21 The test for determining a breach of CD5 is an objective one based on the hypothesis that a reasonable member of the public would discover and so be able to evaluate the conduct in question: see *RC v BSB* (2014) Visitors to the Inns of Court, Unrep., for the approach under the corresponding provision of the old Code of Conduct. This hypothetical member of the public is not unlike the fair minded and informed observer in the law of bias – an extension, unavoidably and necessarily, of the Tribunal's subjective views and collective values.

5.22 Such cases may encompass a broad spectrum of potential allegations.

5.23 As at 2020, there have been quite frequent examples of barristers not disguising their professional status on social media and making controversial or abusive remarks online. It is perhaps paradoxical that the use of electronic disguise is the apparently permissible – and clearly necessary - corollary of the BSB's stance. In one case, a barrister was unmasked by an interloper and the BSB prosecuted him to conviction, even though it appears that he had disguised his barrister status online. That approach seems questionable. The CD5 objective bystander does not have x-ray vision.

5.24 The BSB takes a hard line over anything that is alleged to be offensive on social media. This may include the expression of opinion in political debate. The extent to which a barrister's right to freedom of expression enshrined in Article 10 of the ECHR may be violated by over-ready use of CD5 will be considered in chapter 8 on Human Rights.

Vicarious liability in conduct

5.25 In *Akodu v SRA* [2009] EWHC 3588 (Admin), the Divisional Court held that the doctrine of vicarious liability has no application in professional conduct. Status liability does not apply because professional misconduct is about *personal* fault. This critical point has not been developed in over 10 years of subsequent case law.

5.26. This raises questions for the Bar. When, if ever, should a barrister be liable in conduct for the default of his clerk? When, if ever, should a BSB entity, or its Director, be liable in conduct for the default of one of its employees? These are matters to be worked out.

5.27 If a barrister has been convicted by the SDT *qua* solicitor for the defaults of other solicitors, when the *Akodu* point was not taken on his behalf, and is prosecuted at the BTAS tribunal *qua* barrister for what he did *qua* solicitor and *then* takes the *Akodu* point, does he have a defence?

CHAPTER SIX
TRIAL PREPARATION AND CONDUCT

Pre-trial

The Charges

6.1 The BSB is given up to 10 weeks to serve its charges from the date of the decision to prosecute. Since the Case Examiner drafts charges for the Independent Decision-Making Body, which approves or amends them, it is not understood why the BSB needs so long to serve charges which, in many (if not, most) cases, already exist at the point of the decision to prosecute. Those 10 weeks may be a time of real anguish for the waiting accused. They serve no obvious purpose.

Directions

6.2 A directions hearing will be notified. It should only rarely be treated as a formality. Standard Directions are at Annexe 6 to the Disciplinary Tribunals Regulations. Sometimes, the BSB may try to impose one-sided directions such as a direction that the defence serves its witness statements first. This is because clause 4 of the standard directions is clumsily drafted:

> 4. Within 42 days, ie by [date], the respondent must provide a copy of the documents and a list of witnesses, on which and on whom they intend to rely, and copies of any witness statements on which they intend to rely.
>
> The BSB is to provide copies of any witness statements on which it intends to rely within 42 days, i.e. by [date], if required;

6.3 Given the burden of proof, there is a very strong argument that the BSB should serve its witness statements first. Given what happened in *R ([DM]) v Visitors to the Inns of Court* [2015] EWCA Civ 12, there should never be a direction that enables the BSB to fit its case around that of the defence. So even simultaneity of exchange of witness statements may cause unfairness in a disciplinary case, especially (but not only) where the charges are question-begging.

6.4 The directions are not written in stone. An oral directions hearing may well be desirable, especially if a r.E127 strike-out application or a disclosure application is contemplated.

Better Particulars

6.5 If the Charges are not properly particularised, they should be subjected to a Request for Further & Better Particulars. Clarity is vital. It is sometimes impossible properly to direct testimony, or a disclosure request, or a difficult search for documents, without better particulars of allegations, perhaps made intentionally vague by a prosecutor trying to keep its options open. If the BSB refuses to answer the Request, this should be raised at the directions stage and is a specific reason for an oral directions hearing: see rE118: "…..*an oral hearing [may] be held for the purpose of giving directions and taking such other steps as the Directions Judge considers suitable for the clarification of the issues before the Disciplinary Tribunal.*" It should never be necessary for an accused professional to speculate as to the meaning of allegations, or as to how they are to be proved. In *MS v General Council of the Bar* (2005) Visitors to the Inns of Court, 6th May, Unrep. Lindsay J. said this at [20]:

> It very well may not be right in a case so important to a barrister, his reputation and his livelihood, to require or expect him to jog backwards from the evidence supplied in advance of the hearing (still less to expect him to jog backwards from evidence given at the hearing or from other

sources) in order to understand the fundamentals of the nature of the case intended to be made against him. Nor is it sufficient to say that such was the material supplied to him in advance of the hearing that he could have established the nature of that case. It is, in our view, for the charges themselves to make those fundamentals clear.

6.6 In factually complex cases, where there are many sub-allegations, the defence should ask the BSB to cross-refer its written Opening or Skeleton Argument to the bundle, or even to produce a Scott Schedule: this was done in *BSB v AK* (2020) unrep. If the BSB refuses to do this, that may well reveal a deep-seated problem about its case.

Convening Order

6.7. The President of the Council of the Inns of Court must issue a Convening Order under rE132 in every case. Without it, the tribunal has no lawful authority over the accused barrister. It will name the panel members selected to hear the case. The seminal decision in *R (CR) v Bar Standards Board* [2014] EWCA Civ 163, is reflected in the current rules rE142 and rE143:

rE142

With the exception of judicial Chairs, the persons nominated by the President to sit on a Disciplinary Tribunal must be selected from the pool appointed by the Tribunal Appointments Body.

rE143

In deciding who will sit on the panel, the *President* may have regard to the nature of the charge(s) and/or application(s) being determined and to the identity of the respondent(s) against whom the charges have been made……

Bias challenges

6.8 Under rE133, any panel member may be subject to challenge for good reason. In a relatively small profession, such a good reason might be apparent bias on the footing that the facts are such that the fair-minded and informed observer, having considered the relevant facts, would conclude that there was a real possibility that the tribunal was biased: see *Porter v Magill* [2002] 2 AC 357. But hopeless challenges should not be made. Indeed, even borderline or arguable challenges are high risk: the cost of an interesting bias challenge may be an inwardly or sub-consciously resentful panellist. Amongst veteran New York Attorneys, the philosophy that the advocate should, metaphorically, ensure that he or she can "shoot to kill" in recusal applications, or not "shoot" at all, is a good rule of thumb. That said, even in borderline cases, panellists sometimes err on the side of caution and recuse themselves regardless of the merits of the application. They are under an obligation to make disclosure of any connections that might be seen to undermine their independence. Lord Bingham explained this judicial obligation in *Davidson v Scottish Minsters* [2004] UKHL 24 at [19]:

> It is very important that proper disclosure should be made in such cases, first, because it gives the parties an opportunity to object and, secondly, because the judge shows, by disclosure, that he or she has nothing to hide and is fully conscious of the factors which might be apprehended to influence his or her judgment.

6.9 The issues revealed by the 2013 Browne Report and the changes wrought in the machinery of Bar discipline from 2014, that banned those involved in the work of the Bar Council and BSB from sitting on Disciplinary Tribunals, ought to make bias challenges very rare. But the same could have been said after *Re P (a barrister)* [2005] 1 WLR 3019. Despite the emphatic judgment of Colman J., that a serving PCC member could not lawfully sit on an appeal panel, lessons were still not learnt. By 2011, the

Institute of Legal Executives still conflated the regulatory functions of their representative body with disciplinary offices. So in *R (K) v ILEX* [2012] 1 All ER 1435, the Court of Appeal extended *Re P* and held that it was unlawful for those serving in council roles to sit in judgment as panellists in disciplinary cases. It was submitted successfully that the Vice Chair of ILEX was automatically disqualified as a 'judge in her own cause' (based on Lord Hoffmann's famous disqualification in *Reg. v Bow Street Magistrate, Ex p. Pinochet (No. 2)* [2000] 1 AC 119) and/or the doctrine of apparent bias had that effect. Rix LJ said this at [43]:

> [43] In my judgment Mr Beaumont's submissions are in the main to be preferred.......[44] I am somewhat sceptical that the two doctrines for which *Ex p Pinochet (No 2)* and *Porter v Magill* stand as authority remain to this day separate doctrines. There is force in Lord Hope's observations in [*Meerabux v A-G of Belize* [2005] UKPC 12], that if the *Porter v Magill* development had been available to their Lordships in *Ex p Pinochet (No 2)* then it would have been to that doctrine to which they would more naturally have turned. It remains true, however, that even in *Meerabux's case* Lord Hope continued to give separate treatment to the two doctrines. Nevertheless, in a matter which has everything to do with the necessary perception of justice, it would seem odd to me if the two doctrines rendered different results. They did not in *Re P* (although one result was ratio and the other was fully reasoned obiter dictum), nor did they in *Meerabux's case* itself. Lord Hope in *Meerabux's case* himself suggested that the result in *Ex p Pinochet (No 2)* could have been derived under either doctrine. In my judgment there is also force in Lord Bingham's analysis in *Davidson's case* where as it seems to me he seeks to reconcile the two doctrines in terms of the disqualifying presence of some factor, interest or influence 'which could prevent the bringing of an objective judgment to bear, which could distort the judge's judgment', and where this factor, interest or influence must necessarily be assessed as a

matter of appearances and of perception. As Lord Bingham remarked ([2004] HRLR 34 at [7]): 'In maintaining the confidence of the parties and the public in the integrity of the judicial process it is necessary that judicial tribunals should be independent and impartial and also that they should appear so'. So it was that in *Ex p Pinochet (No 2)*, in the context of an application of the automatic disqualification doctrine, Lord Browne-Wilkinson invoked Lord Hewart's famous dictum about the importance of appearances. It goes without saying that actual bias must disqualify. What is more difficult to define is the test to apply to disqualifying circumstances which may be argued to have the appearance of bias.

[45] In these circumstances, it seems to me that by now it may be possible to see the two doctrines which remain in play in this appeal as two strands of a single over-arching requirement: that judges should not sit or should face recusal or disqualification where there is a real possibility on the objective appearances of things, assessed by the fair-minded and informed observer (a role which ultimately, when these matters are challenged, is performed by the court), that the tribunal could be biased. On that basis the two doctrines might be analytically reconciled by regarding the 'automatic disqualification' test as dealing with cases where the personal interest of the judge concerned, if judged sufficient on the basis of appearances to raise the real possibility of preventing the judge bringing an objective judgment to bear, is deemed to raise a case of apparent bias. I do not think that Lord Bingham regarded the automatic disqualification rule as necessarily technical (although no doubt it could be applied in a formalistic way), but be that as it may Lord Hope showed the way to avoid formalism in *Meerabux's case*, and I note that Lord Bingham sought to avoid technicality by qualifying the disabling personal interest by the phrase 'which is not negligible'.

[46] Therefore I do not see the present case as one where it is necessary to choose between the doctrines. Applying either test, I would conclude that Miss Gordon-Nicholls, the vice-president of ILEX, was disqualified by her leading role in ILEX, and thus her inevitable interest in ILEX's policy of disciplinary regulation, from sitting on a disciplinary or appeal tribunal. Subject to the necessary hesitation that the different opinion of Foskett J engenders, I have by the end of the helpful oral argument in this case really no doubt that the fair-minded and informed observer ought to have and would have concluded that there was here a real possibility of bias. Or to put it in Lord Bingham's terms, he or she would be concerned that there was here the appearance and perception and indeed reality that through Miss Gordon- Nicholls the IAT was not free of an influence which could prevent the bringing of an objective judgment to bear. I note in particular that in *Meerabux's case* Lord Hope cited with approval Shetreet's distinction (Shimon Shetreet *Judges on Trial* (1976) p 310) between 'active involvement in the affairs of an association and mere membership' ([2005] 4 LRC 281 at [24], [2005] 2 AC 513).

6.10 The fair minded and informed observer is a judicial construct, described by Lord Hope in *Helow v Home Secretary* [2008] 1 WLR 2417, in this memorable way:

> 1...the fair-minded and informed observer is a relative newcomer among the select group of personalities who inhabit our legal village and are available to be called upon when a problem arises that needs to be solved objectively. Like the reasonable man whose attributes have been explored so often in the context of the law of negligence, the fair-minded observer is a creature of fiction. Gender-neutral (as this is a case where the complainer and the person complained about are both women, I shall avoid using the word

"he"), she has attributes which many of us might struggle to attain to.

2 The observer who is fair-minded is the sort of person who always reserves judgment on every point until she has seen and fully understood both sides of the argument. She is not unduly sensitive or suspicious, as Kirby J observed in *Johnson v Johnson* (2000) 201 CLR 488, 509, para 53. Her approach must not be confused with that of the person who has brought the complaint. The "real possibility" test ensures that there is this measure of detachment. The assumptions that the complainer makes are not to be attributed to the observer unless they can be justified objectively.

But she is not complacent either. She knows that fairness requires that a judge must be, and must be seen to be, unbiased. She knows that judges, like anybody else, have their weaknesses. She will not shrink from the conclusion, if it can be justified objectively, that things that they have said or done or associations that they have formed may make it difficult for them to judge the case before them impartially.

3 Then there is the attribute that the observer is informed. It makes the point that, before she takes a balanced approach to any information she is given, she will take the trouble to inform herself on all matters that are relevant. She is the sort of person who takes the trouble to read the text of an article as well as the headlines. She is able to put whatever she has read or seen into its overall social, political or geographical context. She is fair-minded, so she will appreciate that the context forms an important part of the material which she must consider before passing judgment.

6.11 The fair-minded and informed observer test gives a judge every opportunity to adopt an objective filter for his or her subjective opinion, that there was no apparent bias on his or her part, or on the part of the judge under appeal. The unavoidable subjective element of this process perhaps explains why most bias challenges fail. In *Locabail (U.K.) Ltd. v Bayfield Properties Ltd* [2000] QB 451 at [25], the Court of Appeal stated:

> It would be dangerous and futile to attempt to define or list the factors which may or may not give rise to a real danger of bias. Everything will depend on the facts, which may include the nature of the issue to be decided. We cannot, however, conceive of circumstances in which an objection could be soundly based on the religion, ethnic or national origin, gender, age, class, means or sexual orientation of the judge. Nor, at any rate ordinarily, could an objection be soundly based on the judge's social or educational or service or employment background or history, nor that of any member of the judge's family; or previous political associations; or membership of social or sporting or charitable bodies; or Masonic associations; or previous judicial decisions; or extra-curricular utterances (whether in textbooks, lectures, speeches, articles, interviews, reports or responses to consultation papers); or previous receipt of instructions to act for or against any party, solicitor or advocate engaged in a case before him; or membership of the same Inn, circuit, local Law Society or chambers (see *K.F.T.C.I.C. v. Icori Estero S.p.A.* (Court of Appeal of Paris, 28 June 1991, International Arbitration Report, vol. 6, 8/91)).

6.12 *Past* BSB or Bar Council members may not be disqualified from sitting in a case prosecuted by the BSB: *Ighalo v Solicitors Regulation Authority* [2013] EWHC 661 (Admin). But each case will turn on its own facts, including the actual role of the former BSB panellist and the number of years that have passed since retirement from office (in *Ighalo*, over 2 years). The Chair of a panel at a re-trial, whose former Pupilmaster was the Chair of the panel at trial that convicted and disbarred the barrister in question, for whom the Chair at the re-trial had natural feelings of respect, affection, gratitude and deference, was not disqualified on the basis of apparent bias: *DM v BSB* [2017] EWHC 969 (Admin).

6.13 The essence of apparent bias is unconscious bias of which the individual decision-maker may not even be aware. As Rix LJ put it in the *ILEX* case at [49]:

> ..the doctrines with which we are here concerned are to guard against the insidious effects of which those concerned are not even conscious.

In what was the leading case in this area before *Porter v Magill, R v Gough* [1993] AC 646, Lord Woolf said this about unconscious bias:

> It must be remembered that except in the rare case where actual bias is alleged, the court is not concerned to investigate whether or not bias has been established. Whether it is a judge, a member of the jury, justices or their clerk, who is alleged to be biased, the courts do not regard it as being desirable or useful to inquire into the individual's state of mind. It is not desirable because of the confidential nature of the judicial decision making, process. It is not useful because the courts have long recognised that bias operates in such an insidious manner that the person alleged to be biased may be quite unconscious of its effect

6.14 The fair-minded and informed observer would be cognisant of the risk of the impugned decision-maker not even being aware of his or her unconscious bias and the mental gymnastics that this entails on the part of the decision-maker, for whom the fair minded and informed observer is an extension of his or her own mind. He or she may perfunctorily think that a recusal application is hopeless, precisely because he or she is not in touch with what he or she does not realise about his or her own prejudices.

An immediate assumption of hopelessness may well itself be a clarion alarm bell that bias has invaded the judge's thinking.

6.15. There are three modern cases concerning the mores of the Bar in this field. In *Watts v Watts* [2015] EWCA Civ 1297, at [28], Sales LJ (as he then was), said this:

> The notional fair-minded and informed observer would know about the professional standards applicable to practising members of the Bar and to barristers who serve as part-time deputy judges and would understand that those standards are part of a legal culture in which ethical behaviour is expected and high ethical standards are achieved, reinforced by fears of severe criticism by peers and potential disciplinary action if they are departed from: *Taylor v Lawrence* [2001] EWCA Civ 119, [33]-[36]; *Taylor v Lawrence* [2002] EWCA Civ 90; .....[61]-[63]....

In *Azumi v Vanderbilt and others* [2017] EWHC 45 (IPEC), a Recorder, sitting as a Deputy High Court Judge, refused an application to recuse himself on the ground that he shared chambers with Counsel for the claimant. He held, applying the test in *Watts*, that a fair-minded observer would have been aware of the professional standards shared between colleagues and would not form a perception of bias (at [16]). In *Siddiqui v Oxford University Chancellor, Masters and Scholars* [2016] EWHC 3451, Kerr J. refused to recuse himself from a university's application to strike out and for summary judgment when: (1) he had attended the university 30 years before, (2) had represented the university in the past when he was junior counsel and (3) until shortly before the hearing had been in the same chambers as leading counsel for the university. Kerr J. held that there was no risk of bias. He had attended the university a long time before and had been in a different college from that of the claimant in the case, with which he was being asked to deal, he could not recall anything of the case which he had done for the university and, as to the third ground, it was, "*commonplace in litigation in these courts for a member of a chambers to appear before a judicial tribunal comprising a former member of that person's chambers*" (at [19]). Kerr J. said at [10]:

> An application of this kind raises important issues. On the one hand, it is fundamental to our system of justice and to the rule of law itself that every party coming before the courts can be confident of an independent and impartial tribunal. Judges swear an oath of office, including a pledge to do justice without fear or favour, affection or ill-will. No-one should feel inhibited about insisting on their right to impartial justice. On the other hand, it is also of public importance that the law and the administration of justice is not undermined or brought into disrepute by a party trying to pick the constitution of the court, in the hope of getting a judge who, the party thinks, will be more likely than the assigned judge to favour that party's cause; or it may be, in the hope that an assigned judge who is asked to stand down on grounds that lack merit, will take the line of least resistance and accede to the request as a matter of listing convenience. The Court of Appeal has emphasised that a judge should not stand down as a matter of convenience where grounds for recusal do not exist.

6.16 None of the above affects cases of actual bias. This is an area of the law that appears to generate strong feelings, sometimes directed towards the defence. In barrister disciplinary cases, the most likely cases of actual bias will arise from excessive judicial statements in the nature of partiality or prejudgment for one side or the other, or apparent hostility towards one party or the other, or perhaps their legal representatives.

6.17 The bias of one panel member is often regarded as capable of tainting all of them: *In re Medicaments and Related Classes of Goods (No.2)* [2001] 1 WLR 700 at [99]. The possibility of this having transpired, must always be thought through on the facts of the instant case. The usual practice in public law is that once apparent bias is found, the taint is held to 'infect' the whole panel.

6.18 Any basis for objection on grounds of bias must be taken when it arises. It cannot be saved up for appeal: *DM v BSB* [2017] EWHC 969 (Admin) at [47]. A conscious decision to do that may well be held to constitute a public law waiver of any right to object to the impugned panellist: *Locabail supra* at [15] and [26].

6.19 The antecedents of panel members are published at https://www.tbtas.org.uk/about-us/who-we-are/panel-members/.
It is always worth researching one's Tribunal, whether or not a bias issue may arise.

Reluctant witnesses

6.20 Thought should be given well before trial as to whether any witnesses are likely to be reluctant to attend the hearing. In the Visitors' appeal in *CR v BSB* (2013) 23rd May, (Wyn Williams J., Chair), it was held at [85], after a BSB concession, that even though the Tribunal has no such power, the High Court has power to order a witness to attend the Disciplinary Tribunal by virtue of CPR 34.4, which provides:

Witness summons in aid of inferior court or of tribunal

(1) The court may issue a witness summons in aid of an inferior court or of a tribunal.

(2) The court which issued the witness summons under this rule may set it aside.

(3) In this rule, 'inferior court or tribunal' means any court or tribunal that does not have power to issue a witness summons in relation to proceedings before it.

Abuse of process

6.21 All disciplinary tribunals have an inherent power to stay proceedings before them on the basis of abuse of process: *R v Metropolitan Police Disciplinary Tribunal ex parte The Police Complaints Authority* (1993) 5 Admin LR 225. Applications for a stay on the basis of abuse of process may be raised either under rE127 at the directions stage, or at the outset of a trial. The criteria were re-stated by Lord Dyson JSC in *R v Maxwell* [2010] UKSC 48 at [13]:

> It is well established that the court has the power to stay proceedings in two categories of case, namely (i) where it will be impossible to give the accused a fair trial, and (ii) where it offends the court's sense of justice and propriety to be asked to try the accused in the particular circumstances of the case.

6.22 Category, (i) might extend to cases where, for example, the BSB's newly minted power to prosecute, apparently without limitation of time, has resulted in the disappearance of witness testimony or the destruction of relevant documents. Another example might be where the BSB's own defective investigation has resulted in the loss of evidence, or in the contamination of witness testimony. This may occur where the function of the prosecutor is misunderstood and a complainant is treated over-sympathetically, not merely as a witness, but as a *de facto* client. Such a mindset might first manifest itself at the tribunal suite in lengthy private discussions between BSB personnel and/or advocates with a key witness of fact. Or there might be internal 'unused material' served by the BSB to similar effect that crosses the line from permissible familiarisation to illegitimate coaching. This was held to be unlawful by the Court of Appeal in *R v Momodou* [2005] 1 WLR 3442, as was showing the witness statements of a defence witness to prosecution witnesses and asking them to comment on them: see Judge LJ (as he then was) at [61] *et seq*. Such principles apply to disciplinary cases: *Regina (Green) v Police Complaints Authority* [2004]

1 WLR. 725 HL. If the prosecutor will not reveal the extent of such contact where there is some good reason to suspect it, then questions can be asked about it in cross-examination, sometimes with illuminating results.

6.23 Even if such an abuse of process application might fall a little short of *Maxwell* (i), the issue of witness contamination might be capable of being worked out as an issue in the trial itself, as going to the weight and reliability of the evidence. In this respect, the absence of corroborative documentation may be significant: see the illuminating discussion by Leggatt J. (as he then was) in the case of *Gestmin SA* v *Credit Suisse (UK) Ltd* [2013] EWHC 3560 (Comm) at paragraphs 16 to 22 of his judgment:

Evidence based on recollection

> 15. An obvious difficulty which affects allegations and oral evidence based on recollection of events which occurred several years ago is the unreliability of human memory.
>
> 16. While everyone knows that memory is fallible, I do not believe that the legal system has sufficiently absorbed the lessons of a century of psychological research into the nature of memory and the unreliability of eyewitness testimony. One of the most important lessons of such research is that in everyday life we are not aware of the extent to which our own and other people's memories are unreliable and believe our memories to be more faithful than they are. Two common (and related) errors are to suppose: (1) that the stronger and more vivid is our feeling or experience of recollection, the more likely the recollection is to be accurate; and (2) that the more confident another person is in their recollection, the more likely their recollection is to be accurate.
>
> 17. Underlying both these errors is a faulty model of memory as a mental record which is fixed at the time of

experience of an event and then fades (more or less slowly) over time. In fact, psychological research has demonstrated that memories are fluid and malleable, being constantly rewritten whenever they are retrieved. This is true even of so-called 'flashbulb' memories, that is memories of experiencing or learning of a particularly shocking or traumatic event. (The very description 'flashbulb' memory is in fact misleading, reflecting as it does the misconception that memory operates like a camera or other device that makes a fixed record of an experience.) External information can intrude into a witness's memory, as can his or her own thoughts and beliefs, and both can cause dramatic changes in recollection. Events can come to be recalled as memories which did not happen at all or which happened to someone else (referred to in the literature as a failure of source memory).

18. Memory is especially unreliable when it comes to recalling past beliefs. Our memories of past beliefs are revised to make them more consistent with our present beliefs. Studies have also shown that memory is particularly vulnerable to interference and alteration when a person is presented with new information or suggestions about an event in circumstances where his or her memory of it is already weak due to the passage of time.

19. The process of civil litigation itself subjects the memories of witnesses to powerful biases. The nature of litigation is such that witnesses often have a stake in a particular version of events. This is obvious where the witness is a party or has a tie of loyalty (such as an employment relationship) to a party to the proceedings. Other, more subtle influences include allegiances created by the process of preparing a witness statement and of coming to court to give evidence for one side in the dispute. A desire to assist, or at least not to prejudice, the party who has called the witness or that party's lawyers, as well as a

natural desire to give a good impression in a public forum, can be significant motivating forces.

20. Considerable interference with memory is also introduced in civil litigation by the procedure of preparing for trial. A witness is asked to make a statement, often (as in the present case) when a long time has already elapsed since the relevant events. The statement is usually drafted for the witness by a lawyer who is inevitably conscious of the significance for the issues in the case of what the witness does nor does not say. The statement is made after the witness's memory has been "refreshed" by reading documents. The documents considered often include statements of case and other argumentative material as well as documents which the witness did not see at the time or which came into existence after the events which he or she is being asked to recall. The statement may go through several iterations before it is finalised. Then, usually months later, the witness will be asked to re-read his or her statement and review documents again before giving evidence in court. The effect of this process is to establish in the mind of the witness the matters recorded in his or her own statement and other written material, whether they be true or false, and to cause the witness's memory of events to be based increasingly on this material and later interpretations of it rather than on the original experience of the events.

21. It is not uncommon (and the present case was no exception) for witnesses to be asked in cross-examination if they understand the difference between recollection and reconstruction or whether their evidence is a genuine recollection or a reconstruction of events. Such questions are misguided in at least two ways. First, they erroneously presuppose that there is a clear distinction between recollection and reconstruction, when all remembering of distant events involves reconstructive processes. Second, such questions disregard the fact that such processes are largely uncon-

scious and that the strength, vividness and apparent authenticity of memories is not a reliable measure of their truth.

22. In the light of these considerations, the best approach for a judge to adopt in the trial of a commercial case is, in my view, to place little if any reliance at all on witnesses' recollections of what was said in meetings and conversations, and to base factual findings on inferences drawn from the documentary evidence and known or probable facts. This does not mean that oral testimony serves no useful purpose – though its utility is often disproportionate to its length. But its value lies largely, as I see it, in the opportunity which cross-examination affords to subject the documentary record to critical scrutiny and to gauge the personality, motivations and working practices of witness, rather than in testimony of what the witness recalls of particular conversations and events. Above all, it is important to avoid the fallacy of supposing that, because a witness has confidence in his or her recollection and is honest, evidence based on that recollection provides any reliable guide to the truth

6.24 *Maxwell* (ii) cases may well be rare. But to the author's knowledge, there have been occasions of heinous prosecutorial misconduct in which *Maxwell* (ii) has been, or might have been, engaged. In the case of the BSB, one recalls for example the suppression of a witness statement in *R ([DM]) v Visitors to the Inns of Court* [2015] EWCA Civ 12, which led Burnett LJ (as he then was) to say this:

15. [M] provided his response to the complaint which in turn was sent to ST [M's ex-client] for comment. The BSB then made preparations for the hearing itself. No statement was ever taken from ST but TA [ST's husband] provided a 49 paragraph statement in June 2010. He did not sign or date it but a decision was taken by the BSB not to disclose it.

The reason was candidly stated in a letter to ST dated 27 July 2010: *"We have decided that we will not disclose Tim's witness statement until shortly before the hearing date. This will remove the possibility of [M] fitting his case around that statement."* The point was repeated in another letter of 26 August 2010.

Instead, directions were agreed which enabled the 'prosecution' case to be presented in a bundle of documents (i.e. the complaint, the responses and the disclosed emails etc) with ST and TA attending for cross-examination, but with provision for the BSB to serve further evidence in advance of the hearing.

[M] was required to serve statements and any documents on which he relied by 31 July 2010.

16. It was in those circumstances that [M] served his detailed statement and bundle without sight of TA's first statement. TA was then provided with a copy of [M's] statement and bundle [nb: a violation of *Momodou*]. TA's second witness statement of 158 paragraphs dated 29 October is an amalgam of evidence properly so called, comment and argument intended to demolish [M's] defence to the charges, rather than to provide unvarnished evidence. It was this document that stood as TA's evidence in chief. The first statement remained undisclosed.

17. What happened was extraordinary. A conscious decision was taken by an official at the BSB which had the effect of subverting the rules which provide for disclosure and furthermore suggested that he was blind to any sense of fairness in the conduct of a disciplinary prosecution. To my mind, that was compounded by inviting a witness to assume the role of surrogate prosecutor by producing a statement of the sort I have described. Moses LJ drew an analogy between disciplinary proceedings of this nature and

criminal proceedings. To my mind that is entirely apt, if not exact, and supports the suggestion that scrupulous standards are required of the BSB acting as prosecutor. This Tribunal was concerned with very serious allegations which had the potential to destroy a professional reputation and bring to an end a professional career, even though its decision could not result in a criminal conviction.

6.25 Irregular conduct may on occasion extend to documents as well as to witness statements or previous inconsistent statements. In the appeal of *AV v Bar Standards Board* [2011] All ER (D) 223, the Visitors to the Inns of Court chaired by Thirlwall J. (as she then was) noted:

Failures of disclosure by the BSB

23. At the hearing on 25th June 2007 the BSB disclosed part of an email to the BSB from Ms Chew, the trainee who had recorded a number of relevant conversations. The rest of the email was disclosed at the beginning of the hearing before us on 19th April 2011 together with an email to Ms Chew from the BSB of 27th June.

24. On 23rd July 2007, i.e. just over a month after the hearing and without explanation the BSB served on [AV] a file note of 27th June 2006 recording discussions between the BSB and Ms Ho.

25. At the start of the hearing before us on 19th April 2011, in addition to the emails to which we refer at paragraph 23 the BSB disclosed to [AV] and his legal team notes of contact between Ms Ho and the BSB on 27 June 2006, 3 July 2006, 19 July 2006, 26 July 2006. This was done on the advice of Mr Elmer [BSB Counsel] after he had gone through the file when preparing for the hearing before us.

> 26. No reason was given by the BSB for the failure to disclose the file notes at the proper time. They plainly should have been disclosed before the hearing before the tribunal. The BSB must ensure that it complies with its disclosure obligations in all cases. They are responsible for the regulation of professionals who are entitled to expect, and indeed demand, that it conducts its own affairs with proper regard for the rules. That failure was unimpressive and unacceptable. It should not be repeated.

6.26 By way of example of *Maxwell* (ii) only, the author conducted a case before a different public regulatory tribunal in 2016 in which it was alleged that the prosecuting regulatory authority had sought, mid-trial, to amend the contract of the overall Chair of Conduct, who was chairing the case, to give him far more limited security of tenure, which apart from violating Article 6 of the ECHR, was said by that Chair in a witness statement to have pressurised him to conduct a "rigged" trial. The resulting abuse of process application under *Maxwell* (ii) led to the remaining charge being withdrawn.

Re-litigation and duplication

6.27 On occasion, those conducting disciplinary proceedings unyieldingly, may try to have a second bite at the cherry, having failed in a first prosecution. The matter may be *res judicata* in an orthodox sense. In *McFadden v UNITE the Union* (2019) UKEAT/0147/19/D, where the Union's position was that it could, in theory, prosecute indefinitely, the Union as prosecutor took such a stance:

> 35. For the Appellant, Mr Beaumont presented a powerful argument that the doctrine of *res judicata* applied to the Union's disciplinary procedures. For the Union, Mr Potter contended that the Certification Officer was right to hold that the doctrine does not apply. In answer to my questions, he acknowledged that the effect of his submis-

sions was that, even if the disciplinary panel had dismissed the charge against the Appellant under rule 27.1.7 (either on the basis that that rule did not apply or on the basis that it was not satisfied that the Appellant did slap the Complainant's bottom), then it would have been open to the Union to bring exactly the same charge before a differently-constituted disciplinary panel in the hope of achieving a different result.

6.28 That case exemplifies an attitude sometimes encountered amongst regulators who may develop over time a somewhat enhanced conception of 'the public interest' as a stated reason for attempted relitgation. But, as Lord Denning MR repeated in *Gouriet v Union of Post Office Workers* [1977] QB 729 at 762

> To every subject in this land, no matter how powerful, I would use Thomas Fuller's words over 300 years ago: "Be you ever so high, the law is above you"…

Cause of action estoppel as a rule of substantive law reflects the operation of the rule of law itself: *Virgin Atlantic v Zodiac Seats* [2014] 1 AC 160 at [25]. The rule of law here steps in through the mechanism of cause of action estoppel to prevent any oppression of the weak by the powerful. The same position obtains under ECHR Article 6. Judicial systems characterised by final judgments that are liable to review are in breach of Article 6 and the doctrine of legal certainty which is a fundamental aspect of the rule of law: *Sovtransavto Holding v Ukraine* [2004] 38 EHRR 44 at [74], [77] and [82].

6.29 The object of the rule of *res judicata* was said by Lord Blackburn in *Lockyer v. Ferryman* (1877) 2 App.Cas. 519, at 530, to be expressed by two principles: (a) *'interest reipublicae ut sit nis litium'* [in the interest of society as a whole, litigation must come to an end] and (b) *'nemo debet bis vexari pro una et eadem causa'* [may no-one be troubled twice for (one and) the same reason]. So the doctrine will palliate the tyranny of the mindset of bodies such as the Union in *McFadden.*

6.30 The doctrine of cause of action estoppel unarguably applies to disciplinary tribunals. Different formulations of charges based on the same underlying factual event will fall foul of the doctrine: *R (Coke-Wallis) v Institute of Chartered Accountants in England & Wales* [2011] UKSC 1. In *R (Mandic-Bozic) v British Association for Counselling & Psychotherapy & UK Council for Psychotherapy* [2016] EWHC (Admin) 3134, the doctrine was applied to prevent regulator B of Psychotherapist X, from proceeding on the same facts with the same complainant against X, when she had already been dealt with at length by regulator A and vindicated on the more serious charges. The doctrine encompasses the wider principle in *Henderson v Henderson* 3 Hare 100. Lord Sumption JSC explained that principle in *Virgin Atlantic v Zodiac Seats* [2014] 1 AC 160 at [18]:

> 18 It is only in relatively recent times that the courts have endeavoured to impose some coherent scheme on these disparate areas of law. The starting point is the statement of principle of Wigram V-C in *Henderson v Henderson* 3 Hare 100, 115. This was an action by the former business partner of a deceased for an account of sums due to him by the estate. There had previously been similar proceedings between the same parties in Newfoundland in which an account had been ordered and taken, and judgment given for sums found due to the estate. The personal representative and the next of kin applied for an injunction to restrain the proceedings, raising what would now be called cause of action estoppel. The issue was whether the partner could reopen the matter in England by proving transactions not before the Newfoundland court when it took its own account. Wigram V-C said, at pp 114—116:
>
> 'In trying this question, I believe I state the rule of the court correctly, when I say, that where a given matter becomes

the subject of litigation in, and of adjudication by, a court of competent jurisdiction, the court requires the parties to that litigation to bring forward their whole case, and will not (except under special circumstances) permit the same parties to open the same subject of litigation in respect of matter which might have been brought forward as part of the subject in contest, but which was not brought forward, only because they have, from negligence, inadvertence, or even accident, omitted part of their case. The plea of *res judicata* applies, except in special cases, not only to points on which the court was actually required by the parties to form an opinion and pronounce a judgment, but to every point which properly belonged to the subject of litigation, and which the parties, exercising reasonable diligence, might have brought forward at the time . . . Now, undoubtedly the whole of the case made by this bill might have been adjudicated upon in the suit in Newfoundland, for it was of the very substance of the case there, and prima facie, therefore, the whole is settled. The question then is, whether the special circumstances appearing upon the face of this bill are sufficient to take the case out of the operation of the general rule.'

19 Wigram V-C's statement of the law is now justly celebrated. The principle which he articulated is probably the commonest form of *res judicata* to come before the English courts. For many years, however, it was rarely invoked. The modern law on the subject really begins with the adoption of Wigram V-C's statement of principle by the Privy Council in *Yat Tung Investment Co Ltd v Dao Heng Bank Ltd* [1975] AC 581. *Yat Tung* was an appeal from Hong Kong, in which the appellant sought to unsuccessfully avoid the exercise by a mortgagee of a power of sale in two successive actions, contending on the first occasion that the sale was a sham and that there was no real sale, and on the second that the sale was fraudulent. Lord Kilbrandon,

giving the advice of the Board, distinguished at pp 589—590 between *res judicata* and abuse of process:

'The second question depends on the application of a doctrine of estoppel, namely *res judicata*. Their Lordships agree with the view expressed by McMullin J that the true doctrine in its narrower sense cannot be discerned in the present series of actions, since there has not been, in the decision in no 969, any formal repudiation of the pleas raised by the appellant in no 534. Nor was Choi Kee, a party to no 534, a party to no 969. But there is a wider sense in which the doctrine may be appealed to, so that it becomes an abuse of process to raise in subsequent proceedings matters which could and therefore should have been litigated in earlier proceedings.'

Lord Kilbrandon referred to the statement of Wigram V-C in *Henderson v Henderson* as the authority for the "wider sense" of *res judicata*, classifying it as part of the law relating to abuse of process.

6.31 The conduct of the prosecutor may generate a legitimate expectation that it will not proceed: *R v Croydon Justices ex parte Dean* [1994] 98 Cr App R 76. The Divisional Court there expressed the strong conclusion that there is a, *"clear public interest to be observed in holding officials of the state to promises made by them in full understanding of what is entailed by the bargain"*. Likewise, in *Postermobile v Brent LBC* (1997) *The Times* 8th December, it was stated by the Divisional Court that the, *"citizen should be able to rely on assurances given by public officials."* In the Crown Court, trials will be stopped as an abuse of process in such circumstances: *R v Robert Thomas* [1995] Crim LR 938. In *R v Bloomfield* [1997] 1 Cr App R 135, the Court of Appeal held that an indication that the prosecution would offer no evidence from which the CPS then tried to resile, would bring the administration of justice into disrepute, i.e. engaging *Maxwell* (ii). A well-recognised badge of abuse of civil process, is the unjust harassment of a party: see

Bradford & Bingley Building Society v Seddon [1999] 1 WLR 1482 at 1492.

Public Law defence

6.32 If the BSB fails to comply with its own rules of investigation in some material way that works to the prejudice of the investigated barrister, then that might amount to a serious procedural irregularity, which could be raised as a substantive defence at trial: see *Boddington v British Transport Police* [1999] 2 AC 143. For example, if it could be shown that there was no proper committee discussion of the barrister's carefully drafted response to the complaint made against him, that might be capable of being argued to be such a defence. Or it might be possible to challenge the legality of the Handbook rule under which the complaint is being considered: see *JH v BSB* (2011) Unrep. Visitors to the Inns of Court, 13th June, *per* Baron J, where it was held that this could, in principle, be done.

Breach of prosecution policy

6.33 From time to time, public authorities issue statements of policy. For example, the BSB has over time issued statements about the relative sanctity of private life. However, recent cases concerning social media seem to be moving away from that statement of policy. If a prosecutor issues proceedings in violation of its own policy, that could be argued to be an abuse of process: *R v Adaway* [2004] EWCA Crim 2831. At [27], the Court of Appeal stated:

> We cannot emphasise too strongly that before criminal proceedings are instituted by a local authority, acting in relation to the strict liability offences created by the Trade Descriptions Act, they must consider with care the terms of their own prosecuting policy.

If they fail to do so, or if they reach a conclusion which is wholly unsupported, as the conclusion to prosecute in this case was, by material establishing the criteria for prosecution, it is unlikely that the courts will be sympathetic..

Trial

6.34 Barrister disciplinary trials are a hybrid: technically civil in nature, but akin to a criminal trial in several key fundamentals. The BSB brings "charges" which are put to the "accused" barrister. A presumption of innocence applies. The burden of proof lies with the BSB. It was judicially described as a "prosecutor" in *Re P (a barrister)* [2005] 1 WLR 3019. A no-case submission may be made at 'half time', emulating the approach of the Crown Court. Some of the conduct alleged may be criminal in nature, or may be based on a criminal conviction.

6.35 Such trials are held in public save where some exceptional factor, such as a medical condition, is germane: rE156. It remains to be seen at the time of writing, whether the national crisis caused by the COVID-19 epidemic will mean that non-public online trials become the norm for a time, despite the clear terms of ECHR Art. 6, which require a trial in public. Some disciplinary trials attract media coverage.

6.36 The usual procedure involves a prosecution opening, then for each witness, prosecution evidence-in-chief, defence cross-examination, re-examination, any judicial examination, a no case to answer submission (if appropriate), defence evidence-in-chief, prosecution cross-examination, defence re-examination and any judicial examination. The parties will make closing speeches, (although the BSB sometimes waives its right to make one), the defence having the final word in any event: rE198. The panel will retire and return with a verdict announced by its Chair. If it makes a finding of guilt, it will hear a plea in mitigation from defence counsel and will retire to consider sanction and then return to pronounce that sanction.

6.37 Trials are held at bespoke premises at Gray's Inn in London. Administration is dealt with by the Bar Tribunals and Adjudication Service. 5-person panels are chaired by retired Circuit Judges with 2 barrister members and 2 lay members. 3-person panels are usually chaired by practising Queen's Counsel, or may be chaired by a retired Circuit Judge, in either case with a barrister member and a lay member. Trials are clerked by independent junior barristers. There is no Legal Assessor.

6.38 It is often difficult to read the mindset of panels. There is anecdotal evidence from those who have served on such panels, that it is the barrister members who can take the most adverse positions in respect of their accused peers. One might have assumed that the lay members would adopt such positions, but apparently this is not so. It is not known whether such attitudes or any preconceptions are explored or tested in the recruitment process, but all panellists should, as one should do with clients, approach the evidence without preconception and with an open mind. Surely the best advice is that of one of our greatest 20th century judges, Sir Robert Megarry in *John v Rees* [1970] 1 Ch 345 at 402:

> As everybody who has anything to do with the law well knows, the path of the law is strewn with examples of open and shut cases which, somehow, were not; of unanswerable charges which, in the event, were completely answered; of inexplicable conduct which was fully explained; of fixed and unalterable determinations that, by discussion, suffered a change.

6.39 An overriding criterion of fairness applies to the proceedings, (1) due to rE165, which applies the rules of natural justice to the proceedings and (2) due to the effect of Article 6 of the ECHR. (2) will be dealt with in chapter 8 on human rights law. As to (1), the rules of natural justice are various and include:

(a) a right to be told the case against an accused: *O'Reilly v Mackman* [1983] 2 AC 237 at 279. It has long been a requirement of natural justice that the charges in disciplinary proceedings must be made clear to the Defendant: *Re King and Co's Trade Mark* [1892] 2 Ch 462 at 482, *per* Lindley LJ. The notice of them must be "fair, adequate and sufficient" to enable the Defendant to defend himself: *Fisher v Keane* (1878) 11 Ch D at 362, *per* Jessel MR. So, in *Bruce v Odhams Press Ltd* [1936] 1 KB 697 at 712-3, *per* Scott LJ, it was held that the particulars of the charge must contain:

> information sufficiently detailed to put the defendant on his guard as to the case he has to meet and to enable him to prepare for [the hearing].

In *Strouthos v London Underground Limited* [2004] EWCA Civ 402, the charge failed to allege dishonesty and the decision to dismiss on grounds of dishonesty was necessarily set aside. Pill LJ held at [12]:

> It is a basic proposition, whether in criminal or disciplinary proceedings, that the charge against the defendant or the employee facing dismissal should be precisely framed, and that evidence should be confined to the particulars given in the charge.

And at [38]:

> ..it does appear to me to be basic to legal procedures, whether criminal or disciplinary, that a defendant or employee should be found guilty, if he is found guilty at all, only of a charge which is put to him. What has been considered in the cases is the general approach required in proceedings such as these. It is to be emphasised that it is wished to keep proceedings as informal as possible, but that does not, in my judgment, destroy the basic proposition that a defendant should only be found guilty of the offence with which he has been charged.

(b) a right effectively to challenge the opposing case against the accused person: *Al-Rawi v Security Service* [2011] UKSC 34 at [89]-[90]:

> 89 As I have observed in the associated case of *Tariq v Home Office* [2012] 1 AC 452, the right to know and effectively challenge the opposing case has long been recognised by the common law as a fundamental feature of the judicial process. I referred in my judgment in that case to various celebrated expressions of that principle and I need not repeat them here. The right to be informed of the case made against you is not merely a feature of the adversarial system of trial, it is an elementary and essential prerequisite of fairness. Without it, as Upjohn LJ put it in *In re K (Infants)* [1963] Ch 381, a trial between opposing parties cannot lay claim to the marque of judicial proceedings.
>
> 90 And so the key nature of this right and its utter indispensability to the fairness of proceedings must occupy centre stage in the debate as to whether it may be compromised to serve the interests which the defendants claim require to be served and which are said to justify a departure from it."

(c) a right to cross-examine: *R (Bonhoeffer) v General Medical Council* [2011] EWHC 1585 at [85][1]; [108] (viii)[2];

---

1 "....fairness requires that in disciplinary proceedings a person facing serious charges, especially if they amount to criminal offences which if proved are likely to have grave adverse effects on his or her reputation and career, should in principle be entitled by cross-examination to test the evidence of his accuser(s) where that evidence is the sole or decisive evidence relied on against him."

2 "In disciplinary proceedings which raise serious charges amounting in effect to criminal offences which, if proved, are likely to have grave adverse effects on the career and reputation of the accused party, if reliance is sought to be placed on the evidence of an accuser between whom and the accused party there is an important conflict of evidence as to whether the misconduct alleged took place, there would, if that evidence constituted a critical part of the evidence against the accused party

[130] ³. This is especially so where there is a conflict of evidence: *R (Evans) v Chief Constable of Sussex* [2011] EWHC 2329. If there is a discretion to allow cross-examination, there may well be a *duty* to consider whether to exercise that discretion: *R v Army Board of the Defence Council ex parte Anderson* [1992] QB 169 at 188 D-F;

(d) a right of access to the evidence on which the case against the accused person is based: *R (British Sky Broadcasting) v Central Criminal Court* [2011] EWHC 3451 at [28];

---

and if there were no problems associated with securing the attendance of the accuser, need to be compelling reasons why the requirement of fairness and the right to a fair hearing did not entitle the accused party to cross-examine the accuser."

3 "In those circumstances, in my judgment, no reasonable Panel in the position of the FTPP could have reasonably concluded that there were factors outweighing the powerful factors pointing against the admission of the hearsay evidence to which I have referred. The means by which the Claimant can challenge the hearsay evidence are, for the reasons I have set out, not in my judgment capable of outweighing those factors. On the contrary, if anything they point in the opposite direction. Nor, for reasons already given, is the diminished value of the hearsay evidence, to which the FTPP appears to have attached importance. The reality would appear to be that the factor which the FTPP considered decisive in favour of admitting the hearsay evidence was the serious nature of the allegations against the Claimant coupled with the public interest in investigating such allegations and the FTPP's duty to protect the public interest in protecting patients, maintaining public confidence in the profession and declaring and upholding proper standards of behaviour. In oral argument Mr Warby QC on behalf of the FTPP submitted that the gravity of the allegations is a factor arguing in favour of admissibility of the hearsay evidence. In my judgment that submission is misconceived. It is of course self-evidently correct that the greater is the gravity of allegations, the greater is the risk to the public if there is no or no effective investigation by a professional body such as the FTPP into them. However, that factor on its own does not in my view diminish the weight which must be attached to the procedural safeguards to which a person accused of such allegations is entitled both at common law and under Article 6 . To the contrary, the authorities to which I have referred suggest the reverse to be the case. The more serious the allegation, the greater the importance of ensuring that the accused doctor is afforded fair and proper procedural safeguards. There is no public interest in a wrong result."

(e) a requirement that the decision-maker will not hear representations behind the back of another party: *Kanda v Government of Malaya* [1962] AC 322 at 337, *per* Lord Denning; [4] [5]

(f) a power to proceed in the absence of the accused, but only with the "utmost care and caution": *R (Raheem) v NMC* [2010] EWHC 2549.

6.40 But the rules of natural justice have also been described as a general duty to act fairly: *Council of Civil Service Unions v Minister for the Civil Service* [1985] AC 374 at 414G-H *per* Lord Roskill [6] and *Wiseman v Borneman* [1971] AC 297 at 308-9, where Lord Morris described the rules of natural justice as "*fair play in action*"; [7] as a duty to comply with the American notion of

---

4 "It follows, of course, that the judge or whoever has to adjudicate must not hear evidence or receive representations from one side behind the back of the other. The court will not inquire whether the evidence or representations did work to his prejudice. Sufficient that they might do so. The court will not go into the likelihood of prejudice. The risk of it is enough. No one who has lost a case will believe he has been fairly treated if the other side has had access to the judge without his knowing."

5 See too *Paice v Harding (Trading As MJ Harding Contractors)* [2015] EWHC 661 (TCC)

6 "The third is where it has acted contrary to what are often called "principles of natural justice." As to this last, the use of this phrase is no doubt hallowed by time and much judicial repetition, but it is a phrase often widely misunderstood and therefore as often misused. That phrase perhaps might now be allowed to find a permanent resting-place and be better replaced by speaking of a duty to act fairly. But that latter phrase must not in its turn be misunderstood or misused."

7 "…the conception of natural justice should at all stages guide those who discharge judicial functions is not merely an acceptable but is an essential part of the philosophy of the law. We often speak of the rules of natural justice. But there is nothing rigid or mechanical about them. What they comprehend has been analysed and described in many authorities. But any analysis must bring into relief rather their spirit and their inspiration than any precision of definition or precision as to application. We do not search for prescriptions which will lay down exactly what must, in various divergent situations, be done. The principles and procedures are to be applied which, in any particular situation or set of circumstances, are right and just and fair. Natural justice, it has been said, is only " fair play in action." Nor do we wait for directions from Parliament. The common law has abundant riches:

"due process": *Neill v North Antrim Magistrates' Court* [1992] 1 WLR 1220 at 1230; [8] and in terms of an acceptance that the categories of natural justice are not closed [9]. This is the modern approach of public lawyers.

6.41 The type of evidence admissible before the Tribunal is governed by rE166:

The Disciplinary Tribunal may:

1 (subject to rE167 below) admit any evidence, whether oral or written, whether given in person, or over the telephone, or by video link, or by such other means as the Disciplinary Tribunal may deem appropriate, whether direct or hearsay, and whether or not it would be admissible in a court of law;

2 give such directions with regard to the admission of evidence at the hearing as it considers appropriate, ensuring that a respondent has a proper opportunity of answering the charge(s) and/or application(s) made against them;

3 exclude any hearsay evidence if it is not satisfied that reasonable steps have been taken to obtain direct evidence of the facts sought to be proved by the hearsay evidence.

---

there may we find what Byles J. called " the justice of the common law " *(Cooper* v. *Wandsworth Board of Works* (1863) 14 C.B.N.S. 180, 194). I approach the present case by considering whether in all the circumstances the tribunal acted unfairly. "

8 Megarry J. in *Fountaine v. Chesterton* (The Times, 20 Aug 1968, 112 S.J. 690 and cited in *John v Rees* at 398 added: "I regard natural justice as a distillate of due process of law."

9 "….lawyers seem to have manifested their classic learnt response to those two cases by treating the categories so far acknowledged in the reactive and exploratory growth of the common law as exhaustive. Rather than try to fit given shapes into pre-formed slots like toddlers in a playgroup…….the courts have to continue the process of working out and refining, case by case, the relevant principles of fairness." See Sedley LJ in *R (Wooder) v Feggetter* [2002] EWCA Civ 554 at [42].

6.42 The equivalent of rE166.3 fell for consideration in *JS v Bar Standards Board* [2016] EWHC 3015 (Admin). S was a family practitioner. Collins J. allowed S's s.24 appeal to the Administrative Court against a decision of a Disciplinary Tribunal that he was guilty of serious professional misconduct relating to his representation of a husband in financial remedy proceedings. S had negotiated a final financial settlement with the wife's legal representatives. Both parties were aged 47. The husband was in full-time employment; the wife was unemployed and in receipt of benefits. The settlement deferred any obligation on the husband to pay any maintenance until the wife obtained full-time employment, which the husband considered unlikely, but included provision for nominal future maintenance after the husband reached 60. The husband, through his solicitors, claimed that S had failed to negotiate a 'clean break' as instructed. S denied having given any such assurance, but the author contended that the deferral clause had protected the husband's position in any event, as the wife had never been re-employed and so no maintenance had ever become payable. The second charge, related to the manner in which S dealt with the solicitors' complaint. Almost 2 years after referral of the complaint, the Legal Ombudsman dismissed the parallel complaint to him. Despite this, the BSB continued with the complaint to it.

6.43 The husband did not give evidence at the hearing. He had indicated to the solicitors that, although his view was unchanged, he did not want to be further involved. The Tribunal admitted written hearsay statements from him, obtained by the solicitors, to the effect that S had orally assured him at court that the Consent Order achieved a 'clean break' – the key issue in the case. It found S's response to the solicitors' initial complaint to have been discourteous. There was no evidence that the BSB had made any effort at all to persuade the husband to attend the Tribunal to give evidence. Despite this, the Tribunal allowed in the key written statement of the husband and then relied on it to find Charge 1 proved.

6.44 Collins J's judgment repays reading. He said this about the dangers of admitting written witness statements, of depriving the defence of cross-examination on essential issues, about the BSB's obligation to conduct the fair and non-delegable taking of witness statements and as to insupportable and irrational findings by a Disciplinary Tribunal:

> 7. The Ombudsman had expressed some confusion as to whether the complaint was made by Mr A or by his solicitors. It was made clear that the solicitors were bringing it on behalf of Mr A. He was concerned that contrary to his understanding and wishes no clean break of maintenance had been made included in the order. The BSB should, accordingly, have appreciated that there was a potential conflict of interest in that the solicitors were vulnerable to an allegation of negligence against them, particularly since a partner of the firm had attended court with Mr S and had been able to see the proposed consent order. There was no doubt that at the very least the solicitor had had it read over to him clause by clause. Thus, it was in the solicitors' interest to put any blame on Mr S rather than on themselves.
>
> 8. It follows in my view that the BSB were seriously at fault in permitting the solicitors to continue to act on Mr A's behalf in pursuing the case and, in particular, in producing Mr A's statement. In fact, there were two statements but the second one merely confirmed the accuracy of the first which supported, in particular, the account given by the solicitor who attended on 31 August, Mr Douglas. He was a partner in the firm. The importance of this will become clear in due course....
>
> ....34. [r.E166], as is apparent, gives a general discretion to admit any evidence in whatever form and by whatever means. But there is a discretion to exclude hearsay under sub-paragraph (3). Furthermore, it is made clear in sub-

paragraph (2) which follows the requirement to apply the rules of natural justice that a defendant must be given a proper opportunity of answering the charges against him.

35. The BSB had not been involved at all with Mr A but had left it to Jennings Solicitors to produce his statements. This was a clear failure to act properly since, as I have said and as Mr Douglas recognised when questioned at the hearing, there was a potential conflict of interest, it being clearly in Jennings' interest to place any blame for the failure to include a clean break, which Mr A says he thought had been included, on [S]. There can be no doubt that to allow Jennings Solicitors to be responsible for producing the statements was a serious error by the BSB.

36. Mrs Jennings accepted that she had supervised the individual in the firm (a legal secretary) who had obtained statements from Mr A. It was of obvious importance to the appellant that Mr A should attend to give evidence since there was a highly material, indeed crucial, issue of fact to be determined, namely what [S] had actually said to Mr A and what Mr A had understood at the hearing in the county court.

37. Further, it would have been necessary to discover what Mr A had been told by his solicitors which may have influenced him in what the statement contained. I have already noted that Mr A's statement referred to Mr Douglas not representing him but being there simply as a note-taker, a role which seems somewhat strange for a partner in the firm. He says that he was absolutely clear from the beginning of the proceedings that he wanted an eventual clean break but that was not put to [S] at the commencement of the negotiations, nor was it contained in the instructions in that form. All that S was informed in his instructions was that Mr A wanted a clean break. But if the overall result was in S's view sufficiently favourable, that

clean break may well not have been required. That was not in the instructions. That was clearly in my view a reasonable approach that S could have taken.

38. Mr A says in his statement:

"Mr [S] absolutely one-hundred per cent assured me that there would be a clean break at 65."

39. Mr A felt he had already given up more capital and a larger share of his pension. It was known to the tribunal that Mr S denied that he had given any such assurance and that, as charge 1 made clear, the assertion that he had was the basis of the charge.

40. On 13 October 2015 Mr Burn, who was dealing with the matter on behalf of the BSB, received a telephone call from Mrs Jennings in which he was told that Mr A would not be attending. Mr Burn's note reads:

"Does not want to be involved, would not be able to give any useful evidence in any event as the lay client."

41. That was an extraordinary observation which led, when Mrs Jennings was cross-examined at the tribunal, to thoroughly unsatisfactory answers being given by her. Mr Burn did nothing; he took no steps to procure or seek to procure Mr A's attendances. At the very least he clearly should have written a letter because he had already been in gross breach of his duty in allowing statements to be taken by Jennings Solicitors and not by a representative of the BSB.

42. Further, it seems that Mr Burn informed Mrs Jennings that it was not vital that Mr A should attend provided that she or Mr Douglas did. If he did so inform Mrs Jennings, that was equally a serious dereliction of duty by him....

...44. Thus no steps were taken to obtain direct evidence of the matters sought to be proved by Mr A's statement.

45. Mr Wilson sought to argue that the evidence of Mr Douglas provided that direct evidence so Mr A's statements could properly be admitted. But that ignores the overriding provision in paragraph rE144 that the rules of natural justice apply. And so the tribunal must be astute to ensure fairness. It is to be noted that a finding of serious professional misconduct is so damaging to a practising barrister that the criminal standard of proof must be applied in deciding on charges of serious professional misconduct. That is laid down in paragraph rE143 of the regulations.

46. It is in my view proper to draw an analogy with the admission of hearsay in criminal cases. The statute and the law makes clear that it is essential that reasonable steps are taken to ensure the attendance of the witness who is to give the evidence even if he is not the only witness who deals with the particular issue. It was all the more necessary in the interests of fairness that Mr A should attend since there were inevitably concerns that his statement may have been influenced by what Mrs Jennings and Mr Douglas wanted him to say, and evidence from the complainant who was independent of his solicitors was essential. The reasons given for admitting the statement are not only jejune but do not meet the facts. The tribunal noted that no steps had been taken by the BSB to write to Mr A or to issue a witness summons. He had at no time been seen by anyone on behalf of the BSB.

47. In giving reasons for admitting the statements as hearsay, this was said, so far as material, by the Tribunal:

"In relation to the steps which had been taken by the Bar Standards Board, it is fair to say that we think that the Board may have perhaps taken further steps by writing a further letter to Mr A inviting him to attend. But within the context of the e-mail that he sent to Jennings Solicitors it is inevitable, it seems, that the response would have been that he would not have been attending today. So even if we thought the Bar Standards Board had not taken reasonable steps - and we do not take that view (the rules of discretion) - it does not say that we should exclude it if the Bar Standards Board had not taken reasonable steps. Looking at the rule itself, we are satisfied that we have jurisdiction to admit the evidence of Mr A, and we do so. We are conscious that he will not be here to be cross-examined but this will go to the weight of the evidence, and it may be, at the end of the day when we consider the matter as a whole, that we will attach no weight to Mr A's evidence. That is a matter for us once we have heard the evidence."

48. That reasoning is truly extraordinary. To say that the view was not taken that the BSB had not taken reasonable steps is clearly perverse. It had taken no steps. It is hardly possible to believe that to take no steps is to take reasonable steps. Further, to say that the weight of his evidence was in effect all that mattered was equally perverse in that it ignored the obvious unfairness which would result and equally ignored the fact that Jennings had an interest in procuring a statement which exonerated them and blamed Mr [S].

49. It is worth noting that in the present approach to litigation involving the drafting and redrafting of statements of witnesses, the latest of which is submitted as his or her evidence, it is often shown in cross-examination that the witness statement does not in truth fully or properly reflect his true evidence. This does not mean that there has been deliberate invention but it is all too easy to persuade a witness that he should put his evidence in a particular way which may turn out not to be entirely accurate.

50. It follows that I have no doubt that the appellant did not receive a fair hearing. The tribunal chose to accept the evidence of Mrs Jennings and Mr Douglas and, further, to accept Mr A's statement because it coincided with their evidence. Cross-examination of Mr A might have shown that the solicitors' account was not reliable. If so, it would have been difficult for the tribunal to have justified their conclusion that Mr S's account was to be rejected because the allegation against him would not have been proved to the criminal standard.

The standard of proof

6.45 As from 1st April 2019, the civil standard of proof applied to barrister disciplinary proceedings, albeit alleged misconduct occurring before that date will still fall to be judged by the criminal standard of proof: rE164. This will include where the same alleged conduct continued beyond 31st March 2019 and forms the basis of a single charge of professional misconduct: rE261A.

6.46 Like the loss of immunity from suit for advocates in 2000[10], the move to the civil standard of proof was politically inevitable. In an ever more accountable world, the special treatment of vested interests is hard to justify. Some would say that the argument was not exactly robustly put to the BSB for retaining the criminal standard. One contention might have been the more general one that any set of disciplinary regulations produced for BTAS as an ostensibly "independent" Tribunal, should be produced by *that* Tribunal (i.e. by COIC), not by way of the prosecutor, with its vested forensic interest in winning cases, appearing to *impose* a lower standard of proof on that Tribunal, as is the case with Bar discipline. The Solicitors (Disciplinary Proceedings) Rules 2007 and 2019 were not made by the Solicitors Regulation Authority, but by the Solicitors Disciplinary Tribunal itself.

---

10 *Arthur J S Hall & Co v Simons* [2002] 1 AC 615

6.47 But it is too late to contend that the rule change, making the civil standard of proof applicable from 1st April 2019, was unlawful. That said, the place of certain dicta remains unclear. The traditional view is reflected in Collins J's remark in *JS v BSB supra*, that:

> It is to be noted that a finding of serious professional misconduct is so damaging to a practising barrister that the criminal standard of proof must be applied in deciding on charges of serious professional misconduct

Another argument runs as follows: lawyers are in a different position to other professionals, such as Doctors, as many of their clients, criminal and civil, have much to gain from mendacity. If that is so, they may well have a vested interest in telling lies about their lawyers to the BSB, the SRA and the Legal Ombudsman. Only the criminal standard of proof can act as a proper safety mechanism against such a serious and frequent occupational risk.

6.48 This may well be why in 2005 the Privy Council could say this in *Campbell v Hamlet* [2005] 3 All ER 1116 at [16] *et seq*:

> [16] That the criminal standard of proof is the correct standard to be applied in all disciplinary proceedings concerning the legal profession, their Lordships entertain no doubt. If and in so far as the Privy Council in *Bhandari v Advocates Committee* [1956] 3 All ER 742 may be thought to have approved some lesser standard, then that decision ought no longer, nearly fifty years on, to be followed. The relevant passage from Lord Tucker's opinion on behalf of the Board in Bhandari's case reads:
>
> 'With regard to the onus of proof the Court of Appeal [for East Africa] said: "We agree that in every allegation of professional misconduct involving an element of deceit or moral turpitude a high standard of proof is called for, and we cannot envisage any body of professional men sitting in

judgment on a colleague who would be content to condemn on a mere balance of probabilities."

This seems to their Lordships an adequate description of the duty of a tribunal such as the Advocates Committee and there is no reason to think that either the committee or the Supreme Court applied any lower standard of proof.' (See [1956] 3 All ER 742 at 744-745)

[17] It has, of course, long been established that there is a flexibility in the civil standard of proof which allows it to be applied with greater or lesser strictness according to the seriousness of what has to be proved and the implications of proving those matters. Lord Bingham of Cornhill CJ pointed this out in the Divisional Court in *B v Chief Constable of the Avon and Somerset Constabulary* [2001] 1 All ER 562 at 573, (para 30) and continued (at para 31):

'In a serious case such as the present [concerning the making of a sex offender order] the difference between the two standards is, in truth, largely illusory. I have no doubt that, in deciding whether the condition ... is fulfilled, a magistrates' court should apply a civil standard of proof which will for all practical purposes be indistinguishable from the criminal standard.'

[18] The same approach has been taken in later cases. In the Court of Appeal in *Gough v Chief Constable of the Derbyshire Constabulary* [2002] EWCA Civ 351 at [90], Lord Phillips of Worth Matravers MR held with regard to the serious consequences of making a banning order under the Football Spectators Act 1989:

'This should lead the magistrates to apply an exacting standard of proof that will, in practice, be hard to distinguish from the criminal standard.'

[19] Most recently, in the House of Lords in *R (on the application of McCann) v Crown Court at Manchester, Clingham v Kensington and Chelsea Royal London BC* [2003] 1 AC 787, Lord Steyn agreed with what Lord Bingham had said in B's case about 'the heightened civil standard and the criminal standard [being] virtually indistinguishable' and concluded:

'In my view pragmatism dictates that the task of magistrates should be made more straightforward by ruling that they must in all cases under s 1 [of the Crime and Disorder Act 1998, providing for anti-social behaviour orders] apply the criminal standard.'

Lord Hope of Craighead similarly recognised that in all these cases 'the civil standard of proof will for all practical purposes be indistinguishable from the criminal standard' and held that 'the standard of proof that ought to be applied in these cases to allegations about the defendant's conduct is the criminal standard' (see [2002] 4 All ER 593 at [83],

[20] Perhaps more directly in point, however, is the decision of the Divisional Court in *Re A Solicitor* [1993] QB 69, concerning the standard of proof to be applied by the Disciplinary Tribunal of the Law Society. Lord Lane CJ, giving the judgment of the court, referred to the Privy Council's opinion in Bhandari's case and continued:

'It seems to us, if we may respectfully say so, that it is not altogether helpful if the burden of proof is left somewhere undefined. between the criminal and the civil standards. We conclude that at least in cases such as the present, where what is alleged is tantamount to a criminal offence, the tribunal should apply the criminal standard of proof, that is to say proof to the point where they feel sure that the charges are proved or, to put it another way, proof beyond reasonable doubt. This would seem to accord with decisions in several of the provinces of Canada.' (See [1993] QB 69 at 81.)

[21] A little later in the court's judgment Lord Lane referred to the provision in the Bar's Code of Conduct requiring the tribunal to apply the criminal standard of proof and observed ([1993] QB 69 at 82) 'it would be anomalous if the two branches of the profession were to apply different standards in their disciplinary proceedings'.

This last observation, of course, clearly warranted the Law Society Disciplinary Committee thenceforth applying the criminal standard in all cases rather than merely in those, earlier referred to, 'where what is alleged is tantamount to a criminal offence'.

6.49 The traditional view that there is a real difference between Barristers and other professionals has much to commend it for another reason. rC29 of the Handbook sets out the so-called 'Cab Rank' rule and provides that:

If you receive instructions from a professional client, and you are: .1 a self-employed barrister instructed by a professional client; or .2 an authorised individual working within a BSB entity; or .3 a BSB entity and the instructions seek the services of a named authorised individual working for you, and the instructions are appropriate taking into account the experience, seniority and/or field of practice of yourself or (as appropriate) of the named authorised individual you must, subject to Rule rC30 below, accept the instructions addressed specifically to you, irrespective of: a the identity of the client; b the nature of the case to which the instructions relate; c whether the client is paying privately or is publicly funded; and d any belief or opinion which you may have formed as to the character, reputation, cause, conduct, guilt or innocence of the client.

Criterion (d) means that barristers are not merely likely to act, but are professionally *obliged* to act for those who may range from the career criminal at one extreme to the desperate businessman at another. The propensity of such people to make dishonest allegations where it serves their interests, or through sheer malice, is uncommonly high.

6.50 Arguably, the civil standard is capable of going some way to accommodate this risk, because the more serious the allegation – and allegations of professional misconduct may be very serious indeed – the more compelling the evidence needs to be: see *In Re H and others (Minors) (Sexual Abuse: Standard of Proof)* [1996] AC 563, per Lord Nicholls at 586:

> The balance of probability standard means that a court is satisfied an event occurred if the court considers that, on the evidence, the occurrence of the event was more likely than not. When assessing the probabilities the court will have in mind as a factor, to whatever extent is appropriate in the particular case, that the more serious the allegation the less likely it is that the event occurred and, hence, the stronger should be the evidence before the court concludes that the allegation is established on the balance of probability. Fraud is usually less likely than negligence. Deliberate physical injury is usually less likely than accidental physical injury. A stepfather is usually less likely to have repeatedly raped and had non-consensual oral sex with his underage stepdaughter than on some occasion to have lost his temper and slapped her. Built into the preponderance of probability standard is a generous degree of flexibility in respect of the seriousness of the allegation. Although the result is much the same, this does not mean that where a serious allegation is in issue the standard of proof required is higher. It means only that the inherent probability or improbability of an event is itself a matter to be taken into account when weighing the probabilities and deciding whether, on balance, the event occurred.

> The more improbable the event, the stronger must be the evidence that it did occur before, on the balance of probability, its occurrence will be established. Ungoed-Thomas J. expressed this neatly in *In re Dellow's Will Trusts* [1964] 1 W.L.R. 451, 455: *"The more serious the allegation the more cogent is the evidence required to overcome the unlikelihood of what is alleged and thus to prove it."* This substantially accords with the approach adopted in authorities such as the well-known judgment of Morris L.J. in *Hornal v. Neuberger Products Ltd.* [1957] 1 Q.B. 247, 266. This approach also provides a means by which the balance of probability standard can accommodate one's instinctive feeling that even in civil proceedings a court should be more sure before finding serious allegations proved than when deciding less serious or trivial matters.

6.51 The move to the civil standard of proof will impact most severely on barristers facing any allegation in which a choice has to be made by the Tribunal as to the irreconcilable evidence about past events presented by a complainant and that barrister. This problem is no more starkly illustrated than in cases of alleged indecent assault, where there are no third-party witnesses. At the time of writing, a series of such cases is being tried at the Solicitors Disciplinary Tribunal. The author achieved an acquittal in one of this series, *SRA v RS* (2019) 28th November, Unrep. where the criminal standard of proof was still applicable, but it must be open to question that the same result would have been achieved on the footing of the civil standard, even applying *Re H*. That is not because of any defect in the *Re H* guidance, but because of the elbow room that the civil standard gives to Tribunals in a climate in which types of allegation become prevalent and their prosecution and punishment takes on a political significance.

Findings of other courts and tribunals

6.52 The rules provide as follows:

rE169

In proceedings before a Disciplinary Tribunal which involve the decision of a court or tribunal in previous proceedings to which the respondent was a party, the following Regulations shall apply:

1 a copy of the certificate or memorandum of conviction relating to the offence shall be conclusive proof that the respondent committed the offence;

2 any court record of the findings of fact upon which the conviction was based (which may include any document prepared by the sentencing judge or a transcript of the relevant proceedings) shall be proof of those facts, unless proved to be inaccurate;

3 the finding and sanction of any tribunal in or outside England and Wales exercising a professional disciplinary jurisdiction may be proved by producing an official copy of the finding and sanction and the findings of fact upon which that finding or sanction was based shall be proof of those facts, unless proved to be inaccurate; and

4 the judgment of any civil court may be proved by producing an official copy of the judgment, and the findings of fact upon which that judgment was based shall be proof of those facts, unless proved to be inaccurate.

Thus the Tribunal adopts the enlightened and realistic stance that it well recognises that other courts and tribunals make mistakes. Their findings are of strong persuasive value, "unless proved to be inaccurate".

6.53 The use by the BSB of r.E169 only applies where the barrister was a party to the other proceedings: rE170. But it is not unknown for judges in civil cases to make rash remarks about professionals who are not parties to those cases, but may be experts or advocates. On closer consideration, such remarks may be unfair and wrong. The regulator takes action and relies on the judgment and/or a transcript. The barrister may tell the story afresh and seek to refute the rash remark without any presumption operating against him or her.

6.54 Where the above provision does apply, it provides the basis of a defence, to be made out following Crown Court practice, on the balance of probabilities (even in cases where the criminal standard of proof still applies).

6.55 Some barristers are dual qualified, as solicitors or as lawyers overseas or in other disciplines such as surveying. If they are subject to disciplinary proceedings by a different regulator, the BSB will rely on r.E169.3. In some cases, where the previous decision was reached many years previously, or in a foreign jurisdiction and documents have been destroyed or lost, it may be a real challenge for the defence to prove that the facts found were inaccurate.

Witnesses of fact

6.56 rE175 provides:

> A witness of fact shall be excluded from the hearing until they are called to give evidence, failing which they will not be entitled to give evidence without leave of the Disciplinary Tribunal

This is a rarely cited, but important provision. As rehearsed in *Momodou* and *Gestmin, supra*, the dangers of witness contamination are ever-present. Hearing the cross-examination of other witnesses before being cross-examined may give witnesses of fact, where certain facts are in issue, an unfair advantage. By the same token and although practices appear to vary, some younger generations of advocates being less punctilious, the view of the author is that such witnesses must never be shown the evidence of the Defendant or of other witnesses for the BSB or the defence. Despite rE175, it is unlikely that the Tribunal would actually stop a witness who had seen and heard the cross-examination of other witnesses from giving evidence. So if it is desired that the nature of the case is such that witnesses should remain out of the hearing room until they give their evidence, then such an application should be made before the case is opened.

Vulnerable witnesses

6.57 The accused barrister is not usually regarded as a vulnerable witness despite his or her state being one of acute vulnerability. It can be galling to read some of the following provisions that may even protect mendacious complainants from being identified:

> rE176
>
> For the purpose of Part 5: Section B, any person falling into one or more of the following categories may be treated by the Disciplinary Tribunal as a vulnerable witness in proceedings before it:
>
> .1 any witness under the age of 18 at the time of the hearing;
>
> .2 any witness with a mental disorder within the meaning of the Mental Health Act 1983;
>
> .3 any witness who is significantly impaired in relation to intelligence and social functioning;
>
> .4 any witness with physical disabilities who requires assistance to give evidence;

.5 any witness, where the allegation against the respondent is of a sexual or violent nature and the witness was the alleged victim; and

.6 any witness who complains of intimidation.

rE177

Subject to hearing representations from the parties, the Chair of the Disciplinary Tribunal or the Disciplinary Tribunal may adopt such measures as it considers desirable to enable it to receive evidence from a vulnerable witness.

rE178

Any witness who is not regarded as a vulnerable witness under rE176 may apply for one or more of the measures set out in rE179 to be put into place on the ground that the measure(s) is desirable to enable the Disciplinary Tribunal to receive the witness's evidence.

rE179

Measures adopted by the Disciplinary Tribunal for receiving evidence from a vulnerable witness may include, but are not to be limited to:

.1 use of video links;

.2 use of pre-recorded evidence as the evidence-in-chief of a witness, provided always that such a witness is available at the hearing for cross-examination and questioning by the Disciplinary Tribunal;

.3 use of interpreters (including signers and translators) or intermediaries;

CHAPTER SIX – TRIAL PREPARATION AND CONDUCT • 137

.4 use of screens or such other measures as the Disciplinary Tribunal consider necessary in the circumstances in order to prevent:

.a the identity of the witness being revealed to the press or the general public; or

.b access to the witness by the respondent

.5 the hearing of evidence (either whole or in part) by the Disciplinary Tribunal in private.

rE180

No respondent charged with an allegation of a sexual or violent nature may cross-examine in person a witness who is the alleged victim, either:

.1 in connection with that allegation, or

.2 in connection with any other allegation (of whatever nature) with which the said respondent is charged in the proceedings.

rE181

In the circumstances set out in rE180, in the absence of the respondent's written consent, BTAS must, no less than seven days before the hearing, appoint a legally qualified person to cross-examine the witness on the respondent's behalf

6.58 In a system which still makes no provision for barristers, all of whom are presumed innocent by law at the point of charge, to be afforded funded defence, (and indeed, has abolished the scheme the author developed in the 1990s[11]), it is noteworthy that

---

11 The Barristers' Complaints Advisory Service

counsel is provided in the interests *of a complainant* who may be genuine, or may not. As at 2020, a barrister may, therefore, *ex hypothesi* face a false charge of sexual or other assault postdating 1.4.19, where there are no other witnesses, where the test is the balance of probabilities, where the complainant may well have lifetime anonymity[12], where the barrister has no anonymity, where the barrister has no insurance cover, so he may be forced to act for himself, but he is not allowed to cross-examine the complainant, where the mere allegations will remain on the internet for all time, where the conviction rate is over 90% and he may be compelled to instruct a "legally qualified person", possibly not of his own choosing, who is in fact under-qualified. There are real grounds for concern that this is a 'perfect storm' of factors that will lead to unsafe convictions.

Hearings in the absence of the accused and re-hearings

6.59 Where the accused barrister has not attended the hearing, the Tribunal may proceed to hear and determine the charges if it considers it just to do so and is satisfied that the accused has been duly served: rE183. If the relevant procedure has not been complied with, but the Tribunal is satisfied that it has not been practicable to do so, the Tribunal may hear and determine the charges in the absence of the barrister, if it considers it just to do so, but subject to compliance with rE234.2 in respect of that barrister if the Tribunal finds any charge proved i.e. that the order must state that the finding and sanction were made in the absence of the Respondent and that he has the right to apply to the Directions Judge for an Order that there should be a new hearing before a fresh Disciplinary Tribunal.

6.60 Where the Disciplinary Tribunal proceeds in the Respondent's absence, the Respondent may apply to BTAS for a Directions Judge, appointed by the President, to consider an application for a fresh hearing before a new Disciplinary Tribunal: rE185. The Respondent's application under rE185 must be supported by a

---

12 Sexual Offences (Amendment) Act 1992, s 1 .

statement setting out the facts and/or circumstances upon which the Respondent relies in support of their application: rE186. The Directions Judge may grant a new hearing if he or she considers it just to do so and is satisfied that: (a) the Respondent submitted the application for a new hearing promptly upon becoming aware of the decision of the Tribunal; and (b) had good reason for not attending the hearing: rE187.

6.61 The position in law was summarised by Holman J. in *Raheem v Nursing and Midwifery Council* [2010] EWHC 2549 (Admin):

> 28. The approach to situations of this kind is now the subject of high authority. I refer first to the decision of Munby J in *Yusuf v The Royal Pharmaceutical Society of Great Britain* [2009] EWHC 867 (Admin), given or handed down on 28 April 2009. As its name indicates, that case concerned an appeal by a pharmacist from a decision of the Disciplinary Committee of The Royal Pharmaceutical Society of Great Britain, but plainly a similar approach must apply to the similar disciplinary committee of the NMC.
>
> 29. In paragraphs 31 to 40 of his judgment, Munby J dealt with the decision of the committee in that case to proceed in the absence of the appellant in that case. At paragraph 33 he quoted a passage from the judgment of Rose LJ in the criminal case of *R v Hayward*, including the words:
>
> "That discretion must be exercised with great care and it is only in rare and exceptional cases that it should be exercised in favour of a trial taking place or continuing, particularly if the defendant is unrepresented."
>
> In the continuing part of the quotation, Rose LJ set out at some length a long list of circumstances or factors that need to be weighed and considered.

30. At paragraph 34, Munby J referred to the observations of Lord Bingham of Cornhill in another criminal case, *R v Jones (Anthony)* [2003] 1 AC 1 that "the discretion to commence a trial in the absence of a defendant should be exercised with the utmost care and caution".

31. At paragraph 36, Munby J said, and I will accordingly accept without further inquiry, that that jurisprudence, albeit developed in the course of criminal cases, was applied to the disciplinary proceedings of professional bodies by the Privy Council in the case of *Tait v Royal College of Veterinary Surgeons* [2003] UKPC 34.

32. At paragraph 38, Munby J dealt with the approach of the committee in the *Yusuf* case on the facts of that case. He said that that committee had "directed itself impeccably in accordance with *R v Jones (Anthony)*" and that the committee "proceeding as it said with the 'utmost caution', was entitled to conclude, and for the reasons it gave, that it was proper for it to proceed in the absence of the appellant."

33. The actual course of the proceedings before the Committee and its ruling in that case was summarised by Munby J in paragraphs 14 and 15. It appears from paragraph 14 that the Society's counsel referred expressly to the decision of the House of Lords in *R v Jones (Anthony)*, whereas I note that no authority was referred to at all in the present case. The reasons of the committee for their decision to proceed in the absence of the appellant in that case apparently ran to "some three pages of transcript". The committee cited from the speech of Lord Bingham of Cornhill *R v Jones (Anthony)*. The chairman rehearsed in considerable detail the facts relating to the application for the adjournment and, in a passage quoted verbatim by Munby J, expressly said:

> "We recognise that the discretion to proceed in his absence is one which must be exercised with the utmost caution, but in this particular instance having considered all the circumstances, we think it is proper for us to proceed in [the appellant's] absence."
>
> 34. Pausing there, it is in my view important to stress that reference by committees or tribunals such as this, or indeed judges, to exercising the discretion to proceed in the person's absence "with the utmost caution" is much more than mere lip service to a phrase used by Lord Bingham of Cornhill. If it is the law that in this sort of situation a committee or tribunal should exercise its discretion "with the utmost care and caution", it is extremely important that the committee or tribunal in question demonstrates by its language (even though, of course, it need not use those precise words) that it appreciates that the discretion which it is exercising is one that requires to be exercised with that degree of care and caution. That is conspicuously lacking from the brief consideration given to the exercise of discretion in the present case…

6.62 In *GMC v Adeogba* [2016] EWCA Civ 162 the CA added this:

> 18 It goes without saying that fairness fully encompasses fairness to the affected medical practitioner (a feature of prime importance) but it also involves fairness to the GMC ……In that regard, it is important that the analogy between criminal prosecution and regulatory proceedings is not taken too far. Steps can be taken to enforce attendance by a defendant; he can be arrested and brought to court. No such remedy is available to a regulator.
>
> 19 There are other differences too. First, the GMC represent the public interest in relation to standards of healthcare. It would run entirely counter to the protection, promotion and maintenance of the health and safety of the

public if a practitioner could effectively frustrate the process and challenge a refusal to adjourn when that practitioner had deliberately failed to engage in the process. The consequential cost and delay to other cases is real. Where there is good reason not to proceed, the case should be adjourned; where there is not, however, it is only right that it should proceed.

20 Second, there is a burden on medical practitioners, as there is with all professionals subject to a regulatory regime, to engage with the regulator, both in relation to the investigation and ultimate resolution of allegations made against them. That is part of the responsibility to which they sign up when being admitted to the profession.

6.63 In *N v BSB* [2014] EWHC 2681, Fulford LJ accepted[13] that the criteria in *R v Jones* applied to barrister cases. The panel had erroneously proceeded without reference to the test of the utmost care and caution. In *Rehman v BSB* [2016] EWHC 2023 (Admin) at [81], Hickinbottom J. said this:

81. In *N* Fulford LJ said that the starting point for disciplinary tribunals in these circumstances is *Jones* which concerned the discretion to commence and proceed with a criminal trial in the absence of a defendant. In *Jones* at [13], Lord Bingham emphasised that the discretion should be exercised "with the utmost care and caution"; and he approved a checklist of factors identified by the Court of Appeal in that case ([2001] EWCA Crim 168 at [22]) to which the court must, in particular, have regard. In *N* Fulford LJ at [55] considered that a disciplinary tribunal, in these circumstances, "must apply those parts of the criteria that are relevant". The relevant criteria are as follows:

i) the nature and circumstances of the defendant's behaviour in absenting himself from the trial or disrupting it;

---

13 In written submissions drafted by the author

and, in particular, whether his behaviour was deliberate, voluntary and such as plainly waived his right to appear;

ii) whether an adjournment might result in the defendant attending;

iii) the likely length of any adjournment;

iv) whether the defendant, though absent, wishes to be legally represented; or whether he has, by his conduct, waived his right to representation;

v) whether the absent defendant's legal representative is able to receive instructions, and present his case;

vi) the extent of the disadvantage to the defendant in not being able to give his account of events;

vii) the risk of drawing an improper conclusion about the defendant's absence;

viii) the seriousness of the offence;

ix) the general public interest, and the interest of victims and witnesses, that proceedings should take place within a reasonable time of the events to which they relate; and

x) the effect of delay on the memories of witnesses.

6.64 As studies have shown[14], the incidence of mental illness in the legal profession is likely to be very significant. At the Bar, the work and lifestyle can be solitary, with little in the way of support structures. When disciplinary proceedings commence, this may lead to an "ostrich" like disengagement. The accused barrister may be fit enough to work but, clinically, not fit to stand trial. With the Bar's continuing failure to provide guaranteed insurance

---

14 See Chapter 1

cover and the Bar Council's (inexplicable) abrogation of BCAS, the advisory panel designed by the author in the 1990s, that solitariness and disengagement may become compounded. Moreover, the prosecution itself may have a profound impact on conscientious practitioners, whose reserves of mental strength are exhausted, even at the point of complaint-making, by a job that requires every ounce of mental energy to be committed to the affairs of clients. That may well be why the author notes that the barrister clients who are least able to cope with the disciplinary process, are so often those who have the most successful practices. Moreover, the disciplinary process itself is known to cause a 'reactive' clinical depression.

6.65 Psychological or psychiatric evidence of any possible unfitness to stand trial and to give instructions to an available legal representative, obtained in good time before trial, may be critical in order to invoke the *Rehman* criteria with any chance of an adjournment. However, the malingerer will get nowhere, not least because, as part of their analysis, good Psychiatrists carry out tests for malingering.

6.66 A GP's note is almost always inadequate: *GMC v Hayat* [2018] EWCA Civ 2796.

Submission of no case to answer

6.67 Such an application may be made at the close of the BSB's case. These are rare, but permitted: rE195. It is good practice to enquire as to whether the BSB has formally closed its case. Its advocate will usually state in open court that it has. Then, but only then, the application may be made. The test is as in *R v Galbraith* [1981] 1 WLR 1039 at 1042 B to D *per* Lane LCJ:

> (1) If there is no evidence that the crime alleged has been committed by the defendant, there is no difficulty. The judge will of course stop the case. (2) The difficulty arises where there is some evidence but it is of a tenuous char-

acter, for example because of inherent weakness or vagueness or because it is inconsistent with other evidence, (a) Where the judge comes to the conclusion that the prosecution evidence, taken at its highest, is such that a jury properly directed could not properly convict upon it, it is his duty, upon a submission being made, to stop the case. (b) Where however the prosecution evidence is such that its strength or weakness depends on the view to be taken of a witness's reliability, or other matters which are generally speaking within the province of the jury and where on one possible view of the facts there is evidence upon which a jury could properly come to the conclusion that the defendant is guilty, then the judge should allow the matter to be tried by the jury

6.68 It will be a matter of judgment as to whether the prosecution witnesses have been so discredited in cross-examination, that a no-case submission might succeed. This judgment call will be influenced by any views, often intuitive, that have been formed about the likely ability of the client to do himself or herself justice in the witness box. The only rule of thumb is that those barrister clients that one expects to be poor witnesses are often excellent performers and *vice versa*. Yet the gains of cross-examination may well be at risk once the barrister gives evidence. And if he does not give evidence, the Tribunal can draw an adverse inference: *BSB v MW* (2014) Unrep. Probably the best no-case submissions are those based on unanswerable strike-out-type points, rather than the evidence, save where a key witness has either not attended the hearing, or has been wholly discredited, or has made startling concessions or admissions.

The Defendant's evidence

Evidence in Chief

6.69 The tribunal should have a witness statement settled by the instructing solicitor, with the assistance of counsel, or by the latter alone in a direct access case. It is the evidence-in-chief of the accused barrister. It must accurately reflect the client's instructions, no more and no less. The very highest standards of integrity are required in drafting witness statements in professional disciplinary cases. There is no substitute for professional, objective drafting of this absolutely vital document. It is no exaggeration that it can make or break the accused barrister's defence.

Cross-Examination of the accused Barrister

6.70 It is not easy to advise a barrister client to behave like a mere witness and not to behave like a barrister. The accused barrister should be advised:

(a) not to try to argue his own case from the witness box;

(b) not to argue with BSB counsel:

(c) to be succinct;

(d) not to speculate;

(e) if something cannot be remembered, then to say so, or express the best of one's recollection;

(f) to be respectful at all times, using correct modes of address (Sir, Madam, etc);

(g) to know his witness statement intimately well;

(h) to be able to navigate around the trial bundle with ease;

(i) to get plenty of sleep before he or she gives his or her evidence;

(j) to dress properly.

6.71 But instruction should be largely limited to the above, because (a) witness coaching is unlawful and (b) a witness should not have his mind cluttered with thoughts of strategy. Those are for defence counsel.

The Tribunal decision (rE199-202)

6.72 At the end of the hearing, the Disciplinary Tribunal must record in writing its finding(s) on each charge or application, and its reasons. That record must be signed by the Chair and by all members of the Disciplinary Tribunal. If the members of the Disciplinary Tribunal do not agree on any charge or application, the finding to be recorded on that charge or application must be that of the majority. If the members of the Disciplinary Tribunal are equally divided, (as may occur, for example, in a 5-person panel if one member drops out, or is recused), on any charge (or application), then, as the burden of proof is on the Bar Standards Board, the finding to be recorded must be that which is the most favourable to the Respondent. But this would be extremely rare.

6.73 The Chair of the Tribunal must announce the Tribunal's finding on the charge(s) and state whether each such finding was unanimous or by a majority. The Tribunal is free to reserve its judgment, but more often announces its decision with short reasons with more detailed reasons to follow. Where the Tribunal dismisses the charge(s), it may give advice about future conduct.

6.74 The rules contemplate majority decisions and so, dissenting judgments. In the appeal in *CR v BSB* (2013) the directions judge, Sir Anthony May, acceded to the application of CR that the reasons of the (numerically secret) dissenting minority should be explained for the assistance of the Visitors on appeal. The judge's direction was conveyed to the dissenting member or members, who replied that he, she or they could no longer remember their reasons for dissent. Nevertheless, the approach in that case means that the defence should always request that panel members who have dissented in what is disclosed to have been a majority decision, should ensure that the reasons for their minority view are fairly represented in the final judgment of the Tribunal and before too much time elapses post-trial.

Reasons

6.75 Judgments of the Tribunal should be fully reasoned: that is an essential feature of the rules of natural justice at common law and ECHR Article 6[15]. The provision of sufficient reasons is an elementary public law standard.

6.76 Historically, there have been some cursory written decisions from the Tribunal. In *O'C v BSB* (2012) Unrep. Collins J as Chair of a Visitors' panel remarked:

> The second point raised relates to the alleged lack of reasons which were given by the Tribunal. There is an obligation under the rules for the Tribunal to give reasons for its decision. Without going into any detail, we are bound to say that the reasoning is singularly unimpressive. *Prima facie,* there is, in our view, considerable force in the submission that the reasons in this case were defective. Again, we have not gone into that in any detail because, in our view, it has not been necessary to do so.

In *AQ v BSB* (2013) Unrep, the Visitors said this about the pronouncement of verdicts with no provision of reasons, *per* Wyn Williams J:

> 40. In our judgment it was incumbent upon the Tribunal to explain its reasoning process in respect of all the documentation to which we have just referred. It did not do so and, in our judgment, it thereby fell into error. In a case of this type with such serious potential consequences for the Appellant it was not sufficient, in our judgment, for the

---

15 *Balani v Spain* (1994) 19 EHRR 565 at [27]

Tribunal to announce verdicts without explaining in some detail the reasoning process which underpinned them.

6.77 In *R v MOD ex parte Murray* [1997] EWHC Admin 1136, Lord Bingham LCJ said this:

> As the late Professor Harold Potter observed (*The Quest of Justice*, 1951, page 13), if there is any truth in the aphorism that justice must not only be done but seen to be done, then a decision without reasons given must always be regarded as undesirable, because it must be suspect since it may be arbitrary".
>
> 55. This observation is not universally true, and the decision in issue here may have been very far from arbitrary. This is, however, an archetypal case in which, without reasons, the subject of the adverse decision cannot be sure, and in a matter of this moment, on the unusual facts here, he is in my view entitled to be sure. An unreasoned decision, followed by unreasoned rejections of applications for review, leaves an uneasy suspicion (which reasons might dispel) that justice may not have been done.

6.78 The extent of reasons need not be onerous, but they must negate any hint of arbitrariness. In *R v Civil Service Appeal Board ex parte Cunningham* [1992] ICR 816, Lord Donaldson MR held:

> 28 I then ask myself what additional procedural safeguards are required to ensure the attainment of fairness. The answer is, I believe, to be found in the judgment of Lord Lane CJ in *R v Immigration Appeal Tribunal ex parte Khan* [1983] QB 790, 794-5 which I do not believe owed anything to the fact that immigration appeal tribunals are required by statute to give some reasons for their decisions:
>
> 'The important matter which must be borne in mind by tribunals in the present type of circumstances is that it must

be apparent from what they state by way of reasons first of all that they have considered the point which is at issue between the parties, and they should indicate the evidence upon which they have come to their conclusions. Where one gets a decision of a tribunal which either fails to set out the issue which the tribunal is determining either directly or by inference, or fails either directly or by inference to set out the basis upon which they have reached their determination upon that issue, then that is a matter which will be very closely regarded by this Court, and in normal circumstances will result in the decision of the tribunal being quashed.

The reason is this. A party appearing before a tribunal is entitled to know, either expressly stated by the tribunal or inferentially stated, what it is to which the tribunal is addressing its mind. In some cases it may be perfectly obvious without any express reference to it by the tribunal; in other cases it may not.

Secondly, the appellant is entitled to know the basis of fact upon which the conclusion has been reached. Once again, in many cases it may be quite obvious without the necessity of expressly stating it, in other cases it may not.'

29 Judged by that standard the Board should have given outline reasons sufficient to show to what it was directing its mind and thereby indirectly showing not whether its decision was right or wrong, which is a matter solely for it, but whether its decision was lawful. Any other conclusion would reduce the Board to the status of a free-wheeling palm tree.

6.79 A *locus classicus* is another judgment of Bingham LJ (as he then was) in *Meek v Birmingham City Council* [1987] IRLR 250 at [8]:

It has on a number of occasions been made plain that the decision of an Industrial Tribunal is not required to be an elaborate formalistic product of refined legal draftsmanship, but it must contain an outline of the story which has given rise to the complaint and a summary of the Tribunal's basic factual conclusions and a statement of the reasons which have led them to reach the conclusion which they do on those basic facts. The parties are entitled to be told why they have won or lost. There should be sufficient account of the facts and of the reasoning to enable the EAT or, on further appeal, this court to see whether any question of law arises..

CHAPTER SEVEN
SANCTIONS

Procedure

7.1 Sanctions are governed by rE203 to rE219 in the BSB Handbook.

7.2 If the Tribunal finds any of the charges or applications proved, it may hear evidence of any previous findings of professional misconduct by a Disciplinary Tribunal or under the determination by consent procedure, any finding of a breach of proper professional standards by the BSB or any other regulator or, where the proved charges concern a BSB entity, in respect of that body or any person employed in the BSB entity directly implicated by the charges.

7.3 The defence then enters a plea in mitigation, trying to attenuate the facts and circumstances of the case, emphasising the accused's contributions to the profession, explaining his domestic circumstances and addressing the most appropriate sanction.

7.4 In preparing for trial, it is almost always essential to obtain good testimonials from other professionals. Sufficient copies of these should be made available as part of the plea in mitigation. They should be agreed with the prosecution before trial, to avoid any need for the referees to be challenged or called.

7.5 After hearing the plea in mitigation, the Tribunal must decide what sanction to impose, taking into account the BTAS sentencing guidance and must record its sanction in writing, together with its reasons. If the members of the Tribunal do not agree on the sanction to be imposed, the sanction to be recorded must be that decided by the majority. If the members of the Tribunal are equally divided on the sanction to be imposed, the sanction to be recorded must be that which is the most favourable to the respondent.

7.6 The Chair of the Tribunal must then announce the Tribunal's decision on sanction and state whether the decision was unanimous or by a majority. In any case where a charge of professional misconduct has been found proved, the Tribunal may decide that no further action should be taken against the barrister. Subject to that power, a barrister against whom a charge of professional misconduct has been found proved may be sanctioned by the Tribunal according to the types of sanction set out in annexes to the Disciplinary Tribunals Regulations ("DTR"). In the case of barristers, sentencing is in accordance with Annexe 1 to the DTR. The sentences for other types of BSB-regulated party are: a BSB authorised body (Annex 2); a BSB licensed body (Annex 3); registered European lawyers (Annex 4); all other BSB regulated persons, (Annex 5). In this text, focus is on Annex 1 alone. Annexes 2 to 5 are available online in the BSB Handbook.

7.7 The sanctions available against barristers are set out at Annexe 1 of the Handbook. They are: disbarment; suspension for a prescribed period; an order that the practising certificate should not be renewed; an order that conditions be imposed on the practising certificate; an order that the barrister be prohibited, either indefinitely or for a prescribed period and either unconditionally or subject to conditions, from accepting or carrying out any public access instructions; an order that authorisation to conduct litigation be removed or suspended, or be subject to conditions; an order to pay a fine of up to £50,000 to the BSB; (or up to £50 million if the charges relate to his or her time as an employee or manager of a licensed body); an order to complete continuing professional development of such nature and duration as the Tribunal may direct; a reprimand; advice about future conduct; an order to attend on a nominated person to be reprimanded or to be given advice about future conduct.

7.8 In any case where a charge of professional misconduct has not been found proved, the Tribunal may still direct that the matter be referred to the BSB for it to consider whether an administrative sanction should be imposed in accordance with the provisions of rE19.3 or rE22.3 of the Enforcement Decision Regulations, where the Tribunal is satisfied there is sufficient evidence on the balance of probabilities of a breach of the Handbook by the respondent and it considers that such referral to the BSB is proportionate and in the public interest. Such a direction is not a disposal or a finding for the purposes of the BSB Handbook.

Referral for sentence

7.9 The sentencing powers of a three-person panel are restricted. It cannot disbar a barrister or suspend a barrister's practising certificate for a period longer than twelve months, or revoke the authorisation or licence (as appropriate) of a BSB entity or suspend it for a period longer than twelve months; or remove a registered European lawyer from the register of European lawyers or impose a sanction of suspension on any BSB regulated person for a prescribed period longer than twelve months; or impose a Disqualification Order on an employee for more than twelve months. However, in the event that a three-person panel considers that a case before it merits the imposition of higher penalties than these, or it otherwise considers that the case is complex enough to warrant sentencing by a five-person panel, the three-person panel must refer the case to a five-person panel. The three-person panel must, in order to help the five-person panel, prepare a statement of the facts as found. The respondent cannot challenge the facts found by the three-person panel; and the three-person panel must direct within what period of time the sentencing hearing before the five-person panel is to be held and make appropriate directions for the parties to provide the President of COIC with their dates of availability.

7.10 There are provisions for convening the 5-person sentencing panel and for sentencing in absence and, in such a case, for an application for a re-hearing.

7.11 There are also discrete sanctions available concerning the undertaking of future legal aid work and the reduction or cancellation of legal aid fees, as well as in connection with pupil supervision.

Suspension procedure

7.12 The period for which a sanction of suspension from practice is expressed to run may be a fixed period or until the respondent has complied with any conditions specified in the order imposing the sanction of suspension. In exceptional circumstances, where the total suspension is three months or less, the Tribunal may postpone the commencement of the suspension for a period as it deems fit.

7.13 Conditions may be imposed on a barrister's practising certificate or on the authorisation or licence of a BSB entity without its being suspended, or to take effect on a barrister's practising certificate or on the authorisation or licence of a BSB entity when a period of suspension ends. Conditions may include: limiting the scope of the respondent's practice (after the end of any suspension, if relevant) to such part as the Tribunal may determine, either indefinitely or for a defined period and/or imposing requirements that the respondent, or in the case of a BSB entity, its managers or employees, undergo such further training and/or prohibiting the respondent from accepting or carrying out any public access instructions; and/or such other matters as the Tribunal may consider appropriate for the purpose of protecting the public and/or preventing a repetition of the conduct in question.

7.14 Under rE225 to 233, the Tribunal has the power to suspend a barrister pending any appeal to the High Court, where he or she has been disbarred, suspended or prohibited from accepting or carrying out any public access work or instructions for more than twelve months. There are equivalent provisions for other categories of BSB-regulated persons and entities. The Tribunal must hear both sides before such an order is made. It can be ordered to start from a given date, i.e. to enable a barrister to complete a part-heard trial. The barrister may apply to vary such an order if there is any change of circumstances.

Sanctions guidance, sentences and principles

7.15. The Bar Tribunals and Adjudication Service publishes Guidance for its panel members both on procedure and on sanctions in *Sanctions Guidance*, (version 5, Oct 2019). This documentation is available on the BTAS website.

7.16 As absurd as it now sounds, the panel guidance was formerly top secret. It was kept under lock and key by the administrator to the Disciplinary Tribunal. It was never shown to the defence despite being the product of the BSB. But its existence did not remain a secret. Eventually, the author procured a copy and, despite inevitable disapproval, cited parts of it in the appeal of *DL v BSB* in 2011. The genie was out of the bottle and the manual was no longer secret. *DL* was a revolutionary event which resulted in far greater transparency. Once BTAS was formed after 2014 the publication of panel manuals became the norm. It is to the credit of BTAS that it has maintained this transparency since its inception.

Bolton

7.17 The most cited dictum in sentencing is the *Bolton* principle, deriving from *Bolton v Law Society* [1994] 1 WLR 512, in which Sir Thomas Bingham MR said this at 518 about sentencing practice by the Solicitors Disciplinary Tribunal:

> It is required of lawyers practising in this country that they should discharge their professional duties with integrity, probity and complete trustworthiness. That requirement

applies as much to barristers as it does to solicitors. If I make no further reference to barristers it is because this appeal concerns a solicitor, and where a client's moneys have been misappropriated the complaint is inevitably made against a solicitor, since solicitors receive and handle clients' moneys and barristers do not…

…It is important that there should be full understanding of the reasons why the tribunal makes orders which might otherwise seem harsh. There is, in some of these orders, a punitive element: a penalty may be visited on a solicitor who has fallen below the standards required of his profession in order to punish him for what he has done and to deter any other solicitor tempted to behave in the same way. Those are traditional objects of punishment. But often the order is not punitive in intention. Particularly is this so where a criminal penalty has been imposed and satisfied. The solicitor has paid his debt to society. There is no need, and it would be unjust, to punish him again. In most cases the order of the tribunal will be primarily directed to one or other or both of two other purposes. One is to be sure that the offender does not have the opportunity to repeat the offence. This purpose is achieved for a limited period by an order of suspension; plainly it is hoped that experience of suspension will make the offender meticulous in his future compliance with the required standards. The purpose is achieved for a longer period, and quite possibly indefinitely, by an order of striking off.

The second purpose is the most fundamental of all: to maintain the reputation of the solicitors' profession as one in which every member, of whatever standing, may be trusted to the ends of the earth. To maintain this reputation and sustain public confidence in the integrity of the profession it is often necessary that those guilty of serious lapses are not only expelled but denied re-admission. If a member of the public sells his house, very often his largest asset, and entrusts the proceeds' to his solicitor, pending re-investment in another house, he is ordinarily entitled to expect that the solicitor will be a person whose trustworthiness is not, and never has been, seriously in question. Otherwise, the whole profession, and the public as a whole, is injured. A profession's most valuable asset is its collective reputation and the confidence which that inspires.

Because orders made by the tribunal are not primarily punitive, it follows that considerations which would ordinarily weigh in mitigation of punishment have less effect on the exercise of this jurisdiction than on the ordinary run of sentences imposed in criminal cases. It often happens that a solicitor appearing before the tribunal can adduce a wealth of glowing tributes from his professional brethren. He can often show that for him and his family the consequences of striking off or suspension would be little short of tragic. Often he will say, convincingly, that he has learned his lesson and will not offend again. On applying for restoration after striking off, all these points may be made, and the former solicitor may also be able to point to real efforts made to re-establish himself and redeem his reputation. All these matters are relevant and should be considered. But none of them touches the essential issue, which is the need to maintain among members of the public a well-founded confidence that any solicitor whom they instruct will be a person of unquestionable integrity, probity and trustworthiness. Thus it can never be an objection to an order of suspension in an appropriate case that the solicitor may be unable to re-establish his practice when the period of suspension is past. If that proves, or appears likely, to be so the consequence, for the individual and his family may be deeply unfortunate and unintended. But it does not make suspension the wrong order if it is otherwise right. The reputation' of the profession is more important than the fortunes of any individual member. Membership of a profession brings many benefits, but that is a part of the price.

7.18 It may be thought ironic that such a great liberal judge as Lord Bingham is cited as the progenitor of such a coercive principle – that punishment may deliberately not fit the offence for some higher reason than the case itself. Whilst in recent years the solicitors' *Bolton* principle has been cited and used in barrister disciplinary sentencing to justify heavier sanctions, so has the European concept of proportionality been cited to qualify such an approach. There are strong tensions between these polar opposite factors.

7.19 Distilling *Bolton*, the Guidance instructs the panels that the purposes of applying sanctions for professional misconduct are: a. to protect the public and consumers of legal services; b. to maintain high standards of behaviour and performance at the Bar; and c. to promote public and professional confidence in the complaints and disciplinary process. These purposes have equal weighting.

Dishonesty and disbarment

7.20 The first rule of thumb is that any finding of barrister dishonesty is likely to be terminal. This is not an invariable rule, but it is the default position for such findings. Where there is strong mitigation, then a good plea in mitigation may persuade the Tribunal to impose a suspension rather than a disbarment.

7.21 Barristers in private practice do not handle client money. But a barrister's honesty is vital for a different reason. His duty to the court is paramount. Judges sitting at all levels of the justice system should be able to trust a barrister's word. Without such trust between judges and advocates, the administration of justice itself could break down. Whilst a barrister's dishonesty may not result in a client losing money, it may result in the erosion of the efficiency, and ultimately the effectiveness, of the justice system.

7.22 Some other examples of dishonest behaviour that may form the basis for charges of professional misconduct include: making a false declaration on Call to the Bar, inflating marks or experience on an application form, falsification of documents, certain types of criminal convictions, such as theft, perjury, or fraud and intentionally false or misleading statements on websites or other promotional material.

7.23 The Guidance about disbarment is that it may be appropriate where the Tribunal is satisfied that one or more of the following factors apply: a. the barrister has engaged in a serious and/or persistent departure or departures from professional standards; b. serious harm has been caused to either the administration of justice, the reputation of the Bar or any person including the individual complainant and there is a continuing risk to the public or the reputation of the profession if the barrister is permitted to continue in practice; c. the barrister has been convicted of a serious criminal offence involving dishonesty, violence or sexual offences; d. the barrister has acted dishonestly regardless of whether it was in connection with a criminal offence; e. the barrister has shown a persistent lack of insight into the seriousness of his/her actions or the consequences for his/her practice, the administration of justice or the reputation of the Bar.

7.24 Panels are advised in the Guidance to take the same line as the SDT, namely that in *SRA v Sharma* [2010] EWHC 2022 (Admin), Coulson J (as he then was) said that save in exceptional circumstances, a finding of dishonesty will lead to a solicitor being struck off the roll, see *Bolton supra* and *Salsbury v Law Society* [2008] EWCA Civ 1285. That is stated to be the "normal and necessary" penalty in cases of dishonesty, but that there will be a small residual category where striking off will be a disproportionate sanction. In deciding whether or not a particular case falls into that category, relevant factors will include the nature, scope and extent of the dishonesty itself; whether it was momentary, such as in *Burrowes v Law Society* [2002] EWHC 2900, or over a lengthy period of time, such as in *Bultitude v Law Society* [2004] EWCA Civ 1853; whether it was a benefit to the accused and whether it had an adverse effect on others.

7.25 The reader may wonder why the Bar has to take heed of the approach in the case of solicitors rather than the converse. The reason for this is that, even today and unlike in the case of the SDT, there is no registry of BTAS decisions from which sentencing (or any other) regularly occurring principles in barrister disciplinary cases can be deduced. This is a serious limitation of the Bar's system. The accumulated wisdom of scores of decisions of the Visitors to the Inns of Court in the 20th Century and beyond has been lost for all time, despite law reporting at that time being more prolific and sophisticated than ever before in the history of the English common law. The Bar's failure to capture, archive and make accessible to all, its own past decision-making, as with other recent serious inefficiencies (see the *CR* litigation) is not merely inexcusable, but could easily become the enemy of justice when the defence is deprived of past, unreported decisions of relevance, that might assist it, which the BSB itself, for the same reason, omits to disclose. Worse still, this prevents the Disciplinary Tribunals, whose members have fixed terms, from inheriting, building on and developing a body of knowledge and expertise.

Perjured evidence

7.26 Where the barrister (or authorised body) is not facing a specific charge alleging dishonest conduct, but the panel nonetheless decides that he/she/it has engaged in dishonest behaviour during the course of the disciplinary proceedings, the panel may refer the matter to the BSB to consider raising a fresh complaint. The panel is instructed by the Guidance only to sanction the barrister in relation to the charges currently before it. That follows the decision of the Visitors in *R v BSB* (2013) Unrep. 19th July, at [16]:

> We have no hesitation in rejecting the submission that the Tribunal was entitled to take account of Mr R's lies to the Tribunal in deciding whether the failure to comply with the court order was discreditable. What he

said to the Tribunal was not part of the circumstances relating to the non payment. If a defendant lies to a Disciplinary Tribunal, that may be a serious matter which can be met with a subsequent charge of dishonest conduct, but it cannot be part of the original offence.

In a case where dishonestly *is* alleged and the barrister is found guilty and disbarred, the perjured evidence becomes irrelevant for obvious reasons, although a successful appeal might trigger a fresh report. It is possible that dishonesty could be alleged, that charge is not proven, but the barrister is found to have lied about something else in the course of giving evidence. In that event, the panel could report the matter to the BSB.

Integrity

7.27 Modern practice has produced the notion of a lack of integrity, or a new word, 'disintegrity'. This is pleaded by regulators, often hand in hand, with 'recklessness', to convey a serious allegation that is less serious than a finding of dishonesty. In such cases, there is greater scope for a successful mitigation to achieve a punishment short of a disbarment or a suspension, although every case will turn on its own facts. A finding of lack of integrity usually carries a lower sanction than a finding of dishonesty: *Adetoye v SRA* [2019] EWHC 707 (Admin),

Suspension – principles

7.28 Suspension is a particularly severe penalty for a barrister in private practice. It inhibits not only work in the period of suspension, but the natural instructions flowing from such work, possibly well beyond the period of suspension. The Guidance advises that suspension should be reserved for cases where the barrister represents a risk to the public which requires that he/she be unable to practise for a period of time and/or the behaviour is so serious as to undermine public confidence in the profession and therefore a signal needs to be sent to the barrister, the profession and the public that the behaviour in question is unacceptable.

7.29 The factors taken into account are not limited to but include: a. actual harm or the risk of harm to the public; b. the seriousness of any breach of the Handbook; c. abuse of position or abuse of trust; d. that the barrister has shown a lack of insight into and understanding of his/her actions and their consequences; e. the barrister has shown a lack of integrity that is not so serious as to warrant disbarment; and f. the behaviour is likely to be repeated or has been repeated since the initial incident.

7.30 It is usual to impose a suspension for a specified period of time. The Disciplinary Tribunal Regulations do not stipulate an upper limit to the period of suspension that a 5-person panel can impose. However, it is believed, arguably wrongly, that very long periods of suspension are tantamount to disbarment and therefore, the Guidance states that where a suspension of more than three years is considered appropriate, the Disciplinary Tribunal should give serious consideration to disbarring the barrister unless the circumstances are exceptional. The Guidance then quotes a 1961 Visitors' decision for this proposition, but there appears to be no transcript of it available. The Guidance surmises that, the longer the period of suspension, the more difficult it will be for the barrister to return to practice as an effective advocate – that may of course depend on the level of experience and on the type of practice. But the reasoning of this argument is crude: it would appear to be tantamount to saying that a sentence of three years of imprisonment is tantamount to a death sentence, so the court might as well execute the convicted Defendant. In any event, for a barrister with any sort of practice, any suspension measured in years would be the equivalent of a substantial financial penalty. Further, if, exceptionally, a period of suspension longer than three years is imposed, it may well be combined with conditions as to retraining so as to ensure that before the barrister returns to practice, appropriate refresher training has been undertaken.

7.31 The Guidance provides banding for suspensions as follows:

Short = up to 3 months;

Medium = over 3 months and up to 6 months

Long = over 6 months and up to three years

7.32 Tribunals are enabled to defer the date when a period of suspension comes into effect. This also applies to suspensions of less than three months in exceptional circumstances.

7.33 When sanctioning non-practising barristers in cases where the Sanctions Guidance recommends a period of suspension, non-practising barristers are prevented from renewing their practising certificate for an equivalent period of time.

Deterrence

7.34 The Guidance further instructs panels that in fulfilling the above purposes it is important to avoid the recurrence of behaviour by the individual or the authorised body as well as to "provide an example" in order to maintain public confidence in the profession, i.e. *pour encourager les autres*. Panellists are instructed in terms that they should also bear in mind that sanctions are preventative and not intended to be punitive in nature, but nevertheless may have that effect. This advice is repeated across the main professions. These high level 18th Century quasi-military concepts are capable of working real injustice.

7.35 Deterrent sentencing is encouraged. This is in order to "send a signal" to the profession where misbehaviour is prevalent. It is not known how, or on what evidential basis, the panel decides if certain misbehaviour is prevalent. The need for deterrence was simply assumed in *FK v BSB* [2018] EWHC 2184 (Admin)

Proportionality

7.36 The effect of the principle of proportionality is that the sanction imposed should be no more onerous than the circumstances require; the lowest proportionate punishment should be imposed in any particular case. Some regulatory systems require panels to conduct a written exercise whereby, in ascending order of gravity, they spell out in terms why each potential sanction is, or is not, applicable, as being proportionate or not as the case may be. Decisions of Bar panels do not tend to do this.

Fines

7.37 Fines are imposed in many cases in their own right and in combination with other sanctions. Traditionally, fines imposed on barristers are less severe than those imposed on solicitors, which often seem very severe indeed. It is thought that this will change, not because barristers are perceived to be better off than formerly – many are not – but because public expectation, as presumably perceived by the strong lay component within the tribunal panel pool, will require barrister and solicitor parity, as with the debate over the move to the civil standard of proof.

7.38 The Tribunal can impose a fine on a barrister of up to £50,000 for acts or omissions that took place on or after 6th January 2014, a fine of up to £15,000 for acts or omissions that took place on or after 31 March 2009 or up to £5,000 for acts or omissions that took place prior to 31 March 2009. It seems remarkable that this available sentence has been enhanced by the BSB tenfold in just 10 years, when, allowing for inflation, the 2020 equivalent of

---

1 "I see the force of Mr Beaumont's submission that the Panel imposed a deterrent sanction, beyond what the individual facts of the case merited, in the absence of evidence that there is or was any systemic problem requiring such deterrence."

£5,000 in 2009, is just £6,751.15. The Guidance suggests that higher fines are reserved for cases where the barrister has profited from his breach. How this might transpire is unclear.

7.39 The maximum fine for a Licensed Body is £250,000. This remains an extraordinary power in the Tribunal's armoury.

7.40 The Guidance provides banding for individual barrister fines as follows:

Low level = up to £1,000

Medium level = over £1,000 and up to £3,000

High level = over £3,000 and up to £50,000

7.41 The Tribunal is obliged as a matter of law to take into account means before imposing a fine: *SRA v Davis & McGlinchey* [2011] EWHC 232 (Admin). The fine and any costs awarded must be aggregated and then discounted to a global sum consistent with the barrister's means: *Matthews v SRA* [2013] EWHC 1525 (Admin). It follows that an accused barrister must make full financial information available to his counsel, so that the Tribunal can, if necessary, be apprised of the barrister's means. BTAS invites such evidence of means to be made available at trial in the event of conviction. The Guidance is clear that a fine should not be increased merely because a barrister can afford it.

7.42 It is possible to ask to pay by instalments but the BSB may oppose this. It may suggest to the Tribunal that this be left to the BSB to agree, but on occasion it proposes payment plans that are not realistic if the barrister is not working. No doubt, the fact that the accounts department of the Bar Council has to police the plan, can be mildly irritating, but there are barristers with modest or no income who genuinely require a great deal of time to discharge fines and costs liabilities. Despite this, the Guidance suggests a maximum instalment period of 12 months.

Reprimands

7.43 The Guidance sees this as a lower end sanction. The public might see a reprimand as the equivalent of punishment by feather duster, but it is not. The Tribunal is mostly sentencing individuals and not firms or corporations. It takes many years for a barrister to build a good reputation. A reprimand may destroy that reputation in the few seconds that it takes to deliver it publicly. Moreover, that reprimand may have to be disclosed in the future in applications for judicial appointment, silk, or to other chambers, employers or in group bids for work. It should never be assumed by anyone that a reprimand is not a very severe sentence indeed for most barristers. Moreover, the outcome of disciplinary cases is published on the internet and in periodicals such as *Legal Futures,* so as to be permanently available to anyone in the world. The reprimand of the barristers of today is not the private ticking off of yesteryear, but a worldwide public humiliation.

7.44 The Guidance provides that relevant positive factors that would indicate that a reprimand is appropriate include, but are not limited to: a. no evidence of loss to any person including the individual complainant; b. appreciation and understanding on behalf of the barrister of the failings; c. the behaviour being isolated; d. the behaviour not being intentional (but this is not applicable in cases of discrimination); e. genuine expressions of regret/remorse; and f. previous good history.

Public Access cases

7.45 The Bar Public Access scheme, introduced in 2004, is a success. The essence of this work is ready access to the public. That access must never be abused. The strong public interest in access to justice at manageable cost relies on the Bar Public Access scheme working for the vast majority of barristers who conduct themselves with competence, efficiency and integrity. However, the small minority who do not, risk jeopardising the scheme for the public and for the rest of the Bar who undertake such work. Consequently, the Tribunal has a sentencing power to ban barristers from doing this work. A ban might be justified if there has been exploitation or serious and repeated maladministration, such as a failure to provide a client care letter setting out the detailed terms of the engagement. But it is all too easy to assert fee exploitation without comparative evidence of rates charged in the marketplace for equivalent work by other barristers and by solicitors dealing directly with the public who, for the most part in many areas of privately paid work, charge more than the Bar. New rules introduced by the Competition and Markets Authority require transparency in fees and, in any event, most direct access clients shop round. But any evidence of exploitation of clients, supported if necessary by expert evidence about fees, ought properly to trigger a *Bolton*-driven ban.

Advice as to future conduct

7.46 This is a valuable means of disposal, albeit one that is open to the BSB itself, so that where it is imposed on its own by the panel, one often wonders whether the proceedings could have been handled less proscriptively by way of such an order at inception.

Combining sanctions

7.47 A combination of sanctions may be appropriate and is permitted in relation to a single breach of the Handbook.

No further action

7.48 This is the Bar's equivalent of an absolute discharge, where there is a technical breach of the Handbook, where the *AW/SH* filter does not assist the barrister, but where the panel is perhaps not comfortable about imposing a sanction at all on an otherwise valuable and conscientious member of the profession.

Testimonials

7.49 The Guidance rather surprisingly enjoins panels to treat testimonials with some caution[2]. It is submitted that this is very wrong indeed and, since the Guidance is just that, a panel that is uncomfortable about a possible sanction against a particularly distinguished and valuable member of the Bar, who has served his or her clients and/or the profession conscientiously for many years, should feel free to give powerful testimonials such weight as they deserve. This may be particularly so if they are capable of persuading the panel to suspend rather than to disbar. Part II, para 7 of the Guidance re-affirms that the Tribunal has complete discretion to impose any sanction which is appropriate to an individual case: the final decision is a matter for decision-makers alone.

Fitness to Practise

7.50 The Tribunal has the power to refer any concerns about a barrister's fitness to practise to the BSB to consider whether to initiate Fitness to Practise proceedings. If there is evidence of mental ill-health or addiction to alcohol or drugs, for example, the extent to which this is deployed as or emphasised in mitigation must be balanced against the risk that it could be used by the BSB to institute a fitness to practise process.

Guidance on specific breaches

7.51 The Guidance contains detailed tables about many (but not all) of the areas of the Handbook and factual scenarios that lead to charges of professional misconduct, with suggested mitigating and aggravating features for each scenario and suggested sanctions and sanction ranges. These should be consulted online from the Sanctions Guidance document itself on the BTAS website. The available sample areas of practice with suggested sanctions and

---

2 In the days when the guidance was secret, this would have been highly objectionable.

types of aggravating and mitigating factors, are: misleading the court (A1); abusing the role of an advocate (A1); conviction for drink driving and related offences (B1); a conviction for assault and violent acts; convictions for drug possession or supply (B3); convictions of BSB Licensed/Authorised Bodies (B4); dishonesty cases (B5); discrimination and harassment (B6); sexual misconduct (B7); breaches of the Public Access Rules (C1); breach of the cab-rank rule (C2); accepting instructions when professionally embarrassed (C3); late withdrawal from a case (C4); failure to comply with a court order or judgment (C5 & C6); misconduct over fees and charging (C7); discourtesy (C8); using barrister status to influence (C9); incompetence (C10); delay (C11); failure to report a criminal charge or conviction promptly to BSB (D1); failure to respond to the BSB (D2); failure to comply with an Order of a BTAS Tribunal, the Legal Ombudsman, the BSB or the Independent Decision Making Body (D3); failure to report bankruptcy or insolvency promptly to BSB (D4); failure to report serious misconduct of themselves or others to BSB (D5); poor practice administration (E1); holding out, (i.e. the barrister has deliberately stated that he/she is entitled to practise and has provided legal services for financial gain when he/she is not entitled to do so); (E2); breach of practising requirements (E3); breach of pupillage rules (E4).

Aggravating factors

7.52 General aggravating factors stated in the Guidance are: premeditation, motive of financial gain, corruption and gross deception, coercion, involvement of others, persistent conduct or conduct over a lengthy period, undermining of the profession in the eyes of the public, attempts to conceal the misconduct, attempting to blame somebody else, the effect on the complainant, the vulnerability of the complainant, any discriminatory behaviour or motivation, any breach of trust, bullying or harassment, position of responsibility within the profession, previous disciplinary findings for similar breaches, previous disciplinary findings for any types of breaches, lack of remorse for having committed the offences, failure to respond promptly to communications from the BSB, inappropriate behaviour frustrating the administration of the complaint, a failure to attend the Tribunal without an explanation, an indication of an element of dishonesty and a lack of insight.

Mitigating factors

7.53 General mitigating factors stated in the Guidance are: admissions, genuine remorse, any willingness to compromise (i.e. in matters such as fees), limited experience in the profession, that the breach was unintentional (irrelevant in cases of discrimination), isolated incident (inapplicable in cases of discrimination), heat of the moment (inapplicable in cases of discrimination), cooperation with BSB, voluntary remedial steps, evidence of financial or other hardship, whether advice was sought and obtained from the Bar Council ethics helpline, the personal circumstances of the accused barrister such as bereavement, relationship breakdown and divorce and the testimonials. To these one should add credit for a guilty plea of one-third in the term of any suspension or the size of any fine: see *FK v BSB* [2018] EWHC 2184 (Admin) at [75].

Publication of sanction

7.54 For most professionals, the publication of even a modest-sounding sanction, is the worst part of the penalty. Long gone are the days when professionals were disciplined in private hearings with the outcome disseminated by word of mouth. The internet has transformed professional discipline from a parochial to a worldwide affair, with news of the outcome spreading to millions of potential readers around the globe in seconds. The destruction of professional reputation by internet is an unofficial punishment far beyond the comprehension of those who cast the original templates of barrister discipline.

CHAPTER SEVEN – SANCTIONS • 173

7.55 At the investigation stage, the BSB does respect confidentiality: rE63. The BSB does this, to its credit, even in the face of enquiries from the media.

7.56 After a decision to charge a barrister is made, charges have been served and a Convening Order has been made, the charges will appear on the BTAS list of forthcoming hearings on its website. Even then, they will not detail the alleged facts, a benign practice not followed by other tribunals.

7.57 After a finding of guilt, the BSB often issues a Press Release. This seems to be *"pour encourager les autres"*. For a defeated Defendant facing an uncertain future, it is often received as the worst kind of triumphalism. Conversely, acquittals are met with no Press Release from the BSB and certainly no apology, even where the case should never have been brought at all. The Press Releases are published in *Legal Futures*, which has a substantial weekly e-mail circulation to solicitors and barristers. In *DM v BSB* [2017] EWHC 969 (Admin) at [56], it was held that the BSB went too far in asserting guilt in a Press Release concerning an impending re-trial:

> 56. The extract from the BSB press release quoted in the legal press stated:
>
> *"Notwithstanding the history of this case, the BSB remains of the view that Mr [M] acted dishonestly and falsified the client care letters during our original investigation. As this is a fundamental breach of the integrity expected from all barristers, it is right that this serious disciplinary matter can be re-heard by an independent disciplinary tribunal."*
>
> 57. The Appellant submitted that this statement deprived him of a fair trial because:

i) the professional regulator was placing improper pressure on the members of the Tribunal to find the charges proved at the re-trial;

ii) it violated the presumption of innocence in Article 6(2) ECHR which also applies in disciplinary proceedings (see *Albert and Le Compte v Belgium* (1983) 5 EHRR 533, at [39]; *Allenet v Ribemont v France* (1995) 20 EHRR 557 ; *Krause v Switzerland* (1978) 13 DR & 73, at pp 75–76; *Clayton & Tomlinson: The Law of Human Rights*, 2nd ed. para 11.487 referring to the principle that public officials must not declare a person's guilt in the absence of a court finding of guilt); and

iii) the prejudicial nature of the comments gave rise to a real possibility (applying the test in *Porter v Magill*) that the Tribunal members would be biased against the Appellant, particularly since the lay members were akin to jurors.

58. In my judgment, in the exceptional circumstances of this case, the BSB was entitled to issue a press release about the outcome of the earlier appeal proceedings, to which it was a party, particularly in the light of the publicity which the case attracted, and the judicial criticisms of its conduct.

59. I also consider that, in its press release the BSB was entitled to express its view that the Appellant ought to face a re-trial, in the light of the seriousness of the allegations against him (dishonesty and fabrication of documents) and the strength of the evidence against him, which had been acknowledged by the Court of Appeal when allowing his appeal because of the risk of unfairness arising from the non-disclosure of the prosecution witness statement. After all, the BSB had already expressed such views in public at the second hearing before the Visitors in July 2015, which took place at the Royal Courts of Justice, and which was

the subject of the press coverage. I agree that the BSB went somewhat further than was proper, in expressing its view that the Appellant had committed the offences with which he was charged. As Mr Counsell QC conceded, it would have been better if the press release had been expressed in more circumspect language, confining itself to commenting on the strength of the evidence against the Appellant.

7.58 All findings, including Determination By Consent ("DBC") reports, remain in the public domain for a minimum of 2 years. Findings that do not result in a sentence involving a period of suspension, disbarment, or removal of the authorisation of an authorised body, cease being placed in the public domain by the BSB after 2 years. Where a finding of a Tribunal involves a period of suspension from practice of 12 months or less, the finding will cease being placed in the public domain by the BSB 5 years after the end of the suspension period. Where a finding of a Tribunal involves a period of suspension from practice of over 12 months, the finding will cease being placed in the public domain by the BSB 10 years after the end of the suspension period. Where a finding of a Tribunal involves a disbarment or removal of an authorisation of an authorised body, even if combined with other lesser sanctions, the full details of the finding will remain in the public domain for a period of 60 years. All findings of professional misconduct remain on a barrister's or authorised body's "record" indefinitely.

7.59 When a charge has been admitted or proved, the findings are posted on the BTAS website in accordance with rE243.1, within 14 days of the finding being made, regardless of whether the sentence has been pronounced or an appeal had been submitted. The Tribunal's report is posted on the BTAS website in accordance with BSB Regulation rE243A within a reasonable time, unless the Tribunal directs that this is not in the public interest. All findings remain on the website for a minimum of 2 years. Findings of Tribunals that do not result in a sentence involving a period of suspension or disbarment will be removed from the website after

2 years. Where a finding of a Tribunal involves a period of suspension of 12 months or less, the finding will be taken down from the BTAS website after 10 years. Where a professional misconduct finding involves a finding that includes a suspension of over 12 months, or a disbarment combined with other orders, the full details of the finding will remain posted on the BTAS website indefinitely.

7.60 As for the BSB's publication policy, rE73 provides that DBC findings are published to the same extent as Disciplinary Tribunal findings, as provided for by rE243 and rE243A. BTAS has no responsibility for publishing findings under the DBC procedure, responsibility for which lies entirely with the BSB. The relevant regulations do not require the BSB to publish Disciplinary Tribunal findings. Responsibility for those lies with BTAS. However, the regulations allow for the BSB to publish findings and sanctions of Disciplinary Tribunals on *its* website. The published information will be posted on the BSB's website, included (possibly emotively) in the barrister's entry on the BSB Register and will be available to anyone on request.

7.61 The Disciplinary Tribunal may order that it is "not in the public interest" to publish the finding and/or sanction: rE243.1. This may apply to proposed BTAS and BSB publications: rE243.2. The onus is on the barrister to apply to the Tribunal to the effect that publication by BTAS and/or by BSB is not in the public interest. Such cases will be rare. But there may, perhaps, be a case for arguing that publication be limited to BTAS. For the convicted in low level matters, a multiplicity of publications must seem like being put in the pillory, but not for a few hours for the amusement of a few passing villagers, to be pelted with unsavoury objects, but for as long as the internet should endure, to be besmirched for eternity. In centuries to come, publication by internet, like the pillory, abolished in England in 1837, will be viewed as an unspeakably cruel punishment to inflict on professionals.

7.62 Where a disciplinary or appeal panel dismisses all the charges against a barrister, details of the outcome will not be put in the public domain save where the barrister requests publication. Therefore, even if the posting in relation to the hearing date remains on the BTAS website after the conclusion of the case, no information will be provided by BTAS about the dismissed charges. An anonymised summary of the case will be placed on the BTAS website, unless the Tribunal directs that this is not in the public interest. Where a charge in front of a Tribunal, or under the DBC procedure, is found not proved, details of the outcome will not be put in the public domain by the BSB unless the relevant person charged so requests.

7.63 All relevant findings are posted on the BSB's website within 7 days of the finding being made, regardless of whether an appeal has been lodged with the High Court. All Tribunal findings are listed initially on the BSB's website as "open to appeal" and such listings remain in place until the 21-day period for the issue of a Notice of Appeal has expired without such a Notice being submitted. Where a Notice of Appeal is issued, the finding is listed as "Subject to Appeal" and this listing will remain on the website until the appeal has been determined by the High Court, at which point it will either be marked as "final" or removed. Where an appeal is successful, the postings on the BSB website and Bar Register will be removed and details of the findings will no longer be put in the public domain by the BSB. However, the BSB and BTAS may choose to post, or provide a link to the High Court appeal judgment on its website, including a covering summary of the case, where the judgment may include points of wider interest. A barrister may request that the fact the appeal has been allowed be published on the BSB's website, however, the entry will not include any details relating to the appeal apart from a statement that it was allowed.

CHAPTER EIGHT
BARRISTERS AND HUMAN RIGHTS

8.1 Article 6 of the Convention for the Protection of Human Rights and Fundamental Freedoms (1950) (the "ECHR") was a reaction by civilised nations against the horrors of the Nazi regime. All of the terrible features of the show trials held by the *Volksgerichtshof*, such as *fait accompli*, secrecy, perfunctoriness, arbitrariness, outside manipulation, judicial placemen and extreme penalties, were rendered unlawful by Article 6.

8.2 Sadly, such traits as arbitrariness and disproportionality of sanction have not been unknown to the English Bar when disciplining its own. Sometimes, incredibly, they are still seen in the way that individual chambers go about investigating and disciplining individual barrister members. The Bar is still a place, where megalomaniacal bullying goes on internally in the running of Chambers.

8.3 It is therefore hardly surprising that this culture is reflected externally, in the name of the Bar Standards Board, an organisation largely designed and run by barristers. Only now, since 1998, any bullies have to contend with the Human Rights Act 1998. Article 6, applicable to the BSB, the Bar Tribunals and Adjudication Service and the Council of the Inns of Court (but not to individual sets of chambers) as "public authorities", renders unlawful any semblance of a return to the bad old days of barrister "kangaroo courts". This is a critical legal check and balance.

8.4 By virtue of Section 6 of the Human Rights Act 1998, it is unlawful for a "public authority" to act in a way which is incompatible with a right set out in the ECHR. These rights are annexed to the 1998 Act and in that way, are part of UK statute law.

8.5 The BSB, the General Council of the Bar, the Council of the Inns of Court and the Bar Tribunals and Adjudication Service are undoubtedly "public authorities" within the meaning of the 1998 Act.

8.6 There are three main features of the ECHR which tend to occur in barrister disciplinary proceedings: the right to a fair trial (ECHR Article 6), the right to a private life and private correspondence (ECHR Article 8) and the right to freedom of expression (ECHR Article 10). There may well be others that do occur and will occur as time passes, but the focus here is on these three.

Fair trial rights

8.7 Article 6 of the ECHR provides:

> Right to a fair trial
>
> 1. In the determination of his civil rights and obligations or of any criminal charge against him, everyone is entitled to a fair and public hearing within a reasonable time by an independent and impartial tribunal established by law.
>
> Judgment shall be pronounced publicly but the press and public may be excluded from all or part of the trial in the interest of morals, public order or national security in a democratic society, where the interests of juveniles or the protection of the private life of the parties so require, or to the extent strictly necessary in the opinion of the court in special circumstances where publicity would prejudice the interests of justice.
>
> 2. Everyone charged with a criminal offence shall be presumed innocent until proved guilty according to law.

3. Everyone charged with a criminal offence has the following minimum rights:

(a) to be informed promptly, in a language which he understands and in detail, of the nature and cause of the accusation against him;

(b) to have adequate time and facilities for the preparation of his defence;

(c) to defend himself in person or through legal assistance of his own choosing or, if he has not sufficient means to pay for legal assistance, to be given it free when the interests of justice so require;

(d) to examine or have examined witnesses against him and to obtain the attendance and examination of witnesses on his behalf under the same conditions as witnesses against him;

(e) to have the free assistance of an interpreter if he cannot understand or speak the language used in court.

8.8 The Court of Appeal stated in *R ([M]) v Visitors to the Inns of Court* [2015] EWCA Civ 12 at [23]:

There is no difficulty in accepting the proposition that the civil limb of article 6 applies to professional disciplinary proceedings including those prosecuted by the BSB: see *Le Compte, Van Leuven and de Meyere v Belgium* (1982) 4 EHRR 1; *P (A Barrister) v General Council of the Bar* [2005] 1 WLR 3019.

8.9 This was tacitly accepted by the 3-judge Court of Appeal in *R (CR) v Visitors to the Inns of Court & Bar Standards Board* [2014] EWCA Civ 1630. The European Commission found that the Bar's disciplinary system engaged the civil limb of Art 6 in *G v*

UK (1988) 55 DR 251. Proceedings before the Solicitors Disciplinary Tribunal have been held not to involve the determination of *criminal* charges (under Art 7): *Brown v UK* [1998] 28 EHRR 233.

8.10 The civil limb of Art 6(1) guarantees untrammelled access to a Tribunal before which guilt and/or sanction are to be determined. The hearing is to be conducted fairly and it must, as a default rule, be in public and within a reasonable time. The Tribunal must be both independent and impartial. It must be, "established by law".

8.11 The Art. 6(2) and 6(3) protections for *criminal* cases are, in effect, incorporated into barrister disciplinary proceedings by way of the application of the rules of natural justice: see rE165.

Fairness

8.12 The fairness guarantee "*is one of the fundamental principles of any democratic society, within the meaning of the Convention*": *Pretto v Italy* [1983] 6 EHRR 182 at [21]. The right to a fair hearing before a tribunal as guaranteed by Article 6(1), must be interpreted in the light of the Preamble to the Convention, which declares the rule of law to be part of the common heritage of the Contracting States: *Brumărescu v Romania* [2001] 33 EHRR 35 at [60]. There can therefore be no justification for interpreting Article 6(1) restrictively: *Moreira de Azevedo v Portugal* [1991] 13 EHRR. 721 at [66].

8.13 Fairness includes having access to the relevant documents in the possession of the administrative authorities: *McGinley & Egan v United Kingdom* [1999] 27 EHRR 1.

8.14 The concept of a fair trial comprises the fundamental right to adversarial proceedings. This is closely linked to the principle of 'equality of arms': *Regner v Czech Republic* [GC] [2018] 66 EHRR 9 at [146]. The requirements resulting from the right to adversarial proceedings are in principle the same in both civil and criminal cases: *Werner v Austria* [1998] 26 EHRR 310 at [66]. Each party must be afforded a reasonable opportunity to present his case – including his evidence – under conditions that do not place him at a substantial disadvantage vis-à-vis the other party: *Regner v Czech Republic supra* at [146]. The desire to save time and expedite the proceedings does not justify disregarding such a fundamental principle as the right to adversarial proceedings: *Nideröst-Huber v Switzerland*. [1998] 25 EHRR 709 at [30]. The right to adversarial proceedings means in principle the opportunity for the parties to have knowledge of and comment on all evidence adduced or observations filed with a view to influencing the court's decision: *Ruiz-Mateos v Spain* [1993] 16 EHRR 505 at [63].

8.15 In recent years, there has, on rare occasions, been an unfortunate tendency for the BSB to send email communications to BTAS without simultaneously copying them to the defence. Even if they are administrative in content, this is a bad practice. The ECtHR holds that it is impermissible for one party to make submissions to a court without the knowledge of the other and on which the latter has no opportunity to comment: *APEH Üldözötteinek Szövetsége v Hungary* [2002] 34 EHRR 34 at [42].

8.16 The denial of legal aid to a party has been held to have deprived the party of the opportunity to present a case effectively before the court against a much wealthier opponent: *Steel & Morris v United Kingdom* [2005] 41 EHRR 22 at [72]. Where an unrepresented barrister faces a prosecution funded by the Bar Council through compulsory subscription income, which now includes payment to BSB counsel, it is submitted that that may breach the equality of arms principle. As a monopoly insurer, Bar Mutual should, but does not, guarantee funding in all disciplinary cases, only those in which there is a concurrent risk of a claim in negligence. But many complaints emanate from sources other than clients, such as lay adversaries, other barristers, solicitors and judges, none of whom would have locus to bring civil claims. The

Bar Council's deliberate abrogation of the defence advisory service BCAS, (founded by the author in the mid-1990s), has compounded the inequality of arms. The matter seems ripe for a legal challenge.

Public hearing

8.17 Litigants have a right to a public hearing because this protects them against the administration of justice in secret with no public scrutiny: *Malhous v Czech Republic* [GC] (2001) *Application no. 33071/96* at [55]. In proceedings before a court of first and only instance, the right to a "public hearing" entails an entitlement to an oral hearing unless there are exceptional circumstances that justify dispensing with such a hearing: *Fredin v Sweden (no. 2)* (1994) *Application no. 18928/91* at [21]-[22]. The exceptional character of such circumstances stems essentially from the nature of the questions at issue, for example in cases where the proceedings concern exclusively legal or highly technical questions: *Koottummel v Austria* [2011] 52 EHRR 9 at [19]. In the context of disciplinary proceedings, in view of the impact of the possible penalties on the lives and careers of those concerned and their financial implications, the ECtHR has held that dispensing with an oral hearing should be an exceptional measure and should be duly justified in the light of its case-law: *Ramos Nunes de Carvalho e Sá v Portugal* [GC] (2018) *Applications nos. 55391/13, 57728/13 and 74041/13* at [208]-[211].

8.18 In a case concerning hearings before the Court of Arbitration for Sport ("CAS"), the Court found that the matters relating to the question whether the sanction imposed on the applicant for doping had been justified, had required a hearing open to public scrutiny. It observed that the facts had been contested and that the penalties which the applicant had been liable to incur carried a significant degree of stigma and were likely adversely to affect her professional honour. It therefore concluded that there had been a violation of Article 6(1) on account of the lack of a public hearing before CAS: *Mutu & Pechstein v Switzerland* (2018) *Applications nos. 40575/10 and 67474/10)* at [182]-[183].

8.19 In March 2020, the UK faced an unprecedented national crisis from the COVID-19 pandemic. Courts and tribunals were closed save for emergency work. Most disciplinary trials ceased. This raised the question whether an online trial would be a "public hearing" under Article 6. Some might say this does not matter in a time of crisis. In fact, it matters even more. The combination of emergency and lack of publicity might be regarded by the accused as more, not less, likely to erode fairness rights. Cutting corners will not do. So long as technology such as "Zoom" enables 'streamed' trials to be viewed by the public at will, or for the public to be notified of the stream in advance so they can log into it, then it is submitted that the pre-requisites of Article 6 will be satisfied. This was the directive of Sir Michael Burton GBE (retired High Court judge) sitting as Chair of Conduct & Appeals at the RICS Disciplinary Tribunal in April 2020.

8.20 Neither the letter nor the spirit of Article 6(1) prevents an individual from waiving his right to a public hearing of his own free will, whether expressly or tacitly, but such a waiver must be made in an unequivocal manner and must not run counter to any important public interest: *Le Compte v Belgium* (1982) 4 EHRR 1 at [59].

Reasonable time guarantee

8.21 In the context of barrister disciplinary proceedings, this is an important safeguard. Some respondents, anxious to prove their innocence, do complain about delays. The BSB takes up to 10 weeks to lay Charges that in many cases are already drafted by the Case Examiner at the stage of a decision to prosecute. One senior barrister recounts that from the time of the first of numerous complaints in a linked series in which he was victimised, to the time that the BSB dropped all Charges against him in 2014, some 10 years had elapsed without any of his cases reaching a trial. In

September 2017, several legal journals carried a story that the BSB issued a public apology, thought to be unprecedented, to a QC who was subject to a hopeless complaint, *inter alia*, about the BSB's unwarranted delay in dealing with it. [1]

8.22 The reasonable time safeguard is designed to prevent a person charged from remaining, *"too long in a state of uncertainty about his fate:" Dyer v Watson* [2004] 1 AC 379, PC *per* Lord Bingham at [50]. It is directed primarily towards excessive procedural delays in the conduct of a prosecution, including any appeal.

8.23 The reasonable time guarantee runs from the moment that an individual is subject to a "charge" within the meaning of the Convention. This is taken to be the time when he is "officially notified" or "substantially affected" by proceedings taken against him. So time runs from the date of being officially alerted to the likelihood of proceedings: *Deweer v Belgium* [1980] 2 EHRR 439 at [42]. In fact, it arguably runs from the date of receipt of a complaint to the BSB: *König v Germany* [1979/80] 2 EHRR 170 at [98]. Certainly, the extent of any pre-charge delay must be relevant to the need for alacrity in the post-charge period.

8.24 Examples of unreasonable delay are courts being inactive for periods of ten months and sixteen months: *Robins v UK* [1997] 26 EHRR 527; four years from trial to appeal (*Robins*); nine years from dismissal on disciplinary grounds to appeal: *Darnell v UK* [1993] 18 EHRR 205; Five and a half years from commencement of proceedings to discontinuance: *Davies v UK* [2002] 35 EHRR 29; eight years, eleven months from commencement of proceedings to termination by agreement: *Eastaway v UK* [2005] 40 EHRR 17; nine years: *Blake v UK* [2007] 44 EHRR 29. The reasonableness of the length of proceedings must be assessed in the light of the circumstances of the case and in accordance with the complexity of the case, the conduct of the parties and what was at stake for the applicant in the dispute: *Comingersoll S.A. v Portugal*

---

1 *"BSB makes unprecedented public apology to QC over investigation failures":* Legal Futures, 20th Sept 2017

[2001] 31 EHRR 31. The ECtHR has condemned delay in cases concerning an applicant's occupational status: *König v. Germany supra* at [111].

8.25 The Court will fashion a remedy that is just and appropriate, in accordance with s. 8(1) of the Human Rights Act 1998.[2] It is to be noted that the section also deals with "proposed" acts of public authorities. The appropriate remedy may be a stay of the proceedings if a fair hearing is no longer possible: *A-G's Reference (No.2 of 2001)* [2004] 2 AC 72. If a fair hearing is no longer possible, the public interest becomes irrelevant: *Brown v Stott* [2003] 1 AC 681 at 708. A breach of the reasonable time requirement combined with material prejudice to the defence, such as the impact of the passage of years on already tenuous evidence, would engage *Maxwell* (i) type abuse of process

8.26 Prejudice may also be personal to the accused. A person awaiting trial is presumed by the law to be in a state of "exquisite agony" resulting in a presumption of prejudice as a result of the passage of time, which it must fall to the prosecution to rebut: see the Canadian case of *R v Askov* [1990] 2 SCR 1199. In that case, proceedings were stayed by the SCC against four accused on the basis of unreasonable delay in bringing them to trial. The time elapsed from charge to trial was two years, ten months, but the court drew the line at six to eight months from committal to trial. In that case it was said that:

> There could be no greater frustration imaginable for innocent persons charged with an offence than to be denied the opportunity of demonstrating their innocence for an unconscionable time as a result of unreasonable delays in their trial. The time awaiting trial must be exquisite agony for accused persons and their immediate family. It is a fundamental precept of our criminal law that every individual is presumed

---

2 "In relation to any act (or proposed act) of a public authority which the court finds is (or would be) unlawful, it may grant such relief or remedy, or make such order, within its powers as it considers just and appropriate."

to be innocent until proven guilty. It follows that on the same fundamental level of importance, all accused persons, each one of whom is presumed to be innocent, should be given the opportunity to defend themselves against the charges they face and to have their name cleared and reputation re-established at the earliest possible time.

Independent

8.27 In context, the independence of the Tribunal panel members means independent from the BSB and the Bar Council, which since the reforms of 2014 on the heels of the Browne Report, has been achieved.

8.28 Compliance with this requirement is assessed on the basis of the manner of appointment of the members of the tribunal, the duration of their term of office and the existence of sufficient safeguards against the risk of outside pressure: *Ramos Nunes de Carvalho e Sá v. Portugal supra* at [153]-[156]. The question whether the body presents an *appearance* of independence is also of relevance (ibid. at [144]).

8.29 In the original Visitors' appeal of *CR v BSB* (2013) Unrep. 23rd May, the Appellant argued based on *Starrs v Ruxton* (2000) SLT 42, that the lay members of the trial panel had not had security of tenure, so were not "independent" within Art 6, because their appointment letters, which had been produced after the trial, stated that they could be removed on an open-ended basis, namely: *"should circumstances arise whereby your suitability for membership of the Panel is in question"* i.e. for any reason, which did not exclude disagreement with their past decisions. Wyn Williams J. said this:

> 116. We turn to Mr Beaumont's third point which relates to security of tenure. As we have set out at paragraph 97 above both lay members were appointed in 2005. In our judgment their letters of appointment make it clear that

they were to be appointed for a term of three years but subject to removal *"should circumstances arise whereby your suitability for membership of the Panel is in question"*. That same letter indicated that the appointment was renewable for a further three year term subject to the proviso just mentioned. The letters of appointment were not signed by the President of COIC but the letters made clear that the appointment was by the President as would be any decision to remove the lay members from the panel.

117. Both lay members were re-appointed by letter dated 11 December 2008 signed by the President of COIC. That letter made it clear that the President of COIC had the right to *"discontinue your Panel membership"*. The letter did not specify the circumstances in which this might occur.

118. We are satisfied that the appointment letter and the re-appointment letter must be read together. We do not consider that there is a realistic possibility that the letter of 11 December 2008 was intended to be read as though the President of COIC was, from that time, entitled to withdraw membership of the panel at his or her whim. By 2008 TAB was in existence with its detailed Rules for appointment and review of members of the panel. Appointment was dependent upon suitability. We have found that the purpose of review was to determine continued suitability. In those circumstances it is inconceivable, in our judgment, that it was ever intended or contemplated that the President of COIC could remove a panel member except in circumstances which related to the member's suitability for office.

119. The issue of membership of the panel is but one aspect of the issue of security of tenure. Membership of the panel did not and does not confer any right to sit as a member of a Tribunal although the expectation was and is that panel members sit from time to time. Once nominated

by the President to sit on a tribunal the circumstances in which a panel member does not sit are set out in the Regulations. Following the making of a convening order the Defendant in the particular proceedings has the right to object to a member of a disciplinary tribunal whereupon the President will determine whether or not the objection is justified – see Reg. 8(3) and (4). Reg. 4(7) empowers the President to cancel a nomination "at any time before the commencement of the substantive hearing". Once a substantive hearing has commenced, however, the President has no power to remove a member from a tribunal.

120. In light of the features which we have highlighted in the preceding paragraphs we are satisfied that the lay members of tribunals enjoy sufficient security of tenure to make the tribunal independent. In summary, the lay members were appointed to the panel for defined periods and were removable from the panel only if their suitability to sit as tribunal members was judged to be impaired by the President of COIC. The President is always a very distinguished judge. There is no suggestion, nor could there be, that the President is not able to discharge this function fairly and independently. That must be right, in our judgment, whether or not, as a matter of fact, the President consults COIC about his decision or seeks no advice of any kind. Once nominated to sit on a particular tribunal and once a substantive hearing has commenced the President has no power to remove a lay member. In our judgment when the principles articulated in [*Findlay v United Kingdom* (1997) 24 EHRR 221], *Starrs and* [*Clancy v Caird* [2000] UKHRR 509] are applied in this case there is no foundation for the suggestion that the lay members of the tribunal which considered the case against the Petitioner were not independent or impartial.

8.30 The author's submission was apparently heretical. In fact, this decision was highly controversial and regarded by many as wrong.

Should a Tribunal judge become an unerringly consistent Defendant's man or woman, an open-ended termination clause could always be used by the Bar's establishment to end tenure.

Guarantees against outside pressure

8.31 Judicial independence demands that individual judges be free from undue influence outside the judiciary and from within. Internal judicial independence requires that they be free from directives or pressures from fellow judges or those who have administrative responsibilities in the court, such as the president of the court or the president of a division in the court. The absence of sufficient safeguards securing the independence of judges within the judiciary and, in particular, vis-à-vis their judicial superiors, may lead to the conclusion that an applicant's doubts as to the independence and impartiality of a court are objectively justified: *Agrokompleks v Ukraine* (2012) Application no. 23465/03) at [137].

Appearance of independence

8.32 In order to determine whether a tribunal can be considered to be independent as required by Article 6(1) appearances are of importance: *Sramek v Austria* [1985] 7 EHRR 351 at [42]. As to the appearance of independence, the standpoint of a party is important, but not decisive. What is more decisive is whether the concern of the applicant can be held to be "objectively justified": *Sacilor Lormines v France* [2012] 54 EHRR 34 at [63]. This brings into play a test of the objective observer: *Clarke v United Kingdom* (2005) Application no. 23695/02. Where a tribunal's members include a person who is in a subordinate position, in terms of his duties and the organisation of his service, vis-à-vis one of the parties, litigants may entertain a legitimate doubt about that person's independence, or the appearance of it. Such a situation seriously affects the confidence which courts must inspire: *Sramek v Austria supra*.

Impartial

8.33 This section should be read in conjunction with the section on the law of bias at common law.

8.34 Given the importance of appearances, the existence of a situation that may give rise to doubts as to impartiality should be disclosed at the outset of the proceedings. In that way, the situation can be assessed in the light of the various factors involved in order to determine whether disqualification is actually necessitated: *Nicholas v Cyprus* [2018] 67 EHRR 40 at [64]-[66].

8.35 Impartiality normally denotes the absence of prejudice or bias and its existence or otherwise can be tested in various ways. The concepts of independence and impartiality are closely linked and, depending on the circumstances, may require joint examination. Where impartiality is disputed on a ground that does not immediately appear to be manifestly devoid of merit, the national court must <u>itself</u> check whether such concerns are justified, so that it can remedy any situation that would breach Article 6(1): *Cosmos Maritime Trading & Shipping Agency v Ukraine* (2019) Application no. 53427/09 at [78]-[82].

Criteria for assessing impartiality

8.36 The existence of impartiality must be determined on the basis of a subjective test, where regard must be had to the personal conviction and behaviour of the particular judge, that is, whether the judge held any personal prejudice or bias in a given case; and an objective test, that is to say by ascertaining whether the tribunal itself and, among other aspects, its composition, offered sufficient guarantees to exclude any legitimate doubt in respect of its impartiality: *Micallef v Malta* [2010] 50 EHRR 37 at [93].

Subjective approach

8.37 In applying the subjective test, the Court has consistently held that, *"the personal impartiality of a judge must be presumed until there is proof to the contrary"*: *Le Compte, v Belgium* (1982) 4 EHRR 1 at [58]. In principle, a judge's personal animosity against a party is a compelling reason for disqualification. In practice, the Court often assesses this question by means of the objective approach: *Rustavi 2 Broadcasting Company Ltd and Others v Georgia* (2019) *Application no. 16812/17* at [359].

Objective approach

8.38 It must be determined whether, quite apart from the judge's conduct, there are ascertainable facts which may raise doubts as to his or her impartiality. When applied to a body sitting as a panel, it means determining whether, quite apart from the personal conduct of any of the members of that body, there are ascertainable facts which may raise doubts as to the impartiality of the panel itself. The ECtHR has emphasised that appearances are of importance and that *"justice must not only be done, it must also be seen to be done"*. What is at stake is the confidence which the courts in a democratic society must inspire in the public. Thus, any judge in respect of whom there is a legitimate reason to fear a lack of impartiality must withdraw: *Micallef v. Malta supra* at [98].

8.39 The question of compliance with the fundamental guarantees of independence and impartiality may arise if the structure and functioning of the disciplinary body itself raises serious issues: *Denisov v. Ukraine* (2018) Application no. 76639/11 at [79]. However, despite the commendable capacity of the 2013 Browne Report for critical self-analysis of the Bar's disciplinary structure and functioning, which led to wholesale reform and a new Tribunal system from 2014, apart from some mild criticism, the judges gave the BSB and the old tribunal system a clean bill of health in the *CR* appeals of May 2013 and late 2014.

8.40 This dichotomy between the Bar's admission of its shortcomings, through Desmond Browne QC's report in 2013 and its reforms and the way in which the judiciary, prompted by the Bar Standards Board, closed ranks and avoided any admissions of default in *CR* and the linked appeals, must seem very strange indeed to observers from all the other ECHR signatory countries.

Established by law

8.41 This was the criterion that figured prominently in argument in *Regina (CR) v Bar Standards Board* [2014] EWCA Civ 1630, dealt with elsewhere. "Established by law" means compliant with the domestic rules that govern the Tribunal's own constitution. In *Zeynalov v Azerbaijan* (2013) Application no. 31848/07 at [30], it was held that:

> 30. The phrase "established by law" covers not only the legal basis for the very existence of a "tribunal" but also compliance by the tribunal with the particular rules that govern it and the composition of the bench in each case....The "law", within the meaning of Article 6(1) of the Convention, comprises not only legislation providing for the establishment and competence of judicial organs, but also any other provision of domestic law which, if breached, would render the participation of one or more judges in the examination of a case irregular...

8.42 The practice of tacitly renewing judges' terms of office for an indefinite period after their statutory term of office had expired and pending their reappointment, was held to be contrary to the principle of a "tribunal established by law": *Volkov v Ukraine* [2013] 57 EHRR 1 at [151].

Remedy

8.43 Tribunals may on occasion not satisfy the requirements of Article 6 in every respect: *Le Compte v. Belgium* (1982) 4 EHRR 1 at

[51]. However, no violation of the Convention will be found if the proceedings before those bodies are "subject to subsequent control by a judicial body that has full jurisdiction", that does provide the guarantees of Article 6: *Bryan v. United Kingdom* [1996] 21 EHRR 342 at [43] *et seq*. Judicial Review may suffice. Art 6 of the Convention does not require access to a level of jurisdiction that can substitute its own opinion for that of the administrative authority: *Ali v UK* [2016] 63 EHRR 20 at [75]-[78]. If there is an Art 6 defect in a barrister disciplinary trial, it will be a question of fact in each case whether this can be cured on a section 24 appeal by the Administrative Court. If the defect is one of substance and means that factual findings are unsafe, then the court will have to quash them. If the defect is one of form or technicality, the appellant will have to show that it has impinged on the findings of fact in a way that cannot be cured by the review powers of the appeal court.

Private life and correspondence

8.44 Despite it now having been stated judicially in *Wingate v Solicitors Regulation Authority* [2018] EWCA Civ 366 at [102] that lawyers need not be paragons of virtue, Barristers are increasingly scrutinised by the BSB for what they say and do in some areas of their private lives. The Handbook itself is not on its face merely concerned with what barristers do in their professional lives. GC27 states that conduct which is not likely to be treated as a breach of Rules rC8 (a barrister must not do anything which could reasonably be seen by the public to undermine your honesty, integrity and independence), rC9 (he must not knowingly or recklessly mislead or attempt to mislead anyone), CD3 (dealing with honesty and integrity), or CD5 (not to behave in a way which is likely to diminish the trust and confidence which the public places in a barrister or in the profession), includes (but is not limited to): minor criminal offences, and conduct in a barrister's private or personal life, unless this involves, abuse of professional position or committing a criminal offence, other than a minor criminal offence.

8.45 As at February 2013, but apparently not now, the BSB stated on its website that it did not usually deal with complaints about barristers' behaviour when they were acting outside their professional role, unless that behaviour had resulted in a criminal conviction or a finding of a court or Tribunal. The notice counselled that if an informant considered that a barrister had committed a criminal offence, he should report the matter to the Police. The BSB added that it would not normally investigate a complaint of misconduct which related to a barrister's private or non-professional life, where there was a clear legal remedy available to the informant, which had not yet been pursued. It was stated to be only in exceptional circumstances that the BSB would deal with complaints about something that a barrister had done in his or her private life. This statement of policy can no longer be found on the BSB's website. Of course, any conviction for anything in a barrister's private life save for a very minor crime, will most likely lead to BSB proceedings, even where the conviction arises from divorce proceedings: see the sad history in *BSB v LC* [2017] EWHC 3101 (Admin).

8.46 CD5 applies "at all times", not merely during professional practice: see rC2. Any behaviour which is likely to diminish the trust and confidence which the public places in a barrister or in the profession, could be investigated by the BSB. There is an obligation to engage with the BSB too, as CD9 (duty to cooperate with BSB) also applies at all times: rC2. This enables the BSB to *investigate* all and any behaviour in private life to discover if CD5 has been breached in private life. Such an investigation could, in theory, be about the most intimate or sensitive matters. A refusal to answer on the basis that the matter is none of the BSB's business, could itself be a breach of the Handbook.

Meaning of private life

8.47 But what is "private life"? Emails may contain electronic signatures. They must also now carry the words *"Regulated by the Bar*

Standards Board". An email sent in bad taste to a friend at a weekend, or after hours, bearing such an electronic signature, may have absolutely nothing to do with professional practice, but might arguably bear upon the reputation of the profession if it falls into the wrong hands. A political or religious speech made anonymously at Speaker's Corner by a barrister is one thing, but a tweet published online about a political matter, where the barrister describes himself as a barrister in his biography, is private conduct arguably bearing on professional status. A Chambers' function is a professional event, but when and in what circumstances does socialising with colleagues become a private event at which the barrister can become intoxicated, swear, tell lewd jokes and generally let his hair down without professional consequences? If a barrister is entitled to hold and express extreme, even discriminatory, opinions in his own home, what if he does so and a window is open through which such offensive views are heard by a neighbour, who happens to know that he is a member of the Bar?

8.48 In practice, if there is any link whatsoever with barrister status, the BSB appears to take the view that the conduct is not within the sphere of private life. The only way to be sure that one has the protection of a private life defence is in private life to conceal barrister status completely, which of course may not be possible if people already know about it, or can easily discover it on the internet.

'Criminal' offences

8.49 The problem of resources suffered by the Police means that much crime is not subject to prosecution. GC27's reference to the commission of criminal offences seems to assume *proven* commission i.e. a prior conviction. But what if a barrister offender is not prosecuted? The BSB's practice appears to be to prosecute such cases regardless of the absence of any prior criminal conviction before a court of record exercising criminal jurisdiction. In *BSB v D* (2016) Unrep. it did just that in a case in which a female barrister was caught on CCTV taking a purse in a nightclub, i.e. very much in the sphere of her private life. The contention that the Tribunal had no jurisdiction *itself* to determine if a serious criminal offence had been committed was rejected by the Tribunal. This topic may have to be revisited. It is difficult to see how an act, clearly occurring in private life, that has not been found to have been criminal by a criminal court can ever be lawfully prosecuted by the BSB. Insofar as its prosecution policy is not to pursue such matters, then an *Adaway* [2004] EWCA Crim 2831 abuse of process application might well lie.

Article 8 defence

8.50 In those cases where the BSB investigates or prosecutes despite the matter arising in or from private life, then it may be that an ECHR Article 8 defence will arise. Art 8 provides:

> *Right to respect for private and family life*
>
> 1. Everyone has the right to respect for his private and family life, his home and his correspondence.
>
> 2. There shall be no interference by a public authority with the exercise of this right except such as is in accordance with the law and is necessary in a democratic society in the interests of national security, public safety or the economic well-being of the country, for the prevention of disorder or crime, for the protection of health or morals, or for the protection of the rights and freedoms of others.

8.51 In *S v General Council of the Bar* [2005] EWHC 844 at [38(i) and (ii)], a panel of 5 Visitors, including 3 High Court Judges, sitting just before the advent of the Bar Standards Board, questioned whether the then regulator should be interceding in private disputes that may attract Art 8 (or Art 10) protection. The panel also doubted whether there could ever be investigations of, say, private occasions of drunkenness, or even adultery. The Visitors counselled circumspection on the part of the then regulator.

Article 8: principles

8.52 Article 8 guarantees a right to 'private life' in the broad sense, including the right to lead a 'private social life', that is, the possibility for the individual to develop his or her social identity: *Bărbulescu v Romania* [2017] IRLR 1032 at [70]. Article 8 secures to individuals a sphere within which they can freely pursue the development and fulfilment of their personality: *A-M.V. v Finland* (2017) Application no. 53251/13 at [76]. Art 8 protects a right to personal development and the right to establish and develop relationships with other human beings and the outside world: *Niemietz v Germany* [1992] 16 EHRR 97 at [29]. Investigations of barristers' private lives and, for example, e-mails, will readily fall within Art 8(1). E-mails are "correspondence": *Copland v United Kingdom* (2007) 45 EHRR 37. A public authority interferes with correspondence and the right to respect for correspondence, if it relies on a communication as a basis for a finding of guilt and a sanction: *FK v BSB* [2018] EWHC 2184 (Admin) at [59] *per* Warby J.

8.53 However, the Art 8(1) right is defeasible if violation: (a) serves a legitimate aim in Art 8(2), such as, "…the protection of the rights and freedoms of others"; (b) is "necessary", in that it corresponds to a "pressing social need" and (c) is proportionate to the legitimate aim pursued: *FK v BSB supra* at [67]. FK sent a Linked-in communication to the spouse (whom he knew) of his former client's putative ex-lover, but FK lost any Art 8(1) protection because, *per* Warby J at [67]:

> A person whose spouse gets caught up in disputes and litigation in which lawyers are instructed on the other side has a reasonable expectation that the other side's lawyers will respect their privacy, and refrain from exploiting what they have learned in that capacity for the purposes of unwanted

intrusions into their lives, with unwelcome comments on inherently hurtful, private and personal matters. Beyond this, again, the facts engage the reputation of the profession at large, and the rights of those who instruct the Bar.

See too *RC v BSB* (2014) Unrep. 30th Jan, Visitors to the Inns of Court, *per* Silber J. at [44].

8.54 "Necessary" in test (b) above, does not have the flexibility of such expressions as "useful", "reasonable", or "desirable": *Piechowicz v. Poland* (2015) 60 EHRR 24 at [212].

BSB Inspections

8.55 The BSB has extensive powers of inspection of Barristers' Chambers: rC70. A barrister must permit the Bar Council, or the Bar Standards Board, or any person appointed by them, reasonable access, on request, to inspect any premises from which he provides, or is believed to provide, legal services; and any documents or records relating to those premises and his practice, or BSB entity. The Bar Council, Bar Standards Board, or any person appointed by them, is entitled to take copies of such documents or records as may be required by them for the purposes of their functions. Anecdotal feedback about the manner of exercise of these powers has not been flattering. Clearly, they are very invasive. The history of the SRA's equivalent powers has been highly controversial.

8.56 It is to be noted that the premises that can be searched could, in theory, extend to the home of a sole practitioner, indeed of any barrister who works from home (and many now do so). The searching party extends to the Bar Council, which exercises no disciplinary functions itself. The power includes a far-reaching power in respect of documents and papers. "Records" would no doubt be argued to include electronic records.

8.57 These powers are extensive on their face and thus may have profound Art 8 implications. The concept of "home" in Art 8(1) embraces not only a private individual's home, but also a lawyer's office or a law firm: *Niemietz v Germany supra* at [30]-[33]. Searches of the premises of a lawyer may breach legal professional privilege: *André v France* (2008) Application no. 18603/03 at [41]. Consequently, such measures must be accompanied by "special procedural guarantees" and the lawyer must have access to a remedy affording "effective scrutiny" to contest them. That is not the case where a remedy fails to provide for the cancellation of the impugned search: *Xavier Da Silveira v France* (2010) Application no. 43757/05 at [37], [42] & [48]. It is not clear what access is afforded to a barrister to contest a BSB request to search his home or Chambers, nor what regulatory procedural safeguards exist, if any.

Freedom of expression

8.58 Article 10 of the ECHR provides:

Freedom of expression

1. Everyone has the right to freedom of expression. This right shall include freedom to hold opinions and to receive and impart information and ideas without interference by public authority and regardless of frontiers. This Article shall not prevent States from requiring the licensing of broadcasting, television or cinema enterprises.

2. The exercise of these freedoms, since it carries with it duties and responsibilities, may be subject to such formalities, conditions, restrictions or penalties as are prescribed by law and are necessary in a democratic society, in the interests of national security, territorial integrity or public safety, for the prevention of disorder or crime, for the protection of health or morals, for the protection of the reputation or rights of others, for preventing the disclosure

of information received in confidence, or for maintaining the authority and impartiality of the judiciary.

8.59 By definition, barristers are people who express themselves through the spoken and written word. Their capacity for speaking and writing does not end with the job. Some enter politics, local or national. Others work part-time in academia. Others, are sought after by the media, whether as journalists or for their views on issues of the day. Many engage in various forms of social media such as Twitter or Facebook and have their own blogs. The Bar should be justly proud of its long tradition of outspoken liberal, and even radical, thought. To impose rules on such extra-curricular activity poses obvious dangers.

Immoral, outrageous or disgraceful behaviour in private life

8.60 In *BSB v RM* (2019), a Disciplinary Tribunal considered the case of a barrister who had been a member of a private, Facebook chat-room. It appears that he used a pseudonym. None of this activity concerned being a barrister. His professional status was apparently concealed. He made some unpleasant remarks about another person. The public front page of the group, which had some 260 members, stated: *"Here you can cuss who you want when you want. You can name and shame too."* His barrister status was somehow discovered. He was reported to the BSB. He was prosecuted and ran Art 8 and Art 10 defences. The Tribunal took the view that immoral behaviour in private life can be prosecuted by the BSB. It found that the comments made by RM were, *"offensive and disparaging, including matters of a sexual and/or violent nature"*. It held that he acted in a way which was likely to diminish the trust and confidence the public places in him or in the profession (i.e. a finding under CD5). The short report of the decision reads that:

> Following Elias LJ in *Remedy UK v GMC* [2010] EWHC 1245 (Admin) the tribunal found that Mr [M's] conduct, although outwith the practice of his profession, was

conduct of a morally culpable or disgraceful kind that brought the profession into disrepute.

8.61 It is true that in *R (Remedy UK Limited) v GMC,* the Divisional Court, founding itself on *Roylance v GMC* [2000] 1 AC 311, accepted that immoral, outrageous or disgraceful conduct in private life, could, in theory, amount to professional misconduct. In *RM* this concept was held to extend to outrageous words of abuse. The profession has every reason to protect its collective reputation through CD5. It is accepted that any barrister behaving immorally, outrageously or disgracefully outside of his professional work or role and using, or tangibly linking to, the status of barrister, should be capable of being prosecuted by the BSB. Likewise, any barrister convicted of a serious criminal offence arising from his or her private life. But on the face of the report, *RM* goes too far. A value judgment about what barristers do or say in their private lives opens Pandora's Box. What is offensive language to a Tribunal may merely be the way that younger people communicate. Men on a football field tend to communicate profanely. A football-playing barrister who is not overtly present *qua* barrister, should be as free to use industrial language as the next player.

8.62 A disciplinary prosecution should not depend on a value judgment about morality. That is not least because the doctrine of legal certainty requires a regulated community to know in advance what is and is not unethical: *R v Rimmington* [2006] 1 AC 459 per Lord Bingham at [32]-[35]. A corollary of RM's case is that any barrister could be prosecuted for adultery or drunkenness, where his professional status is known or even discovered later. This is exactly what the Visitors warned against in *S v Bar Council* [2005] EWHC 844 at [38(i) and (ii)]. There are sound reasons why it is not for the BSB or the Tribunal to try to police the private lives of barristers. Any attempt to do so is fundamentally misconceived. And it is a slippery slope from value judgments about a barrister's personal morality, to value judgments about political allegiance, sexual predilection or personal appearance. Those minded, or even eager, to sit in judgment on morality, would not want to live in a society in which *their* views on politics, sex or beauty were regulated by the state.

Discussing cases with other barristers

8.63 Traditionally, one place in which, especially on Circuit, barristers have been free to 'sound off', is the Robing Room. It is reported that, historically, judges behaved in just the same manner in the Inns' smoking rooms. In *FK v BSB* [2018] EWHC 2184 (Admin), Mr FK attended two different courts in the Midlands asking about the fate of barrister X who, as he had discovered when acting for barrister Y, had been subject to serious allegations by barrister Y. FK was reported to the BSB by an informant linked to the Chambers of barrister X. On one view, his offence was to have engaged in mere robing room gossip. He had certainly been exercising his right to freedom of expression. Warby J. held that Art 10(2) trumped 10(1). He said this:

> 41. Mr Beaumont has advanced a "floodgates" argument, suggesting that if this behaviour is professional misconduct there is a great deal that goes on in the robing room that members of the Bar and Judges could and, on this view, should be sanctioned for. It is a fact, I accept, that barristers are prone to gossip among themselves. The robing room is exclusively for advocates, and is in one sense a sanctuary, though experience shows that it is also a venue for pre-court sparring, including "robing room advocacy" which can sometimes verge on bullying behaviour. There are things that can be said in such a context that count as nothing more than "gossip" or "tittle-tattle". To some extent, professional people of all kinds may need a space in which they can speak freely about their private lives, and their work, to colleagues, without fear that the regulator or an informer is looking over their shoulder, contemplating the instigation of professional disciplinary proceedings. Barristers may speak about their cases. They may use colourful language.

CHAPTER EIGHT – BARRISTERS AND HUMAN RIGHTS • 205

Often there may be nothing wrong with any of this, let alone anything that counts as professional misconduct. Often, the cases spoken about will be – by their very nature – public knowledge. But these considerations do not support the submissions made in the present case, about what this barrister did, in these robing rooms, on these occasions. The robing room cannot be viewed as a "no-go area" for the regulator. All depends on the facts.

...61. Mr Beaumont's argument is that barristers should not be prevented from discussing their cases with other barristers. The exchange of information between professionals is in many ways the very essence of a liberal profession. Those with whom they discuss their cases should not be prevented from receiving the same information (a discrete Art 10 right). There can be no Art 10(2) basis for preventing such discussion, save perhaps in the case of a breach of client confidence. That was not alleged here. Mr Beaumont questions whether the institution of disciplinary proceedings in respect of the robing room charges serves any of the legitimate aims specified in Article 10(2), and submits that in any event it cannot be said to be necessary in a democratic society. It does not correspond to any "pressing social need", nor is it proportionate to any such need

62. A separate strand of the argument emerged in oral submissions: that if, and so far as necessary, the core duties – being subsidiary legislation – should be "read down" by the Tribunal and the Court in accordance with s 3 of the HRA, in order to ensure compliance with human rights law. Mr Beaumont lays particular emphasis on [*Ken Livingstone v Adjudication Panel for England* [2006] EWHC 2533] where the pursuit and imposition of disciplinary sanctions was held to be unlawful. The Mayor of London was disciplined for conduct when leaving an official event. He abused a Jewish journalist by comparing him to a Nazi

prison camp guard. Collins J quashed the decision, holding that the Mayor was off-duty when he spoke, and that the panel's decision relied on an overly broad interpretation of rules against bringing the office of Mayor into disrepute, which could not stand with Article 10. I am invited to adopt similar reasoning in this case.

63. ………In my judgment a, if not the, central function of the BSB's regulatory regime is "the protection of the reputation and rights of others". Core duty 5, which the Tribunal found to have been breached in this case, is expressly aimed at maintaining public confidence in barristers and the profession generally. That is a reputational matter. Other barristers have a proper and legitimate interest in ensuring that their reputations are not tarnished by association with those who misconduct themselves professionally. But this duty is also concerned with the rights of others which include, importantly, the rights of those who employ barristers. They are entitled to expect adherence to high ethical standards. On the facts of this case, the "reputation and rights of others" engaged by the facts also include, prominently, the rights of Mr Jones. His rights under Article 8 were engaged. Further, in this case, the disciplinary measures served the function of "preventing the disclosure of information received in confidence."

65. The question of whether the use or disclosure of such information is or is not legitimate will turn largely on the aims pursued by such use or disclosure, and the application of the tests of necessity and proportionality. Here, the aim of [FK]'s speech is somewhat obscure. It is not, and could not be said, that it served any higher public interest purpose. On the contrary, his case is that it was mere gossip, nothing more. That is speech which ranks low in the hierarchy of free speech values. The need for a compelling justification for interference is correspondingly less. But there was in my judgment a compelling justification.

The disciplinary process served an important purpose by making clear to [FK], to others in the profession, and to the public at large, that disclosures such as these are not an acceptable way to make use of sensitive personal information, with the potential to cause serious reputational harm, which has been imparted to a barrister by a client in confidence, for the sole purpose of enabling him to perform professional services in relation to actual or prospective litigation. This purpose corresponds to a pressing social need and, making all due allowance for the wide parameters of the Article 10(1) right, the pursuit of disciplinary proceedings was a proper and proportionate means of serving those needs. I do not consider this case comes close to [*Ken Livingstone v Adjudication Panel for England* [2006] EWHC 2533].

8.64 *Livingstone* was distinguished, perhaps, because FK was 'on duty', even in the robing room, whereas, when Mr Livingstone uttered his remarks, he had left City Hall for the evening. So in *Livingstone,* Collins J. saw no scope for the operation of the disciplinary regime applicable to the London Mayor, as he had not made his remarks in the course of his professional life. Further, such abusiveness brought Mr Livingstone alone into disrepute, but not the office of Mayor. Moreover, freedom of speech encompassed a right to be abusive, even repugnantly so.

Media comment

8.65 Comment to the media about cases used to be subject to restrictions. In England and Wales, those have been lifted. The BSB guidance requires any media comments not to be such as to appear to undermine a barrister's independence or obligations of client confidentiality. Barristers in direct access cases and/or exercising a right to conduct litigation, may find it to be in a client's interest to make moderate remarks to the press. But as at 2020, the Bar still exercises self-restraint. Overall, media comment in barrister disciplinary cases is unwise and will have no obvious beneficial effect. After a trial or appeal, comment to the specialist press on a point of general interest should present no problems if made with care and with client consent.

Abusiveness

8.66 Barristers are now more frequently investigated and prosecuted by the BSB for what they say on social media. Collins J. said this in *Livingstone* about abusive speech:

> 35……Anyone is entitled to say what he likes of another provided he does not act unlawfully and so commits an offence under, for example, the Public Order Act. Surprising as it may perhaps appear to some, the right of freedom of speech does extend to abuse. Observations, however offensive, are covered. Indeed, as Hoffman, L.J. observed in *R. v Central Television Plc* [1994] 3 All E.R. 641 at 652: 'Freedom means . . . the right to say things which 'right-thinking people' regard as dangerous or irresponsible. This freedom is subject only to clearly defined exceptions laid down by common law or statute . . . It cannot be too strongly emphasised that outside the established exceptions . . . there is no question of balancing freedom of speech against other interests. It is a trump card which always wins.'
>
> 38 ………However offensive and undeserving of protection the appellant's outburst may have appeared to some, it is important that any individual knows that he can say what he likes, provided it is not unlawful, unless there are clear and satisfactory reasons within the terms of Art.10(2) to render him liable to sanctions.

8.67 The right to freedom of expression extends to the right to *"offend, shock and disturb"*: *Vogt v Germany* [1995] 21 EHRR 205. The right extends to painful or distasteful satire, iconoclasm, rudeness, unpopular and unfashionable opinion, banter and humour:

Chambers v DPP [2013] 1 WLR 1833 *per* Lord Judge LCJ; and to the irritating, the contentious, the eccentric, the heretical, the unwelcome and the provocative; and to matters of *"considerable annoyance and irritation"* and to *"inevitable turbulences"*: *Roberts v Bank of Scotland* [2013] EWCA Civ 882, *per* Jackson LJ. A right to express only inoffensive ideas is a right not worth having; of anything unpleasant to read or hear one can say with Sedley LJ in *Redmond-Bate v DPP* (1999) BHRC 375 at [20]:

> "…Nobody had to stop and listen. If they did so, they were as free to express the view that the preachers should be locked up or silenced as the appellant and her companions were to preach … Mr. Kealy was prepared to accept that blame could not attach for a breach of the peace to a speaker so long as what she said was inoffensive. This will not do. Free speech includes not only the inoffensive but the irritating, the contentious, the eccentric, the heretical, the unwelcome and the provocative provided it does not tend to provoke violence. Freedom only to speak inoffensively is not worth having. … From the condemnation of Socrates to the persecution of modern writers and journalists, our world has seen too many examples of state control of unofficial ideas. A central purpose of the European Convention on Human Rights has been to set close limits to any such assumed power. We in this country continue to owe a debt to the jury which in 1670 refused to convict the Quakers William Penn and William Mead for preaching ideas which offended against state orthodoxy."

Since the BSB is the creature of statute, it should never be perceived as trying to exercise *"state control of unofficial ideas"*. It is the challenge of the defence advocate to persuade a sceptical or hostile disciplinary tribunal that these critical principles apply just as much to barristers in their private lives. Their rights are no less than those of ordinary citizens.

Political expression

8.68 Barristers have opinions, often strong ones. They engage in political debate, very often on social media. "Political" has a broad meaning, extending to criticism of public services: *Barthold v Germany* [1985] 7 EHRR 383. Interference with the right of free speech which impedes such political debate must be subjected to particularly close scrutiny: *Sanders v Kingston* [2005] LGR 719. The reasons for this were explained by Lord Bingham in *R v Shayler* [2003] 1 AC 247 at [21] in one of the most important modern judgments in this field:

> *The right to free expression*
>
> 21 The fundamental right of free expression has been recognised at common law for very many years….The reasons why the right to free expression is regarded as fundamental are familiar…..Modern democratic government means government of the people by the people for the people. But there can be no government by the people if they are ignorant of the issues to be resolved, the arguments for and against different solutions and the facts underlying those arguments. The business of government is not an activity about which only those professionally engaged are entitled to receive information and express opinions. It is, or should be, a participatory process. But there can be no assurance that government is carried out for the people unless the facts are made known, the issues publicly ventilated. Sometimes, inevitably, those involved in the conduct of government, as in any other walk of life, are guilty of error, incompetence, misbehaviour, dereliction of duty, even dishonesty and malpractice. Those concerned may very strongly wish that the facts relating to such matters are not made public. Publicity may reflect discredit on them or their predecessors. It may embarrass the authorities. It may impede the process

of administration. Experience however shows, in this country and elsewhere, that publicity is a powerful disinfectant. Where abuses are exposed, they can be remedied. Even where abuses have already been remedied, the public may be entitled to know that they occurred...

The BSB will have little lawful scope for restricting or curtailing by an express or tacit threat of prosecution, debate by barristers, say on social media, on matters of public interest: *Wingrove v UK* [1997] 24 EHRR 1 at [58].

Social Media: the BSB Guidance

8.69 In October 2019, the BSB issued much publicised guidance about barristers' use of social media. The BSB recognises that barristers are likely to want to use social media for a variety of private and professional reasons. It begins by stating that "This applies to you in both a professional and personal capacity". This is said to be since the inherently public nature of the Internet means that anything published online may be read by anyone and could be linked back to one's status as a barrister. The potential for such linkage by a Google search is a new phenomenon for regulation, but, with respect, a barrister who uses a social media pseudonym cannot be so readily traced.

8.70 The BSB instructs the Bar to remember that it is bound by CD5 "at all times" not to behave in a way which is likely to diminish the trust and confidence which the public places in the barrister or the profession. This advice is, without exception, extended to private life.

8.71 Social media use is said to include posting material online, sharing content, promoting "business" as a barrister or networking on sites such as Twitter, content communities such as YouTube, social networking sites like Facebook or LinkedIn and Internet forums.

8.72 The BSB warns that: a. comments designed to demean or insult are likely to diminish public trust and confidence in the profession (CD5); b. it is advisable to avoid getting drawn into heated debates or arguments. Such behaviour could compromise the requirements for barristers to act with honesty and integrity (CD3) and not unlawfully to discriminate against any person (CD8). But this presupposes that barrister status is readily capable of being linked to the comments under scrutiny.

8.73 The BSB states that barristers should always take care to consider the content and tone of what they are posting or sharing. The BSB asserts that comments that a barrister reasonably considers to be in good taste may be considered distasteful or offensive by others.

8.74 The BSB ends by stating that the guidance will be considered by the BSB in any action it takes over concerns about social media use.

8.75 It is of concern that the guidance makes no reference to the right to freedom of expression. No part of private life is ring-fenced. This is unprecedented.

8.76 The greyer areas of this advice may not be *"...prescribed by law..."* within Art 10(2). That criterion means that the law has to be sufficiently foreseeable and precise to enable a citizen to regulate his conduct: *Hashman & Harrup v UK* [2000] 30 EHRR 241 at [36] *et seq*. In that case, bind-overs *contra bonos mores* failed for prospective vagueness. Could the same be said of the prospective impact on free speech of the BSB's social media guidance and CD5? It may well not be clear in advance what kind of statement on social media could sensibly diminish public trust and confidence in the profession. Could this mean, for instance, that a barrister can never criticise a court judgment by way of social media, for fear that the BSB may (even misguidedly) construe this as disrespectful and so a breach of CD5 and could not even do so by way of a Twitter link to his learned article on the topic?

8.77 On Boxing Day 2019, a QC tweeted that he had beaten a trapped fox to death in his garden with a baseball bat in order to save his chickens from distress. His identity as a QC and barrister was overt. He is a well-known, public figure involved in the Brexit litigation. So CD5 may well be relevant. But the matter was plainly part of his private life and engaged his Art 8(1) rights, as well as his Art 10(1) rights. The BSB's policy appears to be to investigate crimes, even absent a conviction by a court, as it did in *BSB v JD* (2016) and to override Art 10(1) rights, as it did in *FK v BSB* (2018) *supra* for the reasons given by Warby J. in that case. Those two cases have placed the BSB in an awkward position. If they were ever to prosecute such a case, they would open themselves up to allegations of interference in private life and/or in the right to freedom of expression from someone much more influential than Ms JD, an unregistered barrister, or Mr FK, a sole practitioner. The problem with invasive laws is that they are often not applied with any consistency. It is understood the BSB took no action against the QC.

Article 10(2)

8.78 In every case in which Art 10(1) rights are relied upon, the BSB will have to persuade the Tribunal that Art 10(2) is engaged on the facts. As Lord Bingham explained in *Shayler supra*:

> Article 10(2)
>
> 23 Despite the high importance attached to it, the right to free expression was never regarded in domestic law as absolute. Publication could render a party liable to civil or criminal penalties or restraints on a number of grounds which included, for instance, libel, breach of confidence, incitement to racial hatred, blasphemy, publication of pornography and, as noted above, disclosure of official secrets.

The European Convention similarly recognises that the right is not absolute: article 10(2) qualifies the broad language of article 10(1)…It is plain from the language of article 10(2), and the European Court has repeatedly held, that any national restriction on freedom of expression can be consistent with article 10(2) only if it is prescribed by law, is directed to one or more of the objectives specified in the article and is shown by the state concerned to be necessary in a democratic society.

"Necessary" has been strongly interpreted: it is not synonymous with "indispensable", neither has it the flexibility of such expressions as "admissible", "ordinary", "useful", "reasonable" or "desirable": *Handyside v United Kingdom* (1976) 1 EHRR 737, 754, para 48. One must consider whether the interference complained of corresponded to a pressing social need, whether it was proportionate to the legitimate aim pursued and whether the reasons given by the national authority to justify it are relevant and sufficient under article 10(2): *The Sunday Times v United Kingdom* (1979) 2 EHRR 245 at [62].

8.79 Any curtailment of freedom of expression has to be, *"convincingly established by a compelling countervailing consideration"*: *McCartan Turkington Breen v Times Newspapers* [2001] 2 AC 277 at 297. Art 10(2) argument must be based on proper evidence from the BSB, not assumptions or assertions: *Kelly v BBC* [2001] Fam 59.

8.80 It is quite impossible to accept that there is a "pressing social need" that all forms of freedom of expression by barristers in their private lives, whether or not their barrister status is concealed from view, should be prevented. One can go further. Absent the commission of a serious crime, or a highly pejorative judicial finding of a civil court, tribunal or quasi-judicial administrative body, there is no pressing social need that the BSB should ensure that barristers are paragons of moral virtue in their private lives. The Court of Appeal said as much in *Wingate supra*. Collins J's enlightened thinking in *Livingstone* at [28] should be applied *mutatis mutandis*:

> ...it is important that the flamboyant, the eccentric, the positively committed—one who is labelled in the somewhat old fashioned terminology, a character—should not be subjected to a Code of Conduct which covers his behaviour when not performing his functions as a member of a relevant authority.

8.81 Within just two days of the first draft of this book being completed, the judgment in *MD v BSB* [2020] EWHC 467 (Admin) appeared online. The facts were that on 14th June 2017, a young black female student at Cambridge University posted on Twitter an open letter to the English Faculty calling for more BME literature on the course. Readers were invited to sign the open letter, to express support for its content and the suggestions it contained. MD is on Twitter. He is a believer in "the Canon of Western literature and culture". He was upset by the open letter, and on 25th October 2017 he responded by tweeting, in reply: *"Read it. Now; refuse to perform cu———-us on shrill ne----ds who will destroy an academic reputation it has taken aeons to build."* The day after the Tweet, Middle Temple referred to the BSB a complaint that MD had used his Twitter account, which was linked to his personal website, to post a racist and sexually explicit slur against a young black Cambridge student. The linkage to the website seems to have been the factor that exposed the tweet, otherwise a vile, but lawful, expression of gratuitous abuse uttered in private life, to the application of CD5. MD was reprimanded and fined £1,000 and his appeal to Warby J, who had heard FK's case in 2018, failed.

8.82 Unlike the fair minded and informed observer in the law of apparent bias who reads more than just the headline[3], the reader on twitter is presumed to read just that, or little more than that:

---

3 *Helow v Secretary of State for the Home Department* [2008] 1 WLR 2416 at [3]

per Warby J at [11] citing *Stocker v Stocker* [2019] UKSC 17 at [25-26] and [42-45]. Warby J held that in social media cases, the BSB is entitled to prosecute on the *Stocker* basis that:

> "The judge tasked with deciding how a …tweet on Twitter would be interpreted by a social media user must keep in mind the way in which such … tweets are made and read.
>
> … it is wrong to engage in elaborate analysis of a tweet … this is a casual medium; it is in the nature of conversation rather than carefully chosen expression; and … is pre-eminently one in which the reader reads and passes on.
>
> … Twitter is a fast moving medium. People will tend to scroll through messages relatively quickly. … The essential message that is being conveyed by a Tweet is likely to be absorbed quickly by the reader."

8.83 This approach is convenient for the BSB. It means that as long as there is some nexus with barrister status such as a link to a barrister's website, the BSB can say that the principles in *Stocker* merely require the tribunal to assess how a hypothetical "ordinary reasonable reader" would be likely to respond to the social media statement under consideration. This is an objective process so it does not require evidence of the reactions of actual readers. Warby J held at [61] that the Panel's task was to read the Tweet, consider such evidence as there was of its context and, applying their common-sense and knowledge of the world, to make an assessment of how the Tweet would be likely to affect the attitudes of ordinary reasonable readers towards the Bar or towards the barrister, or both. And this being so, the BSB did not need to call a single human witness as to the effect on them of the tweet.

8.84 Warby J at [72] did not think that any "bright line" could ever be drawn so as to rule out BSB prosecutions about misconduct in private life:

.....I cannot accept that there is some "bright line" to be drawn between that which falls purely within the private realm, and that which is sufficiently public to engage the disciplinary jurisdiction of the BSB and the COIC tribunals. In my view this is a false point. In the course of argument, I put a hypothetical example to the appellant: a barrister who, on occasions wholly unrelated to his professional practice, committed a number of rapes. The conduct, as opposed to any consequent criminal proceedings, could be characterised as private. The appellant accepted that a bright line could not be drawn on the basis of a distinction between what is private and what is public, but relied on the "criminal offence" exception in gC27. In my judgment, that was to miss the point. Ultimately, the question for the Panel in a case under CD5 is whether the conduct admitted or proved is likely to undermine trust and confidence in an individual barrister (as a barrister) or the profession. That is a question for assessment on the basis of the facts of the individual case. The range of factual scenarios that could properly raise such a question has no theoretical limits. Some public conduct may be too trivial to satisfy this requirement. Some private conduct may clearly cross the line. Some conduct may be hard to categorise as either public or private. A Panel will have to evaluate the conduct in all the circumstances.

But this was *obiter dictum* as it was stated in a case in which there *was* linkage between the conduct in private life and the identity of the tweeter as a barrister. The remark that "Some private conduct may clearly cross the line" is an invitation to the BSB to prosecute any and every perceived infraction in private life committed by a barrister, from the use of profanity, to drunkenness, to adultery. The objective test under the core duties means that the only people whose judgment will matter about this conduct are the BSB case officers (who are not Clergymen, Philosophers or lawyers) and the panels. If they do not like the morals of any particular barrister in his or her private life, that will be "professional misconduct". That cannot be right. And such a system cannot satisfy the doctrine of legal certainty.

8.85 At [73] Warby J said this about linkage:

> It cannot be necessary for a barrister to be immediately or readily identifiable as such, before a charge under CD5 can be brought or made out. Nor can the link to the website in this case be the key factor, that takes the Tweet into the public domain. But I do not believe that is what the Panel was suggesting in its para 32. As it found, the Tweet was in the public domain anyway, as a public tweet, accessible to anybody. The URL, enabling a reader to travel from the Tweet to the appellant's website and identify him as a barrister, is an element of the factual matrix that was relevant to the Panel's assessment of whether his conduct met the test of being "likely to undermine trust and confidence.

This passage too was *obiter* as the barrister *was* identifiable by the URL. With respect, Warby J cannot be right if he meant that if a barrister on social media, or, for that matter, in any social context at all, takes steps not to be identifiable as a barrister and his pseudonym or disguise or the circumstances or setting, enable him to behave uninhibitedly, whether online, or *ex hypothesi* at a fancy-dress party, or one where he or his job are not known, then he is still open to a charge of professional misconduct. The BSB might as well expressly require all barristers to swear an oath on the day of Call to the Bar that they will cease using profane language, stop telling lewd jokes, only watch U-rated films, will have all the gory parts of Shakespeare's plays redacted before purchase and will not read *Lady Chatterley's Lover*. The potential extent of the BSB's invasion of our lives based on paragraph 73 of the judgment of this excellent and highly respected judge is mind-boggling. If behaviour by a person who is a barrister in disguise is so disgraceful that it is criminal, then it is for the Police to investigate it, not the BSB. If it does not reach that threshold then it is lawful and the BSB have no right to investigate it, unless there is some publicly accessible link to barrister status. If Warby J's judgment goes further than that, it is submitted to be *obiter dictum* and/or wrongly decided.

8.86 The dangers of generality are also apparent in Warby's J's analysis of ECHR Art 10(2) and 8(2). In *FK v BSB* he had explained how the Bar and clients have countervailing rights under those provisions. These were held to trump FK's Art 8(1) and Art 10(1) rights. MD fared just as badly, Warby J saying at [96]:

> The appellant's argument that his choice of words was legitimate is best considered in the context of his human rights arguments, which are, in substance, that it was not open to the Panel to regard the legitimate aim of professional regulation as a sufficient justification for the interference with his Convention rights that the sanctions represent. I approach this issue on the footing that the Court's duty under s 6 HRA means that intense scrutiny is required. The submission advanced before me is that this case stands in stark contrast with the facts of *[FK] v BSB*. The appellant was not acting in a professional capacity or in a professional place; he was communicating as a private individual on a topic of legitimate public interest, provoked by the Open Letter. He did not target anyone, defame them, or intrude into their private lives in ways they had gone to law to prevent. All of this is true. But there are countervailing factors…that the public expects, and trusts, members of the profession to exercise judgment, restraint and a proper awareness of the feelings of others.

8.87 Thus it appears that "judgment, restraint and a proper awareness of the feelings of others" must be exercised at all times by barristers in their private lives. No-one would quarrel with that as a moral exhortation. But to the BSB, this is a proscription the breach of which is the basis for a public disciplinary prosecution, public condemnation and the permanent ruination of a professional career and reputation. It is submitted that a regulator has absolutely no legitimate or justifiable role to play in regulating the personal and private lives of professionals who are not acting as professionals, or acting in any way capable of being linked to their professional role or status.

The regulation of advocacy

8.88 The BSB does on occasion prosecute advocacy misconduct. In principle, it is right that it should so. RC7 deals with abuses of the role of an advocate. So barristers must not make statements or ask questions merely to insult, humiliate or annoy a witness or any other person; must not make a serious allegation against a witness whom they have had an opportunity to cross-examine, unless they have given that witness a chance to answer the allegation in cross-examination; must not make a serious allegation against any person, or suggest that a person is guilty of a crime with which a client is charged, unless there are reasonable grounds for the allegation, and the allegation is relevant to the client's case or the credibility of a witness, and where the allegation relates to a third party, the barrister avoids naming them in open court unless this is reasonably necessary; a barrister must not put forward to the court a personal opinion of the facts or the law unless invited or required to do so by the court or by law.

8.89 Whilst such cases are rare, the BSB prosecuted experienced advocates in *AW v BSB* (2013) Unrep, Visitors to the Inns of Court and in *HG v BSB* [2018] EWHC 1409 (Admin). Such cases tend to involve fine interpretations of the justification for momentary statements made or questions asked by experienced advocates in the heat of adversarial contest. Whilst Mr G's appeal failed, Mr W's succeeded. Those so accused might be able to invoke Art 10(1). In *N v Finland* [2004] 38 EHRR 45, it was held that restrictions on counsel's freedom of speech in court may only lawfully be imposed in "exceptional circumstances". Barristers facing unfair threats from judges might also bear this principle in mind.

8.90 Most breaches of rC7 would constitute "exceptional circumstances". But criticisms of matters of subjective interpretation of the law, or of documents, so long as the matters were reasonably arguable, or of a style of advocacy, could not possibly constitute an exceptional reason for violating Art 10(1) rights. Had the BSB brought in regulation of advocacy through its controversial QASA scheme, which it eventually scrapped, that might well have violated Art 10(1) rights. Advocacy, both oral and written, is still an art and not a science. As such, it is vital that its conception and execution remain protected by law.

The Bar and free expression: the future.

8.91 *RM* appears to have been wrongly decided. If it is part of a trend, that trend is inconsistent with the common law and is dangerous. Furthermore, Barristers really need to be men and women of the world. From such hands-on engagement with contemporary life is born an understanding that enriches a barrister's day to day judgment. If the profession is to be genuinely diverse and is not to be seen as stuffy and out of touch, barristers must live full lives among those for whom they provide a service. They should be permitted to do so without excessive interference by the BSB. Tweeting may seem irritating, even foolish to some, but there is much to be said for a modern Bar to appear to be, and to be, accessible, informed, aware and engaged. Just as, in 1985, advertising was not permitted, then *was* permitted, but only in black and white, and, eventually, by 1990, colour brochures were permitted, so technology tends to set its own agenda. In the end, regulation cannot stop human beings from expressing themselves.

8.92 The guidance about use of social media is open to accusations of hypocrisy. Presumably, a ban on using any kind of offensive language means that a barrister engaging in amateur dramatics, even under a stage name, should have the script censored and a barrister who writes a novel, play or film-script, even under a *nom de plume*, should remove any sex, profanity or violence. But such forays into private life are plainly unworkable. At least as a default position, the BSB no more exists to police the content of tweets written by barristers, than it does their plays or novels. To this there may be egregious exceptions of utterly disgraceful behaviour with no artistic, creative or political value at all. MD's case was such a case, decided correctly on its facts, albeit involving some sweeping statements of principle by the court, that were not necessary to the decision in that case and which may be open to misapplication by regulators. But if Parliament has not considered that much of the private behaviour that the BSB may abhor, should trump the statutory right to freedom of expression by way of, for example, the criminal offences created by the Communications Act 2003 or the Protection from Harassment Act 1997, or otherwise, there is no obvious reason why such activity should engage regulatory law.

CHAPTER NINE
COSTS IN DISCIPLINARY CASES

Costs at trial

9.1 Rules E244 to 248 set out the procedure as to costs. A Disciplinary Tribunal may make such Orders for costs, whether against or in favour of a respondent, as it shall think fit. A party who wishes to make an application for costs must, no later than 24 hours before the commencement of the hearing, serve upon any other party and file with BTAS a schedule setting out the costs they seek. Where it exercises its discretion to make an Order for costs, a Disciplinary Tribunal must either itself decide the amount of such costs or direct BTAS to appoint a suitably qualified person to do so on its behalf. Any costs ordered to be paid by or to a respondent must be paid by or to the BSB. All costs incurred by the BSB *preparatory to* the hearing before the Disciplinary Tribunal must be borne by the BSB. That language excludes any brief fee of trial counsel for the BSB. Hitherto those were not paid, but from 2020 will be paid by the BSB to counsel. The BSB will retain a single panel set of chambers to prosecute its cases. This may well lead to costs being claimed by the BSB more frequently than at present.

9.2 However, the rules do not tell the whole story. The discretion as to costs *appears* to be open-ended, but the Tribunal follows the practice of the Solicitors Disciplinary Tribunal and a number of other regulatory jurisdictions. The BSB is to a large extent protected from adverse orders for costs. The leading authority on costs orders against regulators in respect of proceedings before disciplinary tribunals is *Baxendale-Walker v Law Society*. In the Divisional Court at [2006] EWHC 643 (Admin) at [43], Moses LJ said this:

Absent dishonesty or a lack of good faith, a costs order should not be made against such a regulator unless there is good reason to do so. That reason must be more than that the other party has succeeded. In considering an award of costs against a public regulator the court must consider on the one hand the financial prejudice to the particular complainant, weighed against the need to encourage public bodies to exercise their public function of making reasonable and sound decisions without fear of exposure to undue financial prejudice, if the decision is successfully challenged.

9.3 In *Baxendale-Walker* in the Court of Appeal, reported at [2008] 1 WLR 426, at 437, Sir Igor Judge P (as he then was) said this:

Unless the complaint is improperly brought, or, for example, proceeds as it did in *Gorlov's case* [2001] ACD 393, as a shambles from start to finish, when the Law Society is discharging its responsibilities as a regulator of the profession, an order for costs should not ordinarily be made against it on the basis that costs follow the event. The "event" is simply one factor for consideration. It is not a starting point. There is no assumption that an order for costs in favour of a solicitor who has successfully defeated an allegation of professional misconduct will automatically follow. One crucial feature which should inform the tribunal's costs decision is that the proceedings were brought by the Law Society in exercise of its regulatory responsibility, in the public interest and the maintenance of proper professional standards. For the Law Society to be exposed to the risk of an adverse costs order simply because properly brought proceedings were unsuccessful might have a chilling effect on the exercise of its regulatory obligations, to the public disadvantage. Accordingly, Moses LJ's approach to this issue did not go further than the principles described in this judgment.

9.4 In summary, therefore;

  a. there is a wide discretion under the Rules to make a costs order;

  b. the ordinary approach in civil litigation (*prima facie*, that costs follow the event) does not apply to proceedings before disciplinary tribunals;

  c. a tribunal cannot make an order for costs against the BSB merely because the application has failed – there must be good reason to justify such an order;

  d. subject to (b) and (c) above, the tribunal can make a costs order against a regulator if it considers that it is fair to do so and that there is good reason to do so.

9.5 In practice, this means that something more than victory must be prayed in aid by a successful barrister respondent. In barrister cases, whilst it is notoriously difficult to persuade the Tribunal itself to award costs against the BSB, an example of the kind of case that has attracted trial costs being awarded against the BSB retrospectively on appeal, is *JS v Bar Standards Board* [2016] EWHC 3015 (Admin). In that case, Collins J. was scathing of the BSB's failures to ensure: (a) that the ex-client was interviewed by the BSB and not by the conflicted solicitor and (b) that the ex-client attended trial to be cross-examined. He was also scathing of the Disciplinary Tribunal's protection of the BSB from any criticism, although, logically, that error should not have been laid at the BSB's door. Despite *Baxendale-Walker*, Mr S was awarded all of his trial costs. Collins J. said in an unreported ruling:

> That there is power to award costs is not disputed, but the authorities make clear that costs do not follow the event and that a regulator will not be ordered to pay costs [of trial] unless the Judge is satisfied that there was a failure in some way by the regulator or, I would add,

the tribunal which meant that the institution or conduct of the proceedings can be said to have been unsatisfactory in some way. I have no doubt that for the reasons set out in my Judgment both the BSB and the tribunal failed to meet the appropriate standards expected of them…

9.6 Collins J. also criticised the pre-prosecution analysis of the BSB's Case Examiner as a basis for awarding costs. It is always important to compare that report with the final outcome, to determine whether the BSB failed to lend sufficient weight to the barrister's defence and if it subjected him or her unnecessarily or unreasonably to a disciplinary trial. Sometimes a Case Examiner will have produced an impeccable report, only to have been overridden erroneously by the decision-making committee, often on grounds which were never properly recorded or are otherwise Delphic. If that is the case, applying the *Baxendale-Walker* principles, an acquittal ought to be followed by an order for costs against the BSB.

9.7 A system, albeit well entrenched, under which the prosecutor will almost always get its trial costs when it wins, but will almost never pay trial costs when it loses, presents as anomalous, unfair and a violation of the Art 6 'equality of arms' principle. For many respondents paying their own way, it is a reason why they cannot afford to plead not guilty. It is surely an area ripe for review. If the defence is to face such difficulties getting its costs if it wins, then perhaps the fairest reform would be that neither party should ever be able to apply for costs.

9.8 Some barristers act for themselves at the Tribunal. This is generally ill-advised. But on occasion, they win and, on rare occasions, they become entitled to their costs. If so, they are entitled to some compensation for their own time, but the basis set out in CPR Part 46 is not relevant before the Tribunal. It does not even have persuasive value: *R (BSB) v NS* [2016] EWCA Civ 478. The Divisional Court favoured a rate of £60 per hour for the non-practising barrister in that case. One supposes that the rate may depend on the barrister's usual hourly rate and its objective reasonableness if that is challenged.

Costs on appeal

9.9 There is no *Baxendale-Walker* costs protection for a regulator on appeal: see *SRA v Bass & Ward* [2012] EWHC 2457 (Admin). Appeals to the High Court are governed by the costs regime in CPR Part 44 detailed in the notes to the *White Book* and, more generally, are subject to the procedure in CPR Part 52. However, given that most cases are unfunded, a successful appellant will be concerned to recoup his or her costs in the event of success. If he or she is instructing counsel under the Bar's Public Access scheme, he or she will qualify as a litigant in person, as counsel does not usually go on the court record absent conduct of litigation rights: see CPR 46.5(6)(b)(i) which defines a litigant in person as including a self-representing barrister. If so, then the entitlement in CPR 46.5 and the Practice Direction to CPR Part 46 will apply, which, enables the barrister litigant in person to charge £19.00 per hour for his litigant in person time, in addition to instructed direct access counsel's fees and any disbursements and court fees. These items should be set out and filed with the Administrative Court Office and served 24 hours in advance of the appeal in a Form N260 Statement of Costs for the purposes of summary assessment by the appeal court.

9.10 On appeal to the Administrative Court, it is useful to have in mind CPR Part 52.19:

> (1) Subject to rule 52.19A, in any proceedings in which costs recovery is normally limited or excluded at first instance, an appeal court may make an order that the recoverable costs of an appeal will be limited to the extent which the court specifies.
>
> (2) In making such an order the court will have regard to—

(a) the means of both parties;

(b) all the circumstances of the case; and

(c) the need to facilitate access to justice.

(3) If the appeal raises an issue of principle or practice upon which substantial sums may turn, it may not be appropriate to make an order under paragraph (1).

(4) An application for such an order must be made as soon as practicable and will be determined without a hearing unless the court orders otherwise.

If the Disciplinary Tribunals continue to make no order as to the BSB's costs despite the move towards paying BSB counsel a brief fee from 2020, or make only partial awards of the BSB's costs, then that would engage CPR 52.19(1) in most appeals by barristers to the Administrative Court.

9.11 The practice of the BSB on appeal is not consistent. In some cases, counsel is instructed not to ask for costs if the BSB succeeds. In others, the BSB does seek costs if it succeeds, or a *pro bono* costs order under CPR Part 46.7, payable to charity. The view of the BSB may, it seems, sometimes be influenced by whether the defence is acting *pro bono*. It also seems to be influenced by a given case officer's subjective opinion of a given Appellant's behaviour or by the merits of the underlying case.

Offers to settle

9.12 There is no reason why offers to settle headed 'without prejudice save as to costs', or even open offers, should not be made in regulatory proceedings. The former will usually be respected by the BSB and not shown to the Tribunal. That said, the BSB is often not amenable to negotiation. It does not have the same financial concerns or reputational sensibilities as a commercial or private litigant. The BSB is not spending its own money. This being so, the psychological dimensions of negotiation do not operate in the way that they can in civil litigation. In *AQ v BSB* (2013) Unrep. Visitors to the Inns of Court, Wyn Williams J. and his colleagues were influenced by the barrister appellant's invitation to the BSB to concede the barrister's appeal, in ordering the BSB to pay the costs of the appeal:

> …in this case there are factors which pointed clearly in favour of making an order for costs. Almost as soon as this appeal was launched the Appellant's legal advisers invited the [BSB] to concede the appeal on the ground which has succeeded. That offer was repeated, most recently, shortly before the hearing. In our judgment there was always a very good prospect that the appeal would succeed for the reasons which we have articulated yet the [BSB] decided to contest the appeal with vigour.
>
> There can be little doubt from the information available that funding this appeal has been difficult for the Appellant. In the context of this appeal we took that consideration into account.
>
> Unhesitatingly, we were of the view that justice demanded that the [BSB] should pay the Appellant's costs of and incidental to the appeal.

Other contexts

9.13 An Independent Decision-Making Panel may not make an award of costs when dealing with an allegation under the determination by consent procedure: rE43.

9.14 In an appeal from an administrative sanction, the panel has no power to award costs: rE6

CHAPTER TEN
CONSENT ORDERS

Determination by consent procedure

10.1 In contrast to the usual obduracy of the BSB about settling cases at trial, there is a sophisticated determination by consent procedure, which is available only whilst the Independent Decision-Making Panel has it in mind to refer a matter to a Disciplinary Tribunal. Where the Commissioner or an Independent Decision-Making Panel is satisfied that the requirements of rE33 are met, namely the evidential and the public interest tests, an allegation which the Commissioner or an Independent Decision-Making Panel is otherwise intending to refer to the Disciplinary Tribunal may, with the consent of the barrister against whom the allegation is made, be finally determined by an Independent Decision-Making Panel. This is referred to as the "determination by consent procedure": rE34.

10.2 The Commissioner or an Independent Decision-Making Panel must, in deciding whether to refer an allegation to the determination by consent procedure, consider all the circumstances. However, the Commissioner or an Independent Decision-Making Panel may only make the allegation subject to the determination by consent procedure if the applicable person submits to the jurisdiction of an Independent Decision-Making Panel; and the Commissioner or an Independent Decision-Making Panel considers that there are no substantial disputes of fact which can only fairly be resolved by oral evidence being taken; and having regard to the regulatory objectives, it is in the public interest to resolve the allegation under the determination by consent procedure; and the potential professional misconduct or disqualification condition, if proved, combined with the applicable person's previous disciplinary history, does not appear to be such as to warrant a period of suspension or disbarment, the withdrawal of an authorisation or licence (as appropriate) or the imposition of a disqualification order (or equivalent by another Approved Regulator): rE35.

10.3 The standard of proof to be applied is the civil standard of proof, but the Commissioner or an Independent Decision-Making Panel must apply the criminal standard of proof when deciding charges of professional misconduct where the conduct alleged occurred prior to 1st April 2019, including where the same alleged conduct continued beyond 31st March 2019.

10.4 Where the Commissioner or an Independent Decision-Making Panel has decided to refer an allegation to the determination by consent procedure, the Commissioner or an Independent Decision-Making Panel may terminate the procedure at any time if it no longer considers that the requirements of rE35 are satisfied, or for any other good reason: rE39. If the determination by consent procedure ends other than by a finding and sanction, then an allegation may be referred to a three-person Disciplinary Tribunal.

10.5 An Independent Decision-Making Panel may impose on an applicable person against whom a charge of professional misconduct has been found proved under the determination by consent procedure any one or more the following: a fine, the imposition of any conditions on a licence or authorisation, a reprimand, advice as to future conduct, and an order to complete continuing professional development.

10.6 In determining what sanction, if any, to impose under the determination by consent procedure, an Independent Decision-Making Panel shall have regard to any relevant policy or guidelines issued by the BSB and/or by the Council of the Inns of Court from time to time.

10.7 An Independent Decision-Making Panel may not make an award of costs when dealing with an allegation under the determination by consent procedure.

10.8 The Commissioner must publish any finding and sanction resulting from the determination by consent procedure to the same extent as such publication would have taken place on a finding and sanction by a Disciplinary Tribunal, as provided for in the Disciplinary Tribunal Regulations.

10.9 If the barrister accepts the outcome of the determination by consent procedure, neither party may appeal against it.

Plea bargains

10.10 Once charges are laid and defence counsel instructed, the imminence of trial may be the first time both that an independent view has been fully brought to bear on the case, and that the accused's mind has been focused so intensely on the potential prospects of success, the risks and the financial implications of fighting on.

10.11 It is desirable too from the BSB's standpoint that there is a vehicle for cases to settle at such a late stage. This saves Tribunal time and saves prosecution witnesses the ordeal of cross-examination. From 2020, it will save the profession the costs of prosecution counsel.

10.12 Regrettably, whilst some prosecution counsel are willing to engage in negotiation, others are not. Some may be perfectly willing to do so, only to be instructed by the BSB Case Officer that on no account is the matter to be resolved by negotiation. This is very unsatisfactory indeed to the point of being sub-optimal practice. Despite lobbying hard for the civil standard of proof, the BSB clearly does not like *all* of the trappings of civil procedure.

10.13 Its practice is, however, not even consistent with regulatory law. The RICS, was until, 2018, very cool towards regulatory settlements containing an agreed proposed sanction, but now enters into such agreements containing the following preface, co-drafted by the author:

This procedure in substance follows the practice in the Nursing and Midwifery Council and the Solicitors Disciplinary Tribunal, where parties may ask a panel to approve a consensual panel disposal. It was adopted in *RICS v Wells* (2018) and *RICS v Kelly* (2019). It is also allied to the procedure adopted in the criminal courts where the judge may provide an indication of sentence based on provisional admissions. In our submission, it represents a proportionate and appropriate attempt between the parties to resolve this case in a way which ensures the public interest in the good repute of the profession is upheld and that formal findings are made, but that considerable tribunal time and costs are saved.

The Panel has the power to approve the proposed approach. In the case of *Hill v Institute of Chartered Accountants in England and Wales* [2013] EWCA Civ 555, the Court of Appeal endorsed a permissive approach by regulators to the interpretation of their rules, as it did in the case of solicitors in *Virdi v Law Society* [2010] 1 WLR 2840, CA at [31]. In short, in the absence of a prohibition, the Panel has the power to exercise its discretion, regulate its own procedure and consider the submissions within this document. The case of *Regina v Goodyear* [2005] 2 Cr. App. Rep. 20 demonstrates a well-established, analogous approach in the criminal courts.

10.14 It is quite clear that by analogy with *Re Carecraft Construction Company Limited* [1994] 1 WLR 172, a party willing to agree to a sanction such as a disbarment or its equivalent should not be put through the ordeal of a pointless hearing. Likewise, the parties may agree on a *Regina v Goodyear*[1] basis, to a sanction, subject to the tribunal's approval, on the strictly contingent basis that if the panel does not approve the sanction, or otherwise declines to engage, that the proposed sanction and any admissions or concessions, are to stand withdrawn. The formula in the set-

---

1 [2005] 2 Cr. App. Rep. 20

tlement agreement then has to agree that the panel falls to be recused. The BSB has agreed to a *Goodyear* formula in the past, but in recent years has refused to do so. This inconsistency has no rational basis. All disciplinary panels have the flexibility to fill gaps in their procedures with pragmatic solutions designed to conduce to greater efficiency and flexibility: *Virdi v Law Society* [2010] 1 WLR 2840, CA.

10.15. The BSB has nothing like the Solicitors (Disciplinary Proceedings) Rules 2019. Rule 25 provides:

> Agreed Outcome Proposals
>
> 25.—(1) The parties may up to 28 days before the substantive hearing of an application (unless the Tribunal directs otherwise) submit to the Tribunal an Agreed Outcome Proposal for approval by the Tribunal.
>
> (2)   An Agreed Outcome Proposal must— (a) contain a statement of the facts that are agreed between the relevant parties; (b) set out the agreed proposed penalty and an explanation as to why the penalty would be in accordance with any guidance published by the Tribunal on sanctions imposed by the Tribunal; (c) be signed by the relevant parties; and (d) comply with any relevant practice direction made by the Tribunal in respect of Agreed Outcome Proposals.
>
> (3)   If the Tribunal approves the Agreed Outcome Proposal in the terms proposed it must make an Order in those terms. The case must be called into an open hearing and the Tribunal must announce its decision.
>
> (4)   If the Tribunal wishes to hear from the parties before making its decision the Tribunal may direct that there be a case management hearing which the parties to the proposed Agreed Outcome Proposal must attend for the purpose of

making submissions before a final decision is reached. The case management hearing must be heard in private.

(5) Where the Tribunal is not satisfied that it is appropriate to make an Order in accordance with paragraph (3) it must provide reasons to the parties who may then submit a revised proposal. If the Tribunal is satisfied with the revised proposal, it must make an Order in accordance with it.

(6) Some or all of the same members of the panel appointed in respect of the application may consider the initial Agreed Outcome Proposal, any submissions made at a case management hearing and any revised proposal but may not subsequently participate in the panel for the substantive hearing (if there is one).

(7) If on considering a submission under this rule the Tribunal decides not to make an Order in accordance with paragraph (3) it must make directions for the substantive disposal of the matter by a panel consisting of members who were not on the panel which considered the submission.

(8) If on considering a submission under this rule the Tribunal decides not to make an Order and the Tribunal does not publish that decision or announce it in an open hearing, no information will be published or announced about the submission save that the Agreed Outcome Proposal was not approved.

10.16 The Bar is lagging behind the solicitors' profession and the RICS tribunals in how it approaches regulatory settlements. This is surprising and baffling. It is the source of much acrimony on the part of the prosecuted barrister community. It is in the interests of all protagonists to embrace and streamline a procedure for agreeing findings and, in particular, sanctions.

10.17 None of the above should alter the fact that the default setting for an innocent man or woman is a plea of not guilty.

CHAPTER ELEVEN
APPEALS

Appeals to the High Court

11.1 Until 2014, appeals lay from the Disciplinary Tribunals to the Visitors to the Inns of Court. The last iteration of the Visitors, comprised a Chair, who was a High Court Judge, a practising barrister and a pre-vetted lay person. Visitors' decisions could in principle be challenged by way of judicial review. The long history of the Visitors' jurisdiction, spanning hundreds of years, was explored in the *CR* litigation: see *R (CR) v Visitors to the Inns of Court* [2014] EWCA Civ 1630 at [11]-[24] and *Re S (a Barrister)* [1970] 1 QB 160. The Visitors were the agents of the monarch and those sitting represented all of the High Court Judges who, historically, had exercised powers of discipline over the Bar.

11.2 Centuries of legal history were swept away with the enactment of Section 24 of the Crime and Courts Act 2013, which provides:

> 24 Appeals relating to regulation of the Bar
>
> (1) Section 44 of the Senior Courts Act 1981 (extraordinary functions of High Court judges) ceases to have the effect of conferring jurisdiction on judges of the High Court sitting as Visitors to the Inns of Court.
>
> (2) The General Council of the Bar, an Inn of Court, or two or more Inns of Court acting collectively in any manner, may confer a right of appeal to the High Court in respect of a matter relating to—
>
> (a) regulation of barristers,

(b) regulation of other persons regulated by the person conferring the right,

(c) qualifications or training of barristers or persons wishing to become barristers, or

(d) admission to an Inn of Court or call to the Bar.

(3) An Inn of Court may confer a right of appeal to the High Court in respect of—

(a) a dispute between the Inn and a member of the Inn, or

(b) a dispute between members of the Inn;

and in this subsection any reference to a member of an Inn includes a reference to a person wishing to become a member of that Inn.

(4) A decision of the High Court on an appeal under this section is final.

(5) Subsection (4) does not apply to a decision disbarring a person.

(6) The High Court may make such order as it thinks fit on an appeal under this section.

(7) A right conferred under subsection (2) or (3) may be removed by the person who conferred it; and a right conferred under subsection (2) by two or more Inns of Court acting collectively may, so far as relating to any one of the Inns concerned, be removed by that Inn.

Limited route to the Court of Appeal

11.3 Sub-sections 24(4) and (5) on their face emasculated the pre-2014 rights of barristers to seek permission to appeal to the Court of Appeal from the High Court within the judicial review jurisdiction. Now the Court of Appeal (or Supreme Court) will only *ever* hear a barrister's disciplinary appeal if he or she has been disbarred. A barrister suspended for 2 or 3 years, perhaps with the loss of hundreds of thousands of pounds of fee income, or fined many thousands of pounds, or reprimanded wrongly with widespread adverse publicity, will have no right to seek permission to appeal to the Court of Appeal against even the most egregiously unfair decision of the Administrative Court. The late CR, whose leading case of *R (CR) v Visitors to the Inns of Court* [2014] EWCA Civ 1630 was the most important case concerning barrister discipline since *Re P a Barrister* in 2005, would now not be able to take such a case to the Court of Appeal, as she was suspended and not disbarred. It is not possible to understand how section 24 was some progressive reform, because it was not.

11.4 Such a blanket restriction on barristers arising from s.24, works to the advantage of just one litigant – the Bar Standards Board. So it is interesting to delve a little into how it came into being. In the House of Lords, the provision about appeals was, it appears, introduced by Baroness Deech. She was then also the incumbent Chair of the BSB. There appears to have been no opposition. It is recorded in *Crime and Courts Bill* (HL) Bill No. 115 of 2012/13, Research Paper 13/4, 9th January 2013, that:

> *The Bill*
>
> On Report in the House of Lords, the crossbench peer Baroness Deech, who is Chair of the Bar Standards Board (which regulates barristers) moved an amendment to introduce a new clause to deal with appeals relating to the regulation of the Bar.

The new clause would abolish the jurisdiction of High Court judges to sit as Visitors to the Inns of Court and would confer on the Bar Council and the Inns of Court the power to confer rights of appeal to the High Court in relation to the matters that were covered by the Visitors' jurisdiction.

Baroness Deech said that this transfer of the Visitors' jurisdiction "is something that the senior judiciary and the Bar Standards Board have been working towards for a number of years". [1]

168 Replying for the Government, Lord Ahmad of Wimbledon said that the Government supported the amendment and agreed that the practice of High Court judges sitting as Visitors to the Inns of Court was inappropriate[2]. He said that the proposal to abolish the role of judges sitting as Visitors was supported by the Lord Chief Justice, the Bar Standards Board, the General Council of the Bar and the Inns of Court. Enabling appeal to the High Court instead would "improve administrative efficiency and transparency, and at the same time make the appeal arrangements for barristers more consistent with those for solicitors".

169 The amendment was agreed without vote and is now Clause 22.

11.5 In fact, the claimed need for consistency with appeals by solicitors was wrong. With a few narrow exceptions, Solicitors who have not been struck off the roll at the Solicitors Disciplinary Tribunal were (and are) not barred by section 49 of the Solicitors Act 1974

---

1 This claim is arresting. There is no evidence that "the senior judiciary" were working towards such a repeal, let alone "for a number of years."

2 The historic practice was not "inappropriate" at all. It had lasted since the 13th Century.

from seeking permission to appeal to the Court of Appeal. Barristers who have not been disbarred *are* now so restricted by s.24. Under the old system abrogated by s.24, barristers were able to bring judicial review proceedings to challenge the decisions of the Visitors. The BSB clearly did not like this. That meant that cases could, if appropriate, be taken further to the Court of Appeal, or, in theory, beyond. That right of appeal had nothing to do with the nature of the sanction imposed by the Disciplinary Tribunal. The reason why solicitors have a second right of appeal is surely that the CA's own permission filter for second appeals is a tough enough threshold to weed out vexatious appellants: see CPR Part 52.7. Section 24's protection of the BSB from such vexation was unnecessary and potentially unfairly disenfranchises those barristers, other than those who are disbarred, who are dealt an unfair hand in the High Court. It may well be that a High Court judge who knows that he or she is not accountable to the Court of Appeal is more likely to be unpersuaded by the Appellant.

11.6 It was argued in *D v BSB* [2018] EWHC 2762 (Admin), that s. 24 was incompatible with the rights of barrister access to the Court of Appeal, an appeal structure already provided for within the machinery of civil justice, but now denied for the first time to the majority of appellant barristers on arbitrary grounds which violated Article 6. D sought a Declaration of Incompatibility under s. 4 of the Human Rights Act 1998. Higginbottom LJ said this:

> Mr Beaumont submitted that, if we were to refuse the appeal, we should make a declaration of incompatibility under section 4 of the Human Rights Act, on the basis that section 24(4) and (5) of the Crime and Courts Act 2013 are incompatible with article 6 of the European Convention on Human Rights ("the ECHR"). By those provisions in the 2013 Act, a decision of this court on an appeal from a BSB Disciplinary Tribunal is final and cannot be appealed further, except where there is a decision

to disbar when there is an appeal to the Court of Appeal (Civil Division).

Mr Beaumont submits that it is irrational and arbitrary to allow an appeal from this court where the sanction is disbarment, but not where it is (e.g.) a suspension for a lengthy period or large fine which may in practice have a devastating if not fatal effect on a barrister's livelihood. Indeed, he submitted that any sanction – even a reprimand – might have a salutary effect on the career of a particular barrister. Furthermore, he relied upon the fact that second appeals from the Solicitors' Disciplinary Tribunal and other disciplinary tribunals are not limited in this way. He referred to debates in Parliament suggesting that, at least some in that place considered that appeals from these two branches of the legal profession should be brought more closely together. He submitted that by allowing second appeals from all complaints against barristers would not open any floodgate, because they would be required to obtain permission on the basis of the strict second appeals criteria.

However, in my view, section 24(4) and (5) is [sic] clearly not incompatible with the ECHR. Mr Beaumont did not rely on article 14 (discrimination), quite rightly, as being a barrister in this context does not fall within any of the protected characteristics. Nor it [sic] incompatible with article 6. Whilst article 6 guarantees an individual a right to a fair trial, where an article 6-compliant decision is made by a court, it is trite law that article 6 does not guarantee a right of appeal (see, e.g., *Porter v United Kingdom* [1987] Application No 12972/87). Of course, if a right of appeal is granted, any appeal itself has to be compliant with article 6: *Andrejeva v Latvia* (2010) 51 EHRR 28 and *Delcourt v Belgium* (1970) 1 EHRR 355, upon which Mr Beaumont relied, support that different proposition. He attempted to distinguish the cases in which there was no machinery for an appeal, from this in which there is machinery but Parliament has chosen to limit the cases which might avail themselves of it; but in my view they cannot be distinguished.

As Ms Padfield submitted, in respect of individuals in the situation of the Appellant (i.e. who have not been disbarred), Parliament has determined that there should be no further appeal from this court; and therefore, the first appeal being article 6-compliant, article 6 is not further engaged. Of course, she did not concede that the differentiation of disbarment cases from those with a lesser sanction is either arbitrary or disproportionate: she submitted that it is in fact principled, understandable and proportionate. In my view, there is force in each element of that submission; but it is unnecessary to make any findings in that regard…

11.7 It is submitted that this regime is a blemish on our civil justice system and an insult to the Bar, clearly engineered by the BSB through its influence in the House of Lords. A barrister *in extremis* should be treated with respect by the courts and, subject to obtaining permission to appeal, must surely be entitled to access to the Court of Appeal and, if appropriate, to the Supreme Court. There is no justification for affording greater appeal rights to suspended, fined or reprimanded solicitors than are afforded to barristers subject to equivalent sanctions.

11.8 It is also to be noted that there is not a single body representing the Bar that would be likely to make representations to Government about this topic. The Bar Council regards itself as the approved regulator under the Legal Services Act 2007, so would be unlikely to assist the Bar to gain parity with solicitors in terms of access to the Court of Appeal. It regards itself as predominantly having conceived the BSB, its progeny. The lack of pure Trade Union representation for the Bar results in many injustices for barristers of which this is but one.

Appeals by the BSB

11.9 The appeal rules in the Handbook provide:

rE236

In cases where one or more charges of professional misconduct have been proved, and/or a disqualification order has been made, an appeal may be lodged with the High Court in accordance with the Civil Procedure Rules:

.1 by the respondent against finding and/or sanction;

.2 with the consent of the Commissioner, by the Bar Standards Board against sanction.

rE237

In any case where any charge of professional misconduct or application to disqualify has been dismissed, the Bar Standards Board may (with the consent of the Commissioner) lodge an appeal with the High Court in accordance with the Civil Procedure Rules.

rE238

Where a respondent lodges an appeal against a disbarment or Disqualification Order or the revocation of a licence or authorisation, they may at the same time lodge with the High Court an appeal against any requirement imposed under rE227 to rE229 as appropriate.

But these rules are silent as to the enabling power in s. 24(2) of the 2013 Act. The General Council of the Bar, an Inn of Court, or two or more Inns of Court acting collectively in any manner, may confer a right of appeal to the High Court in respect of a matter relating to the regulation of barristers. In

BSB v LC [2017] EWHC 3101 (Admin), it was submitted that there was no evidence that any such powers had ever been conferred on the BSB, which had appealed to the High Court against a sanction imposed on LC.

11.10 Higginbottom LJ held that he was "just" persuaded that such a power had been conferred on the BSB. In fact, this is not understood. There was no evidence that it had been. He said:

> 31. Section 24 of the 2013 Act abolished the jurisdiction of judges of the High Court sitting as Visitors to the Inns of Court to review decisions of such a tribunal. However, it provided that the General Council of the Bar, an Inn of Court, or two or more Inns of Court acting collectively in any manner, may confer a right of appeal to the High Court in respect of a matter relating to the regulation of barristers (section 24(2)(a)).
>
> 32. Rights of appeal to this court have been provided in the 2014 Regulations, which form part of the BSB Handbook. Mr Speaight accepted that, if the Handbook had been properly adopted, then the 2014 Regulations which form part of it do confer jurisdiction on this court to hear appeals, including appeals by the BSB against sanction. However, the Respondent and those representing him repeatedly requested evidence that the BSB has formally adopted the Handbook, without any satisfactory response; and so, in my view understandably, Mr Speaight submitted that this court had no such jurisdiction. Before us, relying upon the minutes of a meeting of the BSB on 21 March 2013, Mr Clarke submitted that the BSB Handbook was approved in draft form at that meeting; and, although that draft did not purport to confer any appellate jurisdiction on this court, the meeting also agreed to delegate responsibility for the agreement of any further amendments to the Handbook Working Group which, we were told, in due course agreed amendments to include the provisions to

appeal to this court now found in regulation rE183 and rE185 of the 2014 Regulations which came into force on 6 January 2014. Unfortunately, Mr Clarke said, a search for a document confirming that the Working Group had approved such amendments had drawn a blank; but, he submitted, as the relevant rules have now appeared in the BSB Handbook for four years, we could safely assume that they had been properly agreed and adopted by the Group.

33. In my view, given the terms of section 24 of the 2013 Act, it is far from satisfactory for the jurisdiction of this court to be based upon less than the clearest evidence of the right of appeal being properly conferred by an appropriate body. It is even less satisfactory that the Respondent's perfectly legitimate enquiry about the source of jurisdiction met with no full response until the day of the appeal hearing itself. However, I am satisfied – just – that the evidence shows that the BSB Handbook (of which the 2014 Regulations form part) confers jurisdiction upon this court to hear appeals from a Disciplinary Tribunal.

11.11 With effect from 1st November 2017, a revision in the form of the Disciplinary Tribunals Regulations 2017 came into force. On this occasion, the minutes of the BSB did provide a proper record of the adoption of the new Regulations.

11.12 *BSB v LC* also concerned the old rE185. That rule provided that the BSB may lodge an appeal (against sentence or dismissal) on judicial review-type grounds, i.e. where it considered that the Disciplinary Tribunal had taken into account irrelevant considerations, failed to take into account relevant considerations, reached a decision that was wrong in law, or reached a decision which no reasonable Tribunal could properly have reached. After LC's case in December 2017, in which the BSB was heavily criticised for failing to articulate proper grounds for its appeal against LC's sanction, it proceeded to repeal rE185, arrogating to itself an unfettered right to appeal to the High Court. COIC objected, but was overridden by the BSB.

Principles on appeal – dynamic review

11.13 Whether the Appellant to the High Court is the barrister or the BSB, it is important to identify the relevant principles governing the attack on the decision of the Disciplinary Tribunal. Currently, they spring from CPR Part 52.21, formerly CPR Part 52.11. It provides as follows:

> (1) Every appeal will be limited to a review of the decision of the lower court unless—
>
> (a) a practice direction makes different provision for a particular category of appeal; or
>
> (b) the court considers that in the circumstances of an individual appeal it would be in the interests of justice to hold a re-hearing.
>
> (2) Unless it orders otherwise, the appeal court will not receive—
>
> (a) oral evidence; or
>
> (b) evidence which was not before the lower court.
>
> (3) The appeal court will allow an appeal where the decision of the lower court was—
>
> (a) wrong; or
>
> (b) unjust because of a serious procedural or other irregularity in the proceedings in the lower court.

(4) The appeal court may draw any inference of fact which it considers justified on the evidence.

(5) At the hearing of the appeal, a party may not rely on a matter not contained in that party's appeal notice unless the court gives permission.

11.14 There have been a number of statements of the relevant principles in recent years, but the following by Lang J. in *SH v BSB* [2017] 4 WLR 54 at [15] is perhaps the most comprehensive:

> 16 An appeal against the decision of a disciplinary tribunal is by way of review, not rehearing. However, the nature of an appeal by way of review under rule 52.11 is flexible and differs according to the nature of the body which is appealed against, and the grounds upon which the appeal is brought. In *EI Dupont de Nemours & Co v ST Dupont* [2006] 1 WLR 2793, Aldous LJ said, at paras 92–94, 96:
>
> "92. CPR Pt 52 draws together a very wide range of possible appeals. It applies, not only to the Civil Division of the Court of Appeal, but also to appeals to the High Court and county courts … it applies to a wide variety of statutory appeals where the nature of the decision appealed against and the procedure by which it is reached may differ substantially …
>
> "93. It is accordingly evident that rule 52.11 requires, and in my view contains, a degree of flexibility necessary to enable the court to achieve the overriding objective of dealing with individual cases justly. But as Mance LJ said on a related subject in *Todd v Adams and Chope* ..[2002] EWCA Civ 509; ..it cannot be a matter of simple discretion how an appellate court approaches the matter.
>
> "94. As the terms of rule 52.11(1) make clear, subject to exceptions, every appeal is limited to a review of the

decision of the lower court. A review here is not to be equated with judicial review. It is closely akin to, although not conceptually identical with, the scope of an appeal to the Court of Appeal under the former Rules of the Supreme Court. The review will engage the merits of the appeal. It will accord appropriate respect to the decision of the lower court. Appropriate respect will be tempered by the nature of the lower court and its decision making process. There will also be a spectrum of appropriate respect depending on the nature of the decision of the lower court which is challenged. At one end of the spectrum will be decisions of primary fact reached after an evaluation of oral evidence where credibility is in issue and purely discretionary decisions. Further along the spectrum will be multi-factorial decisions often dependent on inferences and an analysis of documentary material. Rule 52.11(4) expressly empowers the court to draw inferences …"

"96. Submissions to the effect that an appeal hearing should be a rehearing are often motivated by the belief that only thus can sufficient reconsideration be given to elements of the decision of the lower court. In my judgment, this is largely unnecessary given the scope of a hearing by way of review under rule 52.11(1). Further the power to admit fresh evidence in rule 52.11(2) applies equally to a review or rehearing.

The scope of an appeal by way of review, such as I have described, in my view means that the scope of a rehearing under rule 52.11(1)(b) will normally approximate to that of a rehearing 'in the fullest sense of the word' such as Brooke LJ referred to in .. [*Tanfern Ltd v Cameron-MacDonald* (Practice Note)] [2000] 1 WLR 1311, para 31]. On such a rehearing the court will hear the case again. It will if necessary hear evidence again and may well admit fresh evidence. It will reach a fresh decision unconstrained by the decision of the lower court, although it will give to the decision of the lower court the weight that it deserves. The circumstances in which an appeal court hearing an appeal from within the court system will decide to hold such a rehearing will be rare, not least because the appeal court has power under rule 52.10(2)(c) to order a new trial or hearing before the lower court."

17 In *Assicurazioni Generali SpA v Arab Insurance Group* (Practice Note) [2002] EWCA Civ 1642 Clarke LJ said at paras 13–16 and 23:

"13 ... I observe that CPR r 52.11.1(4) expressly gives the appeal court ... power to draw any inference of fact which it considers justified on the evidence. There is no suggestion that that rule applies only to appeals by way of rehearing under rule 52.11(1)(b), so that the court has that power when conducting a review. In these circumstances, it seems to me that in the type of appeal in which the court is asked to reverse findings of fact based upon the credibility of the witnesses, the same approach should be adopted in this court whether the appeal is by way of review or rehearing.

"14. The approach of the court to any particular case will depend upon the nature of the issues ... determined by the judge ... In some cases the trial judge will have reached conclusions of primary fact based almost entirely upon the view which he formed of the oral evidence of the witnesses. In most cases, however, the position is more complex. In many such cases the judge will have reached his conclusions of primary fact as a result partly of the view he formed of the oral evidence and partly from an analysis of the documents. In other such cases, the judge will have made findings of primary fact based entirely or almost entirely on the documents. Some findings of primary fact will be the result of direct evidence, whereas others will depend upon inference from direct evidence of such facts.

"15. In appeals against conclusions of primary fact the approach of an appellate court will depend upon the weight to be attached to the findings of the judge and that weight will depend upon the extent to which, as the trial judge, the judge has an advantage over the appellate court; the greater that advantage the more reluctant the appellate court should be to interfere. As I see it, that was the approach of the Court of Appeal on a 'rehearing' under the Rules of the Supreme Court and should be its approach on a 'review' under the Civil Procedure Rules 1998.

"16. Some conclusions of fact are, however, not conclusions of primary fact of the kind to which I have just referred. They involve an assessment of a number of different factors which have to be weighed against each other. This is sometimes called an evaluation of the facts and is often a matter of degree upon which different judges can legitimately differ. Such cases may be closely analogous to the exercise of a discretion and, in my opinion, appellate courts should approach them in a similar way…"

18 In *Assicurazioni* Ward LJ set out the test which the appellate court should apply under rule 52.11, in circumstances where the lower court has heard the witnesses, at para 197:

"Bearing these matters in mind, the appeal court conducting a review of the trial judge's decision will not conclude that the decision was wrong simply because it is not the decision the appeal judge would have made had he or she been called upon to make it in the court below. Something more is required than personal unease and something less than perversity has to be established. The best formulation for the ground in between where a range of adverbs may be used—'clearly', 'plainly', 'blatantly', 'palpably' wrong, is an adaptation of what Lord Fraser of Tullybelton said in *G v G (Minors: Custody Appeal)* [1985]

1 WLR 642, 652, admittedly dealing with the different task of exercising a discretion. Adopting his approach, I would pose the test for deciding whether a finding of fact was against the evidence to be whether that finding by the trial judge exceeded the generous ambit within which reasonable disagreement about the conclusion to be drawn from the evidence is possible. The difficulty or ease with which that test can be satisfied will depend on the nature of the finding under attack. If the challenge is to the finding of a primary fact, particularly if founded upon an assessment of the credibility of witnesses, then it will be a hard task to overthrow. Where the primary facts are not challenged and the judgment is made from the inferences drawn by the judge from the evidence before him, then the Court of Appeal, which has the power to draw any inference of fact it considers to be justified, may more readily interfere with an evaluation of those facts. The judgment of the Court of Appeal in *The Glannibanta* (1876) 1 PD 283, 287 seems as apposite now as it did then: 'Now we feel, as strongly as did the Lords of the Privy Council in the cases just referred to [*The Julia* (1860) 14 Moo PC 210 and *The Alice* (1868) LR 2 PC 245], the great weight that is due to the decision of a judge of first instance whenever, in a conflict of testimony, the demeanour and manner of the witnesses who have been seen and heard by him are, as they were in the cases referred to, material elements in the consideration of the truthfulness of their statements. But the parties to a cause are nevertheless entitled, as well on question of fact as on questions of law, to demand the decision of the Court of Appeal, and that court cannot excuse itself from the task of weighing conflicting evidence and drawing its own inferences and conclusions, even though it should always bear in mind that it has neither seen nor heard the witnesses, and should make due allowance in this respect.

11.15 Despite the appeal being a review rather than a re-hearing, it should be impressed on the judge that it is a dynamic review and is a hearing very much 'on the merits'. The switch from the Visitors to a statutory format of appeal should not make a difference. Collins J. put it in this way in *O'C v BSB* (2012) Unrep. Visitors to the Inns of Court:

> The second point raised relates to the alleged lack of reasons which were given by the Tribunal. There is an obligation under the rules for the Tribunal to give reasons for its decision. Without going into any detail, we are bound to say that the reasoning is singularly unimpressive. *Prima facie,* there is, in our view, considerable force in the submission that the reasons in this case were defective. Again, we have not gone into that in any detail because, in our view, it has not been necessary to do so. The reason why we say that is because, even if we were persuaded that our *prima facie* view was indeed correct, we are hearing the matter anew. We consider the charges on their merits and will reach a conclusion based upon their merits. This is not a review, as was made abundantly clear by the Court of Appeal in *R v Visitors to the Inns of Court, ex parte [RC]* [1994] QB 1. That involved an appeal from a judicial review of a decision of the Visitors. In that case, the Visitors had approached the matter on the basis that their responsibility was to review rather than consider the application on its merits. It is clear now that we do consider the matter entirely on its merits. In the course of his judgment in *ex parte* Calder, Stuart Smith LJ made it clear that we as Visitors, since we are able to hear the matter entirely on its merits, will give the necessary protection to an appellant and it is not necessary for the matter to be remitted for a further consideration by the tribunal which was either in breach of fairness or failed to give proper reasons. That follows from the decision of the House of Lords in *Lloyd v McMahon* [1997] AC 625.

11.16 Ms O'C won her appeal and sued the BSB for race discrimination. The Claim was struck out and she took the appeal to the Supreme Court and won. The Supreme Court observed this about the earlier Visitorial appeal in *O'C v BSB* [2017] UKSC 78 at [35]:

> (6) On an appeal the Visitors were required to look afresh at the matters in dispute and to form their own views. They were required to consider whether the charge had been made out to their satisfaction, to the requisite standard of proof. The proper approach was that of an appellate court rehearing the case on its merits. (*R v Visitors to the Inns of Court, Ex p [RC]* [1994] QB 1 per Sir Donald Nicholls V-C at pp 42D-F, 42H; per Stuart-Smith LJ at pp 61H - 62D. See also *[AL] v Daniels* [1962] 1 QB 237, per Devlin LJ at p 256.)

> (7) It was open to the Visitors to correct procedural defects and to remedy procedural unfairness before the Disciplinary Tribunal. As Sir Andrew Collins observed in delivering the judgment of the Visitors in the present case, the Visitors were able to hear the matter entirely on its merits. They would give the necessary protection to an appellant and it was not necessary for the matter to be remitted for further consideration by the Tribunal.

11.17 In *ex parte RC supra* Sir Donald Nicholls V-C said this at 42:

> I can see no reason to doubt that an appeal to the judges as visitors is precisely that: an appeal. It is so described in the authorities. In *[AL]* v. *Daniels* [1962] 1 Q.B. 237, 256, Devlin L.J. referred to it as "a rehearing on appeal." Thus the visitors will look afresh at the matters in dispute and form their own views.

11.18 Before the Visitors in *CR v BSB* (2013) Unrep. Wyn Williams J. said this at [17] having followed *O'C v BSB* (2012) and *ex parte RC*:

> That said the appellate courts are, generally, slow to allow an appeal against a decision of a lower court which is founded upon the exercise of discretion. In *G v G (Minors: Custody Appeal)* [1985] 1 WLR 647 at 652 Lord Fraser said- "....the appellate court should only interfere when they consider that the judge of first instance has not merely preferred an imperfect solution which is different from an alternative imperfect solution which the Court of Appeal might or would have adopted, but has exceeded the generous ambit within which a reasonable disagreement is possible."
>
> In *Phonographic Performance Ltd v AIE Rediffusion Music Ltd* [1999] 1 WLR 1507 at 1523 Lord Woolf MR explained:
>
> "Before the court can interfere it must be shown that the judge has either erred in principle in his approach or has left out of account or has taken into account some feature that he should, or should not, have considered, or that his decision was wholly wrong because the court is forced to the conclusion that he has not balanced the various factors fairly in the scale."
>
> 18. In so far as the decisions of the Tribunal which are impugned in this case are founded upon the exercise of discretion we propose to adopt the approach which is encapsulated in *G* and *Phonographic Performance Ltd*.

11.19 It is possible to discern two strands of authority. Lang J's judgment in *SH*, for all of its comprehensiveness, does not appear to have benefited from citation of *ex parte RC*, *O'C*, *CR*, or any other authorities concerning the pre-section 24 approach applicable to appeals by barristers. Sir Andrew Collins in *O'C* described a dynamic merits-based form of review. Lang J., by the time of *SH*, operating under s.24 of CCA 2013, described a more conservative and technical approach akin to the way in which appeals are argued in the Court of Appeal, Civil Division. But, in reality, it does not matter which approach is correct. For a ground of appeal against conviction to succeed, it will have to assert serious unfairness likely to have had a material effect on the outcome of the trial. That will only very rarely involve fresh evidence. By the time of *S v BSB* in late 2016, 4 years on from his judgment in *O'C* speaking of a "re-hearing" *qua* Chair of a Visitors' panel, Sir Andrew Collins now had to grapple with CPR Part 52 having replaced the Hearings before the Visitors Rules. He said this at [17]:

> 17. In dealing with this appeal, I must apply the approach which is set out in CPR 52.11. This means that the appeal is limited to a review of the tribunal's decision. CPR 52.11 (3) provides: "(3) The appeal court will allow the appeal where the decision of the lower court was - (a) wrong; or (b) unjust because of a serious procedural or other irregularity in the proceedings in the lower court. (4) The appeal court may draw any inference of fact which it considers justified on the evidence."

> 18. Mr Treverton-Jones QC [and Mr Beaumont], who appeared for the appellant, [rely] on both aspects of CPR 52.11(3), submitting that the decision was wrong in that the tribunal should not have found on the evidence before it that either charge was proved. The negligence which is charged was, he submitted, not established and even if it was would not be regarded as constituting serious professional misconduct. The manner in which the appellant had dealt with the complaint did not breach the Code and any shortcomings, if they existed, again could not be regarded as serious.

> 19. Further, there was an attack on some of the findings of fact and in particular on the judgment of the tribunal in accepting the evidence of the solicitors against that of the appellant.
>
> 20. I am of course aware that in respect of this last attack it is rare for an appellate court to overturn a factual finding based upon the tribunal having seen and heard the relevant witnesses. Nonetheless, if any finding is in all the circumstances unreasonable it cannot stand. But the hurdle to be surmounted by an appellant who seeks to show that a finding of fact made by the tribunal or court which has heard and seen the witnesses on either side is a high one.

11.20 In *S v BSB* the unfairness perpetrated by the BSB and by the trial panel, was so egregious, as found by Collins J, that both the dynamic review approach and re-hearing approach would have led to the same outcome before that fair-minded and humane judge. It is, however, a sad reality, that those judges who are most likely to dismiss appeals against conviction brought by barristers and other professionals, will do so whichever test they are urged to apply. And it is very difficult to conceive of any successful appeal that is not based on the kind of grounds that would be likely to commend themselves to a judge sitting in the Civil Division of the Court of Appeal, in other words, review type grounds.

Appeals against sanction

11.21 The litmus test for manifest excessiveness was described by Jackson LJ in *Salsbury v Law Society* [2008] EWCA Civ 1285 as being whether the sanction was "clearly inappropriate":

> From this review of authority I conclude that the statements of principle set out by Sir Thomas Bingham MR in *Bolton v Law Society* [1994] 1 WLR 512 remain good law, subject to this qualification. In applying the *Bolton* prin-

ciples the Solicitors Disciplinary Tribunal must also take into account the rights of the solicitor under articles 6 and 8 of the Convention. It is now an overstatement to say that "a very strong case" is required before the court will interfere with the sentence imposed by the Solicitors Disciplinary Tribunal. The correct analysis is that the Solicitors Disciplinary Tribunal comprises an expert and informed tribunal, which is particularly well placed in any case to assess what measures are required to deal with defaulting solicitors and to protect the public interest. Absent any error of law, the High Court must pay considerable respect to the sentencing decisions of the tribunal. Nevertheless if the High Court, despite paying such respect, is satisfied that the sentencing decision was clearly inappropriate, then the court will interfere. It should also be noted that an appeal from the Solicitors Disciplinary Tribunal to the High Court normally proceeds by way of review: see CPR r 52.11 (1).

11.22 In *FK v BSB* [2018] EWHC 2184 (Admin), it was submitted that the effect in lost fee income of a 7-month suspension imposed by the Disciplinary Tribunal was tantamount to a fine of over £140,000. FT had no other equivalent means of earning his living and had a school-age family. Applying the test in *Salsbury*, suspension for merely asking about the fate of another barrister in two robing rooms, was "clearly inappropriate" because it was manifestly excessive and so a "disproportionate" interference with the Article 8 right to practise a profession without undue interference by a public authority. Warby J held:

> 69. I take a different view, when it comes to sanction. As Mr Goudie QC has fairly and rightly reminded me, it is not the function of the Court on an appeal of this kind to substitute its own view for that of the expert disciplinary tribunal. Appropriate deference should be paid to the experience and expertise which that tribunal enjoys; there is a high threshold for interference: see *Salsbury v Law Society*

[2009] EWCA Civ 1285 [2009] 1 WLR 1286 [30] (Jackson LJ).

70. That said, the need for deference of this kind is somewhat less when it comes to judicial scrutiny of sanctions imposed on legal professionals. This is a profession which the Court knows something about. Further, there is little room for deference so far as evaluation of the facts is concerned. The facts were all agreed, and no other facts were relied on by the Tribunal. Its Judgment does not disclose any inferential conclusions of fact, which this Court might perhaps hesitate to disturb. Mr Goudie concedes that the sanction "could be viewed as being at the higher end of the scale". In my judgment, it goes further. Making all due allowance for the advantages enjoyed by the Tribunal, the sanction in this case was manifestly excessive and should be set aside.

11.23 The reduction of the suspension of FK from 7 months to 3 months by Warby J, engaged a number of principles and approaches. Warby J's approach below is useful for those seeking to work out a way of formulating grounds of appeal against sanction:

72. Page 32 of the Sanctions Guidance identifies categories of suspension. The "long" category is "over 6 months and up to three years." A "medium" suspension is "over 3 months and up to 6 months", and a "short" one is "up to three months". Pages 33 and following of the Sanctions Guidance give illustrative examples of appropriate starting points and ranges for a variety of disciplinary offences. The Tribunal did not expressly refer to these pages in its Judgment, but I infer that it had them in mind. The first example is "recklessly misleading the Court", for which the suggested starting point is a reprimand. Other examples include "recklessly making allegations of fraud", the appropriate sanction range for which is said to be a "medium

level fine to short suspension". A "medium level fine" is "£1,000 and up to £3,000". A "high level" fine is more than "£3,000 and up to £50,000". For "A conviction for an act of violence causing injury" is given a starting point of a "medium level suspension". For harassment over a prolonged period, the Guidance suggests a starting point of "a high level fine and a short suspension". For discourtesy, in the form of "high level" discourtesy with a "significant impact on the victim", the Guidance recommends a "reprimand accompanied by a medium to high level fine."

73. At the hearing, the BSB presented a Note on Sanction which highlighted two possible analogies: discourtesy and abusing the position of the advocate (as, for instance, by reckless allegations of fraud).

74. The Panel had regard to the Sanctions Guidance, including the guidance on the applicability of suspension, and on illustrative sanctions. It considered the aggravating factors. These were "premeditation" on all three dates; persistent conduct over a lengthy period; and previous disciplinary findings against Mr [FK]....By this process the Tribunal arrived at a global starting point. It then considered the mitigating factors: Mr FK's early admissions; the apology he had made for his "inappropriate" behaviour; and the undertaking he gave when asked for one by Mr Jones' lawyers. It thus arrived at the global sanction of 7 months' suspension, concurrent. In the Judgment, the Panel said this:

"Bearing in mind the Sanctions Guidance and the breaches as summarised in Version 4, we have come to the unanimous view that Mr [FK's] conduct and behaviour is so serious as to undermine public confidence in the profession and therefore a signal needs to be sent to Mr [FK] the profession and the public, that the behaviour in question is unacceptable.

... the relevant factors to be taken into account if we are thinking of suspension are not *limited* to but include the following: "(b) the seriousness of any breach of the Handbook" and "(e) the barrister has shown lack of integrity that is not so serious as to warrant disbarment" but (and these are our words) serious enough to warrant suspension whether the charges admitted are taken together or individually.

... We have looked at the Guidance given at page 32 and, in our judgment, for the reasons that I have just given, and the seriousness we take of Mr [FK's] actions, whether considered individually or collectively, this conduct and behaviour – unacceptable as it is – falls into the higher level of suspension, recognising that the allegation made by [Ms McBride and Mr Jones], at the time that these things were said, were unproven. We have taken a period of time looking at the levels of suspensions at the higher level which has a range of over six months and up to three years. That is the band we feel that Mr [FK's] case falls into.

We started with a period of suspension of nine months. Taking into account of his admission, his remorse and apology, the undertaking that he gave near the time of the offending behaviour, that starting point of nine months should be reduced to seven months to reflect these features and the other mitigation that we have heard."

75. I have no doubt that it was appropriate for the Tribunal to consider these three separate offences in the round, and to impose a single penalty to reflect the totality of the misconduct. I have concluded that the Tribunal was entitled to conclude that suspension was the appropriate penalty. The sanctions exercise in this case was not straightforward, as the offending was not easy to compare with any of the illustrative examples. But in my judgment the Tribunal fell into error in at least four ways, the combin-

ation of which led to a penalty that was well beyond what was proportionate.

(1) I see the force of Mr Beaumont's submission that the Panel imposed a deterrent sanction, beyond what the individual facts of the case merited, in the absence of evidence that there is or was any systemic problem requiring such deterrence.

(2) Secondly, the Tribunal's reasoning shows no evidence that it considered the impact of suspension on [Mr FK]. Mr Beaumont has submitted that this was tantamount to a fine of over £140,000 and thus represents an unprecedented sanction, of "breathtaking" severity. The figure is supported by a statement from Mr [FK]. Means are relevant to financial penalty, but I agree with Mr Goudie that assessment of the precise financial impact is not the right "metric" by which to assess suspension. However, a Tribunal must give at least some consideration to the impact on the barrister. Whatever the scale of his or her practice, to prevent a barrister from practising and earning a living is a serious matter, impinging – as Mr Beaumont points out – on the barrister's Convention rights.

(3) The third point is or may be linked to the second. Although I find that the Tribunal was right to view this offending as meriting suspension, I consider the starting point of 9 months' suspension to be clearly excessive. Even with the aggravating features of the case, a suspension of 9 months represents – to any self-employed individual – a very severe penalty indeed. The charges, though serious in nature, were not so serious as to call for the deprivation of the right to practise one's profession for as long as that. Comparison with the illustrative examples leads me to the conclusion that these sanctions were out of kilter with the guidance.

(4) Fourth and finally, the Tribunal failed to give sufficient credit for [FK]'s early acceptance of guilt and the other mitigation that was available to him. A discount of 2 months is a mere 20%. The early guilty plea alone merited more than this. It would be hard to justify credit of less than one third for these matters, taken together...

..77. In my judgment, the appropriate global starting point for all three charges, after consideration of aggravating features and applying the principle of totality, could not have exceeded 5 months' suspension. After due allowance for mitigation, and an appropriate discount for [FK]'s early admissions, the sanction which I substitute is one of 3 months' suspension on each of the robing room charges, to run concurrently, and 5 weeks' suspension on the LinkedIn Charge, also concurrent. That, in my judgment, is amply sufficient to mark the seriousness of the matter, and to send an appropriate signal to the profession and the public

Former Chairs of the Bar

11.24 Most barrister appeals are heard by a single judge with an Administrative Court 'ticket'. Cases perceived to raise a difficult or important point of practice, may be listed before a two (or even three) judge Divisional Court. Know your judges once the lists are published online from 14:30 on the day before an appeal. Research their careers and backgrounds. There are at any one time a number of former Chairs of the Bar Council serving as High Court Judges. If asked to recuse themselves, most, if not all, will withdraw from an appeal concerning the Bar Standards Board, given that the Bar Council, the BSB's parent body, is the approved regulator under the Legal Services Act 2007. That said, a particularly highly regarded and fair-minded former Chair of the Bar Council may be a desirable tribunal.

Dissenting judgments

11.25 An appeal from a majority decision poses a unique advantage. One panel member (if it was a 3-person tribunal) or two panel members (if it was a 5-person tribunal) will have found in the Appellant's favour below, either on guilt or on sanction, or both. The rules contemplate majority decisions and so, dissenting judgments. In the appeal in *CR v BSB* (2013), the directions judge, Sir Anthony May, acceded to the application of CR that the reasons of the (numerically secret) dissenting minority should be explained for the assistance of the Visitors on appeal. The judge's direction was conveyed to the dissenting member or members, who replied that he, she or they could no longer remember their reasons for dissent. Nevertheless, the approach in that case means that the defence should always request that panel members who have dissented in what is disclosed to have been a majority decision, should ensure that the reasons for their minority view are fairly represented in the final judgment of the Tribunal and before too much time elapses post-trial. As soon as a decision to appeal has been made, the Tribunal should be asked to procure these reasons from the dissenting member or members and to secure them for the assistance of the Appellant and the High Court and to provide them to the Appellant once they are to hand. It is possible both that the Tribunal will refuse to do this and the BSB will refuse to assist. If so, the Appellant should seek an early direction from the Administrative Court.

Appeals after a guilty plea at the Tribunal

11.26 There have been several cases in recent years, in which barristers have pleaded guilty at the Tribunal. Many may have had no representation or free representation. In the majority of cases, there has been no ground for complaint. But in some, the representation and advice has been sub-par. In such circumstances, it is desirable that the appeal court should be able to revisit the merits of the case, set aside the guilty plea and send the matter back for a trial. In principle at least, this is possible: see the cases summarised in *FK v BSB supra* at [16]-[24]. The bar is inevitably a high one. The jurisprudence concerning false confessions by those accused of crime is an accepted part of the law of evidence. Barristers too may be swayed to admit charges against them for the same or similar reasons: out of fear; to remove severe pressure; to avoid public embarrassment; to save money. If young, they may be the type of people who are unusually attuned to accepting opinions and rulings within the command structure of a chambers. They could be peculiarly likely to accept the advice of a senior barrister, even if it is wrong.

Judicial Review challenges against directions orders

11.27 Under the old Disciplinary Tribunals Regulations, there was a power to seek a review against directions made by Directions Judges. The matter would be heard by a High Court Judge. This was a valuable jurisdiction. But it did lead to delays. It has been abolished. Yet it is possible, in theory at least, that a particularly bad direction, could be challenged by way of judicial review. There have been sets of directions drafted by the BSB in which the BSB has procured that the defence serves its witness statements before the BSB. It is difficult to think of anything that offends one's sense of fair play more acutely than such a direction. That might be challenged by way of judicial review if it has no rational foundation. Or an application to strike out under rE127.2 rejected without proper reasons, might also be taken further in this manner. Neither of these examples could be faulted on the basis of the availability of an alternative remedy.

Suspension of practising certificate pending appeal

11.28 The Disciplinary Tribunal Regulations give Disciplinary Tribunals the power to order that the BSB suspend a barrister's practising certificate pending the outcome of an appeal where the sanction imposed is one of more than one year's suspension or disbarment. This power is different from imposing a sanction of suspension or disbarment, in that suspension of a practising certificate only affects the barrister's ability to provide legal services as a barrister. Only the Inns of Court have the ability to disbar barristers. The need for a provision that allows the BSB to suspend the right to have a practising certificate arises because sanctions imposed by Tribunals will not be implemented until after the outcome of any appeal is known. Where a Tribunal considers that the barrister represents an immediate risk to the public which warrants a lengthy suspension or disbarment, it might be wrong to allow the barrister to continue practising, or to be eligible to obtain a practising certificate, merely because an appeal has been submitted. The Regulations stipulate that a Tribunal should order that the barrister's practising certificate be suspended pending appeal unless there is good reason not do so.

Service

11.29 CPR PD 52D provides for barrister appeals under s. 24 of the CCA 2013. It states that Notices of Appeal must be served on *both* the BSB and on COIC, which, one assumes, means, the BTAS. The time for appeal is (an extendable) 21 days: see CPR Part 52.12.

CHAPTER TWELVE
THE LEGAL OMBUDSMAN

12.1 Few now may recall the Extraordinary Meeting of the Bar in 1995 at a packed Quaker's Hall, known as "Friend's House", in London's Marylebone Road. It was selected because no building at the four Inns of Court could accommodate the angry hordes of barristers who wanted to protest about what the Bar Council had in store for them. The EGM presaged a new type of complaint against barristers about poor service. The public interest, apparently demanded this.

12.2 Friendly, that evening, the House was not. The general mood lay somewhere between outrage and mutiny, just about assuaged by the smooth advocacy of the then Bar Chairman, Peter Goldsmith QC. The criminal bar, in particular, feared an onslaught of complaints from incarcerated prisoners with nothing better to do than to complain relentlessly about the rudeness of their barristers. But the real fears impressively expressed that unforgettable night by barristers at all stages of their careers, did not deter the Bar Council's legislators.

12.3 Springing from that meeting was a new system of complaints, which became known as "inadequate professional services" or "IPS". It was administered by the Bar Council side by side with graver matters of "professional misconduct" until 2006 with the advent of the Bar Standards Board.

12.4 A challenge to exculpatory IPS findings lay to an external statutory body, the "Legal Services Ombudsman" or the LSO, set up under s.21 of the Courts and Legal Services Act 1990. The IPS process would then be gone through all over again by the LSO, a process which could add months more to the original IPS process.

12.5 The BSB administered both of the species of complaints until 6th October 2010, when a new system, created by the Legal Services Act 2007, came into force. That Act created the Office for Legal Complaints to deal with 'service complaints', a new description for inadequate professional services. This set up the Legal Ombudsman or (avuncular sounding) "LeO". The (unpopular) LSO was abolished by s. 159 of the 2007 Act.

12.6 LeO applies to barristers as it applies to solicitors. LeO is not a first instance scheme. This means that a former client must invoke and exhaust a barrister's complaints procedure first before LeO can have any jurisdiction. LeO must decline jurisdiction if an approach to it is premature: s. 126(1) of the LSA 2007. But a complainant can use the Legal Ombudsman if the complaint has not been resolved to the complainant's satisfaction within 8 weeks of being made to the barrister, or an Ombudsman considers that there are exceptional reasons to consider the complaint sooner, or without it having been made first to the barrister, or where an Ombudsman considers that in-house resolution is not possible due to an irretrievable breakdown in the relationship between the barrister and the person making the complaint: Scheme Rules 4.2.

12.7 Time Limits: the complainant has 6 months to refer the matter to LeO from the date of the Barrister's response: Scheme Rules 4.4. Whilst the system is not intended to resemble a civil cause of action, where that might assist the barrister (see below), in terms of limitation, where that might assist the complainant, it does. Scheme Rules 4.5 to 4.7 provide that ordinarily the act or omission, or when the complainant should reasonably have known there was cause for complaint, must have been after 5th October 2010; and the complainant must refer the complaint to the Legal Ombudsman no later than 6 years from the act/omission or 3 years from when the complainant should reasonably have known there was cause for complaint. Where a complaint is referred by a personal representative or beneficiary of the estate of a person who, before he/she died, had not referred the complaint to the Legal Ombudsman, the period runs from when the deceased should reasonably have known there was cause for complaint; and when the complainant (or the deceased) should reasonably have known there was a cause for complaint will be assessed on the basis of the complainant's (or the deceased's) own knowledge, disregarding what the complainant (or the deceased) might have been told if he/she had sought advice. If an Ombudsman considers that there are exceptional circumstances, he/she may extend any of these time limits to the extent that he/she considers fair. For example an Ombudsman might extend a time limit if the complainant was prevented from meeting the time limit as a result of serious illness and is likely to extend a time limit where the time limit had not expired when the complainant raised the complaint with the barrister.

12.8 LeO is manned by case officers. They are often not legally qualified. They engage with complainants chiefly by email, but also by telephone. The emphasis seems in the initial phase to be on conciliation, rather like ACAS, as well as due process, even where these functions are irreconcilable. Some might say that they are always irreconcilable.

12.9 In the early stages, an offer to settle will be well received – but a barrister may feel that the complaint is about a small sum of money and is akin to blackmail along the lines of, *'this complaint will cause you hundreds of hours of work and worry, unless you repay most or all of your modest fee'*, where the complaint itself is unfounded. Barristers trained to look at merits before remedy will not appreciate a case officer who reverses that logic. That is in spite of the breadth of s. 137(1) of the 2007 Act, which provides that:

> A complaint is to be determined under the ombudsman scheme by reference to what is, in the opinion of the ombudsman making the determination, fair and reasonable in all the circumstances of the case.

12.10 One might think that a repayment of fees or a payment of compensation that has no basis in law cannot be fair and reasonable. However it is provided by s. 137(5) that:

> The power of the ombudsman to make a direction under subsection (2) [i.e. for refunds of fees or compensation] is not confined to cases where the complainant may have a cause of action against the respondent for negligence.

12.11 BMIF can be generous in their support for barristers who are subject to complaints to LeO, in contrast to their approach to the usually much more serious disciplinary complaints to the BSB. This is anomalous.

12.12 Section 136 of the 2007 Act provides for complaint costs. The cost of a complaint to LeO is £400. But this is not payable by the complainant, however vexatious, but, by way of presumption, <u>by the barrister</u>. That seems designed to put pressure on the barrister from day 1, to settle, or pay £400, even if exonerated. It is not payable if the complaint is abandoned or withdrawn, but most are not, nor if a complaint is settled, so that is a signal to a barrister to refund fees, even where there is no good reason to do so. Nor is the £400 payable if the complaint is resolved or determined in favour of the barrister, but what does that mean? Does it mean *unconditionally* resolved in favour of the barrister? There is almost always something to criticise and the case officers can be highly subjective in the things that they choose to criticise about the Bar. But if LeO is satisfied that the barrister took all reasonable steps, under his/her complaints procedures, to try to resolve the complaint, the £400 may be waived. Again, this appears to mean, offering money. So if a barrister has charged £500, unless he offers to return a complainant £100 for no material reason, he will pay the £400 fee even if exonerated, and may make a net £100 from a £500 fee, even *if* exonerated. The hidden message to the Bar from LeO is: 'in any case where the client is a potential complainant to LeO: add £400 to the fee'. The losers from this scheme are the vast majority of sensible clients who do not make vexatious complaints, but still find themselves paying higher fees. In truth, LeO often (albeit unpredictably) waives the £400 fee if the barrister is exonerated, but the intention behind this presumption is universally reviled by the Bar (and one presumes, solicitors) and should be abolished. Why should costs not follow the event as under the CPR?

12.13 There appears to be a great deal of assistance given by case officers to complainants to formulate and re-formulate their complaints. This happens unbeknown to barristers. It may go on for weeks or even months. It may happen even after the complaint has been fully and decisively answered by the barrister. If the barrister has BMIF-funded representation and a complete, carefully drafted letter of response has been sent to LeO, yet another formulation of the response may emerge. The cost of this exercise at the fee rates that BMIF is willing to pay to its panel firms in the City of London, when complainants are willing or indeed, encouraged, to make the most wounding but misconceived, allegations of dishonesty, fraud or severe incompetence against barristers with impunity and without costs consequences, can run into many tens of thousands of pounds, or even more. It appears that LeO has absolutely no conception of the damage that it does, or the cost that it runs up, by over-indulging vexatious complainants in this manner.

12.14 LeO appears to be willing to consider repeat complaints from the same complainant who has spent months attacking a barrister without any success and running up a huge costs bill for BMIF. LeO does not understand, or chooses not to understand, the rules of cause of action estoppel dealt with elsewhere in this book. The cause of action estoppel doctrine is a vital protection against harassment from repeat complainants indulged by LeO.

12.15 LeO is obliged to disclose to the barrister its communications with the complainant about the complaint. The BSB itself now observes such an obligation. However, the practice of LeO in this respect is inconsistent. In *BSB v JS* (2014), S refused to engage with LeO until they made disclosure of such material, and the Disciplinary Tribunal sympathised to such an extent, that he was acquitted of a charge of non-cooperation with LeO.

12.16 LeO's record in the Administrative Court is at best mixed. If a barrister is being treated unfairly or in breach of the LeO's rules, very often a threat of proceedings in the Administrative Court will lead to early compliance. The grant of permission to move for judicial review, often leads to compliance by LeO without the need for a final hearing. But the threshold for interference is set high: see *R (LC, a barrister) v Legal Ombudsman* [2014] EWHC 182 (Admin):

> In exercising powers of review, this court does not put itself in the position of the Ombudsman and test the reasonableness of the decision against the decision the Court would make. It does not review the merits of the decision as if it were exercising the statutory powers itself. To do so would be to subvert the intention of Parliament in vesting the Ombudsman with the function of administering the scheme. His decision may only be overturned as unreasonable if it is unreasonable in the Wednesbury sense (*Associated Provincial Picture House Ltd v Wednesbury Corporation* [1948] 1 KB 223). There are a number of different formulations of this well-known and oft-applied test. A common modern formulation is that the decision must be outside the range of reasonable responses open to the decision maker (see e.g. *Boddington v British Transport Police* [1992] 2 AC 143 at 175H per Lord Steyn). This is a high threshold, particularly in the context of a scheme intended to resolve complaints swiftly and informally in which the decision maker is afforded a wide discretion to do what he thinks is fair and reasonable in all the circumstances. One way in which a decision may pass the threshold is if it is irrational in the proper sense of the word, that is to say if its reasoning is not logically capable of supporting the conclusion (see e.g. *R v Parliamentary Com-*

missioner for Administration, ex parte Balchin [1998] 1 PLR 1, 13E-F per Sedley J and *R (Norwich and Peterborough Building Society) v Financial Ombudsman Service Ltd* [2002] EWHC 2379 (Admin) at [59] per Ouseley J).

12.17 LeO must only consider the complaint actually made. Neither the case officer nor the Ombudsman should stray into considering matters that have not been raised by the complainant and/or have not first been put to the barrister for comment: *R (AR, a barrister) v Legal Ombudsman* [2014] EWHC 601 (Admin). LeO is subject in this respect to the principles of natural justice: *R (JS, a barrister) v Legal Ombudsman* [2016] EWHC 612 (Admin).

12.18 The case officers must be careful to behave professionally. In the AR case *supra*, there was this internal memorandum about the barrister:

> Ears but does not listen; eyes but cannot see; a tongue that probably never stops; and an everlasting supply of ink!

Needless to say, AR did not receive this well and it formed the basis of a submission that the LeO investigation was biased. That submission failed but on another occasion might very well succeed.

12.19 Under Scheme Rule 5.7, LeO may dismiss or discontinue all or part of a complaint if, in its opinion:

> a) it does not have any reasonable prospect of success, or is frivolous or vexatious;

> b) the complainant has not suffered (and is unlikely to suffer) financial loss, distress, inconvenience or other detriment;

c) the authorised person has already offered fair and reasonable redress in relation to the circumstances alleged by the complainant and the offer is still open for acceptance;

d) the complainant has previously complained about the same issue to the Legal Ombudsman (unless the Ombudsman considers that material new evidence, likely to affect the outcome, only became available to the complainant afterwards);

e) a comparable independent complaints (or costs-assessment) scheme or a court has already dealt with the same issue;

f) a comparable independent complaints (or costs-assessment) scheme or a court is dealing with the same issue, unless those proceedings are first stayed (by the agreement of all parties or by a court order) so that the Legal Ombudsman can deal with the issue;

g) it would be more suitable for the issue to be dealt with by a court, by arbitration or by another complaints (or costs-assessment) scheme;

h) the issue concerns an authorised person's decision when exercising a discretion under a will or trust;

i) the issue concerns an authorised person's failure to consult a beneficiary before exercising a discretion under a will or trust, where there is no legal obligation to consult;

j) the issue involves someone else who has not complained and the Ombudsman considers that it would not be appropriate to deal with the issue without their consent;

k) it is not practicable to investigate the issue fairly because of the time which has elapsed since the act/omission;

l) the issue concerns an act/omission outside England and Wales and the circumstances do not have a sufficient connection with England and Wales;

m) the complaint is about an authorised person's refusal to provide a service and the complainant has not produced evidence that the refusal was for other than legitimate or reasonable reasons;

n) there are other compelling reasons why it is inappropriate for the issue to be dealt with by the Legal Ombudsman.

12.20 The system operates on a two-tier basis. The case officer makes a case decision. If either party disagrees with it, the matter is sent for an Ombudsman's final decision: Scheme Rule 5.19. If neither party disagrees with the case decision within a stated time limit for a response, it will be final.

12.21 Paras 5.36 to 5.54 of the Scheme Rules deal with the range of outcomes. An Ombudsman will determine a complaint by reference to what is, in his/her opinion, fair and reasonable in all the circumstances of the case. In determining what is fair and reasonable, the Ombudsman will take into account (but is not bound by): a) what decision a court might make; b) the BSB's rules of conduct at the time of the act/omission; and c) what *the Ombudsman* considers to have been good practice at the time of the act/omission. This may be idiosyncratic and controversial.

12.22 The Ombudsman's determination may contain one or more of the following directions to the barrister in favour of the complainant:

a) to apologise; b) to pay compensation of a specified amount for loss suffered; c) to pay interest on that compensation from a specified time; d) to pay compensation of a specified amount for inconvenience/distress caused; e) to ensure (and pay for) putting right any specified error, omission or other deficiency; f) to take (and pay for) any specified action in the interests of the complainant; g) to pay a specified amount for costs the complainant incurred in pursuing the complaint; h) to limit fees to a specified amount. There is a limit of £50,000 on the total value that can be awarded by the determination of a complaint.

12.23 The determination requires the complainant to notify the Ombudsman, before a specified time, whether the complainant accepts or rejects the determination. Under para 5.49 of the rules, if *the complainant* tells the Ombudsman that he/she accepts the determination, it is binding on both parties and final. Or under rule 5.54, it may be rejected by the complainant. So after perhaps months of the LeO procedure (funded by the Bar Council and the Law Society) and after, say, up to £100,000 of BMIF expenditure on the particular case, the barrister and BMIF are still in the hands of the complainant even if the LeO determination is <u>against</u> the complainant. The rules enable the complainant, who has spent not a penny, to veto an adverse determination and to start legal proceedings if so desired. But the barrister has no such veto at all.

12.24 It is submitted that the profligacy of this system requires urgent legislative reform. The outcome of a system of ADR, like Arbitration, should bind both parties, if consensual, or neither, if it is not. For the Bar, LeO is not consensual. Most barristers want it no more than they did in 1995. But we respect and accept that we are bound by adverse findings. Yet ex-clients are not so bound. That is inherently irrational and unfair. What kind of biased contest is it in which, if one party loses, they lose and if the other loses, they can scrub out the loss? And what kind of perverse signal does this send out to the barrister contestant from the start of the contest – 'this is a contest in which if you lose, you <u>will</u> lose, but if you win, you <u>may not</u> win'.

12.25 If, but only if, a determination becomes binding and final, neither party may start or continue legal proceedings in respect of the subject matter of the complaint. If the complainant does not tell the Ombudsman (before the specified time) that he/she accepts the determination, it is treated as rejected, unless the complainant tells the Ombudsman (after the specified time) that he/she accepts the determination and the complainant has not previously told the Ombudsman that he/she rejects the determination and the Ombudsman is satisfied that there are sufficient reasons why the complainant did not respond in time.

12.26 If the LeO proceedings disclose misconduct by the barrister, LeO will refer it to the BSB, who will commence a disciplinary investigation. This means that after a long LeO investigation, there may then be, say, another 2 years of BSB and tribunal proceedings (or even more).

12.27 LeO decisions are published online on LeO's website. There were just over 100 published barrister decisions as at 1st March 2020 out of 1654 published LeO decisions. Two of those concerned barristers who had recently been promoted to the bench, one to the High Court. Much of the data concerned those against whom there had been a complaint, but no outcome save exoneration. The fact that such information ought to remain confidential because it is embarrassing and professionally damaging and encourages further vexatious complaints, is lost on those who regard publication as interesting. That said, it is submitted that the publication of data for a short time about those who let the Bar down, in particular those who exploit the public financially with grossly inflated fees when dealing directly under the Bar Public Access scheme, is probably entirely justified.

MORE BOOKS BY LAW BRIEF PUBLISHING

A selection of our other titles available now:-

'A Practical Guide to the General Data Protection Regulation (GDPR) – 2nd Edition' by Keith Markham
'Ellis on Credit Hire – Sixth Edition' by Aidan Ellis & Tim Kevan
'A Practical Guide to Working with Litigants in Person and McKenzie Friends in Family Cases' by Stuart Barlow
'Protecting Unregistered Brands: A Practical Guide to the Law of Passing Off' by Lorna Brazell
'A Practical Guide to Secondary Liability and Joint Enterprise Post-Jogee' by Joanne Cecil & James Mehigan
'A Practical Guide to the Pre-Action RTA Claims Protocol for Personal Injury Lawyers' by Antonia Ford
'A Practical Guide to Neighbour Disputes and the Law' by Alexander Walsh
'A Practical Guide to Forfeiture of Leases' by Mark Shelton
'A Practical Guide to Coercive Control for Legal Practitioners and Victims' by Rachel Horman
'A Practical Guide to Rights Over Airspace and Subsoil' by Daniel Gatty
'Tackling Disclosure in the Criminal Courts – A Practitioner's Guide' by Narita Bahra QC & Don Ramble
'A Practical Guide to the Law of Driverless Cars – Second Edition' by Alex Glassbrook, Emma Northey & Scarlett Milligan
'A Practical Guide to TOLATA Claims' by Greg Williams
'Artificial Intelligence – The Practical Legal Issues' by John Buyers
'A Practical Guide to the Law of Prescription in Scotland' by Andrew Foyle
'A Practical Guide to the Construction and Rectification of Wills and Trust Instruments' by Edward Hewitt
'A Practical Guide to the Law of Bullying and Harassment in the Workplace' by Philip Hyland

'How to Be a Freelance Solicitor: A Practical Guide to the SRA-Regulated Freelance Solicitor Model' by Paul Bennett
'A Practical Guide to Prison Injury Claims' by Malcolm Johnson
'A Practical Guide to the Small Claims Track' by Dominic Bright
'A Practical Guide to Advising Clients at the Police Station' by Colin Stephen McKeown-Beaumont
'A Practical Guide to Antisocial Behaviour Injunctions' by Iain Wightwick
'Practical Mediation: A Guide for Mediators, Advocates, Advisers, Lawyers, and Students in Civil, Commercial, Business, Property, Workplace, and Employment Cases' by Jonathan Dingle with John Sephton
'The Mini-Pupillage Workbook' by David Boyle
'A Practical Guide to Crofting Law' by Brian Inkster
'A Practical Guide to Spousal Maintenance' by Liz Cowell
'A Practical Guide to the Law of Domain Names and Cybersquatting' by Andrew Clemson
'A Practical Guide to the Law of Gender Pay Gap Reporting' by Harini Iyengar
'A Practical Guide to the Rights of Grandparents in Children Proceedings' by Stuart Barlow
'NHS Whistleblowing and the Law' by Joseph England
'Employment Law and the Gig Economy' by Nigel Mackay & Annie Powell
'A Practical Guide to Noise Induced Hearing Loss (NIHL) Claims' by Andrew Mckie, Ian Skeate, Gareth McAloon
'An Introduction to Beauty Negligence Claims – A Practical Guide for the Personal Injury Practitioner' by Greg Almond
'Intercompany Agreements for Transfer Pricing Compliance' by Paul Sutton
'Zen and the Art of Mediation' by Martin Plowman
'A Practical Guide to the SRA Principles, Individual and Law Firm Codes of Conduct 2019 – What Every Law Firm Needs to Know' by Paul Bennett
'A Practical Guide to Adoption for Family Lawyers' by Graham Pegg
'A Practical Guide to Industrial Disease Claims' by Andrew Mckie & Ian Skeate
'A Practical Guide to Redundancy' by Philip Hyland
'A Practical Guide to Vicarious Liability' by Mariel Irvine

'A Practical Guide to Applications for Landlord's Consent and Variation of Leases' by Mark Shelton
'A Practical Guide to Relief from Sanctions Post-Mitchell and Denton' by Peter Causton
'A Practical Guide to Equity Release for Advisors' by Paul Sams
'A Practical Guide to Unlawful Eviction and Harassment' by Stephanie Lovegrove
'A Practical Guide to the Law Relating to Food' by Ian Thomas
'A Practical Guide to Financial Services Claims' by Chris Hegarty
'The Law of Houses in Multiple Occupation: A Practical Guide to HMO Proceedings' by Julian Hunt
'A Practical Guide to Unlawful Eviction and Harassment' by Stephanie Lovegrove
'A Practical Guide to Solicitor and Client Costs' by Robin Dunne
'Occupiers, Highways and Defective Premises Claims: A Practical Guide Post-Jackson – 2nd Edition' by Andrew Mckie
'A Practical Guide to Financial Ombudsman Service Claims' by Adam Temple & Robert Scrivenor
'A Practical Guide to the Law of Enfranchisement and Lease Extension' by Paul Sams
'A Practical Guide to Marketing for Lawyers – 2nd Edition' by Catherine Bailey & Jennet Ingram
'A Practical Guide to Advising Schools on Employment Law' by Jonathan Holden
'A Practical Guide to Running Housing Disrepair and Cavity Wall Claims: 2nd Edition' by Andrew Mckie & Ian Skeate
'A Practical Guide to Holiday Sickness Claims – 2nd Edition' by Andrew Mckie & Ian Skeate
'Arguments and Tactics for Personal Injury and Clinical Negligence Claims' by Dorian Williams
'A Practical Guide to QOCS and Fundamental Dishonesty' by James Bentley
'A Practical Guide to Drone Law' by Rufus Ballaster, Andrew Firman, Eleanor Clot
'A Practical Guide to Compliance for Personal Injury Firms Working With Claims Management Companies' by Paul Bennett
'A Practical Guide to the Landlord and Tenant Act 1954: Commercial Tenancies' by Richard Hayes & David Sawtell

'A Practical Guide to Dog Law for Owners and Others' by Andrea Pitt
'RTA Allegations of Fraud in a Post-Jackson Era: The Handbook – 2nd Edition' by Andrew Mckie
'RTA Personal Injury Claims: A Practical Guide Post-Jackson' by Andrew Mckie
'On Experts: CPR35 for Lawyers and Experts' by David Boyle
'An Introduction to Personal Injury Law' by David Boyle
'A Practical Guide to Claims Arising From Accidents Abroad and Travel Claims' by Andrew Mckie & Ian Skeate
'A Practical Guide to Chronic Pain Claims' by Pankaj Madan
'A Practical Guide to Claims Arising from Fatal Accidents' by James Patience
'A Practical Approach to Clinical Negligence Post-Jackson' by Geoffrey Simpson-Scott
'Employers' Liability Claims: A Practical Guide Post-Jackson' by Andrew Mckie
'A Practical Guide to Subtle Brain Injury Claims' by Pankaj Madan
'A Practical Guide to Costs in Personal Injury Cases' by Matthew Hoe
'The No Nonsense Solicitors' Practice: A Guide To Running Your Firm' by Bettina Brueggemann
'The Queen's Counsel Lawyer's Omnibus: 20 Years of Cartoons from The Times 1993-2013' by Alex Steuart Williams

These books and more are available to order online direct from the publisher at www.lawbriefpublishing.com, where you can also read free sample chapters. For any queries, contact us on 0844 587 2383 or mail@lawbriefpublishing.com.

Our books are also usually in stock at www.amazon.co.uk with free next day delivery for Prime members, and at good legal bookshops such as Wildy & Sons.

We are regularly launching new books in our series of practical day-to-day practitioners' guides. Visit our website and join our free newsletter to be kept informed and to receive special offers, free chapters, etc.

You can also follow us on Twitter at www.twitter.com/lawbriefpub.

Lightning Source UK Ltd.
Milton Keynes UK
UKHW020016150620
364850UK00007B/456